Don
1-

Stephen Davey

WISDOM COMMENTARY SERIES

TITUS

CHARITY HOUSE
PUBLISHERS

Wisdom Commentary Series: Titus

Author: Stephen Davey
Editor: Lalanne Beale Barber
Cover Design and Body Layout: Grace Gourley
Cover Photo: Ancient shipyard in Crete that existed in the days of the Apostle Paul
Photo of Stephen: Sam Gray Portraits, Raleigh, NC (samgrayportraits.com)
ISBN 978 0 9908050 7 6

Published by Charity House Publishers

Charity House Publishers, Inc.
2201 Candun Street
Suite 103
Apex, NC 27523-6412
USA
www.wisdomonline.org

With incredible gratitude for my sons
~Benjamin and Seth~
who inspire me by their courageous commitment
to live out the Gospel,
persuading anyone who will listen to follow them,
as they follow their Lord and Savior, Jesus Christ.

CONTENTS

(Continued on next page)

(Continued)

Paul, a bond-servant of God and an apostle of Jesus Christ . . . ⁴to Titus, my true child in a common faith: Grace and peace from God the Father and Christ Jesus our Savior.

–Titus 1:1*a*, 4

CHAPTER ONE

FROM ONE SLAVE TO ANOTHER

Titus 1:1a, 4

DEFINING THE NAME

For twenty-one years during Rome's Golden Age (AD 98–AD 180), Marcus Aurelius was emperor. Christianity had become illegal and the spilling of Christians' blood was in season. The penalty for following Jesus Christ included imprisonment, torture, and death.

Human language cannot describe the suffering believers were made to endure in hope of making them admit the impious things charged against them, such as murder, incest, and cannibalism.

In AD 177, there existed a Christian community within the empire in southern France. Sanctus was a deacon in the church in the town of Vienne and was on trial for the *crime* of Christianity. As he stood before the Roman governor, his life literally was hanging in the balance.

According to ancient Church historian Eusebius, who recorded the events of the trial, Sanctus was resolved—no matter what—to remain true to Christ. When it became obvious that he would not renounce his faith, he was condemned to a public death in the amphitheatre. On the day of his execution, he was led into the arena where he was forced to sit on a red-hot chair; metal plates were applied to his body until he no longer looked like a man. Still, he would not yield. For every question put to him, he had but one answer: "I am a Christian."[1]

Throughout his torture, Sanctus remained resolute; his answer was unchanging. The watching crowd realized that his resistance couldn't be broken. They eventually grew tired of hearing of his loyalty to Christ, and his throat was cut.[2]

For Sanctus, his entire identity—his name, citizenship, and social status—was bound up in Jesus Christ. What defined him above and beyond everything else was the designation *I am a Christian.*

But the term *Christian* wasn't just a title . . . it was a way of thinking; it was a new way of living.[3]

MAINTAINING THE NAME

More than ever, the Church is in need of going back to the biblical drawing board and answering this question: What exactly does it mean to be a Christian . . . to live and act like one?

In our world today, the term *Christian* has become so broad, so elastic, that one size now fits all.

Today you can claim the title *Christian*, even if you don't care about Christ. You can claim the Name and yet deny:

- the deity of Christ;
- the virgin birth of Christ;
- the coming judgment of the world by Christ;
- a future kingdom whose King is Christ;
- a heaven for those who believe in Christ;
- a hell for those who don't believe in Christ.

You can be a Christian leader today and deny the need for Christ's atoning death on the cross. In fact, a growing number of people who call themselves Christians now believe that salvation doesn't really need to involve the cross of Christ. You can be a Christian today and conclude the Gospel is way too restrictive and the Bible is far too intolerant.

A Pew Forum on Religion and Public Life found that sixty-five percent of people polled said they believed the basic message of the Bible, while at the same time saying they believe in the legitimacy of other religious tenets, which included everything from reincarnation to astrology.

Every so often, I read from what are considered Christian—even, evangelical—journals and magazines, and I am more and more amazed at how quickly the undertow of secular thought is sweeping the Church into a sea of moral uncertainty and doctrinal confusion.

Many churches and denominations today are convinced that our commission as Christians is as much about saving the planet as it about saving people. In fact, more than ever, you are likely to be considered *unchristian* if you don't buy into the politically correct perspective of the environmentalists and the abortionists and the gay activists.

I was in an audience where a mainline denominational leader was debating an evangelical leader on the biblical basis for homosexuality and same-sex marriage. I expected the rather usual arguments. But what surprised me was the denominational leader's insistence that allowing homosexual marriages was nothing less than a *core value* of Christianity.

A local newspaper in my county interviewed a pastor from a mainline Protestant church in our city. He was asked, "What would you say to someone who's thinking about giving your church a try?" The pastor responded, "I would say that they would all be welcome regardless of who they are and regardless of their belief system." He then went on to add, "We don't try to convert anybody."

The reporter asked, "Well, what exactly is your church known for?" to which the pastor admitted, "We are known for having a positive spiritual message so that we can feel better when we leave than when we came in."

What a nice way of effectively saying, "We believe in nothing!" In other words, no matter what you believe or how you might behave, church is all about feeling better about yourself by the time you dismiss for lunch.

I get advertisement cards from churches and they all seem to say the same thing:

LOOKING FOR A CHURCH THAT RELATES TO YOU?
COME AS YOU ARE!
THE COFFEE'S GREAT!
THE MUSIC'S COOL!
THE SERMONS ARE SHORT and DYNAMIC!

. . . which is to be interpreted: "We're not gonna *bother* anybody."

Today you can believe just about anything you want to believe and feel pretty good about your position and opinion . . . until you open the Bible.

The Bible has a way of messing all that up because the Gospel isn't interested in relating *to* the world but in saving people *from* the world—and at the same time, renewing the mind of the believer who is constantly being influenced *by* the world.

The truth is we *need* to be provoked. Preachers and parishioners alike *need* to be challenged to live for somebody rather than themselves *(Hebrews 10)*:

Here's a personal confession of what *I* need:

- I need my mind renewed and transformed so that it doesn't justify *any* sin *(Romans 12)*.

- I need the Bible to act as a sword to cut through the façade of my motives, because I'm good at fooling myself *(Hebrews 4)*.

- I need the fellowship and accountability of other believers who passionately love and follow Jesus Christ *(Hebrews 10)*. (I love to hear one particular friend in the ministry pray because it stuns me to know how poorly I pray.)

- I need to be exposed to unfiltered, unpolished truth from God's Word, which is profitable—telling me where I'm wrong and where I'm right and how to believe and how to behave *(2 Timothy 3)*.

- I need to have my mission in life *continually* redefined.

REDEFINING THE ROLE

In twenty-five sentences or less, the Apostle Paul is going to stick his nose into just about everybody's business. In this extremely brief letter to a church leader named Titus, Paul will *redefine*:

- spiritual maturity;
- true leadership;
- godliness for men and women;
- the priority of the home;
- wholesome, sacrificial relationships;

- sexual purity;
- credibility and public testimony;
- the Gospel.

Never before have we so needed these issues clarified, redefined, and restated.

Paul's Exhortation: An Epistle

Paul wrote several letters to men who were serving as pastor-teachers—and that's why we refer to these letters as the Pastoral Epistles or, simply, Letters to Pastors. We know them as First and Second Timothy and Titus.

They were not exclusively for the benefit of the pastor-teachers but also for the congregations they led. These were Spirit-inspired letters to be added to the New Testament for the good of every New Testament church.

In fact, as early as the third century, the letter to Titus was included in a list of apostolic letters considered *necessary* for the life of the Church.[4]

Most believe that Paul wrote this brief letter to Titus in between his pastoral letters to Timothy. Paul would affectionately refer to both of these young pastors as his sons in the faith.

As his letter to Titus opens, it begins differently from the way we write letters or emails today—it begins with the name of the writer: ***Paul***.

We typically *end* our letters with our signature—but not in New Testament times. In those days, whenever you opened a letter, you immediately knew who the author was.

The name ***Paul*** is from the Latin *Paulus*, which means *small* or *little*. He had been born a Roman citizen and Paul was his Gentile Roman name.[5] His middle name, so to speak, was the Hebrew name *Saul*; his Jewish parents had more than likely named him after the first king of Israel.

However, throughout his ministry, he would choose to be known not by the name of a former king but by the common name of a Gentile—a name without any particular Jewish regality or tradition. And since Paul referred to himself as *an apostle of Gentiles (Romans 11:13)*, he would choose this common Gentile name throughout his ministry.

By the time he wrote to Titus, Paul was a veteran missionary, church planter, pastor-teacher, and theologian.

In His wonderful publication entitled *Insights*, Chuck Swindoll writes that when Paul sent this letter to Titus, he had experienced just about everything:

- He had survived years of misunderstanding, controversy, slander, betrayal.

- Disciples had thrilled him and then failed him.

- Friends had come and gone.

- Churches he had planted had thrived but flirted with apostasy.

- Congregations had looked to him for guidance but rejected his authority or questioned his integrity.

- He was accused of boasting in his success.

- He was dismissed as a failure when imprisoned.

No one knew better than Paul how rewarding, yet how frustrating, ministry could be. He had suffered repeated disappointment in people; the scars he had received over the years would be his gift to Titus, who needed these reminders as he struggled to stabilize churches on the unruly island of Crete.[6] Frankly, there was no one better to prepare Titus for the mountain climb of ministry on Crete than the aged apostle.

Crete is located in the middle of the Mediterranean Sea. It was the midway port to the continents beyond and a melting pot of everything and anything. During the days of Titus, there were up to a million residents occupying a hundred bustling cities along its coastline. The citizens were aggressive and materialistic. They had even earned a reputation for deception and vice.

In fact, if you said that someone was *Cretising*, that meant he was lying. The expression "playing a Cretan with a Cretan" meant that you tricked a trickster—you got the better of a deceiver by out-deceiving him.[7]

The very name of the island had come to symbolize corruption and deception and just about every form of vice. Talk about a mission field. Talk about pressure for any young pastor. Titus is going to need inspired instruction—words of direction from a wise and seasoned shepherd.

He would need something like the words of Hudson Taylor, a veteran missionary pioneer to China in the 1800s, who delivered to his staff on one occasion: "It doesn't matter how *great* the pressure is, what really matters is *where* the pressure lies—whether it comes *between* you and God or presses you *nearer* to the heart of God."[8]

What great mentoring from a veteran mountain climber.

In this letter Paul will effectively pull up a chair beside Titus—and to everyone who truly means it when they say, "I am a Christian"—and he will mentor us *all* in:

- how to stand for Christ;

- how to handle the pressure;

- how life is redefined for those passionate about the Body of Christ and the glory of God.

Paul's Obligation: A Slave

Actually, the very first aspect which Paul will redefine for us is our view of *ourselves*. The letter opens: ***Paul, a bond-servant of God*** (Titus 1:1*a*).

In addition to *Christian*, the Bible calls believers by a number of different names: children of God, citizens of heaven, ambassadors, branches, infants, joint-heirs, and more. And all of these titles help us understand a little better what it means to *be* a Christian.[9]

However, the Bible uses one term more frequently than any other—in fact, nearly forty times in the New Testament—and it comes from the original Greek *doulos*, which should be translated *slave*.

In other words, the overriding description of the Christian's relationship to Jesus Christ throughout the New Testament is a relationship between a master and his *slave*.

Unfortunately, most Christians read the term *bond-servant* more often than not. And that's simply because as far back as the *King James Version* and the *Geneva Bible* that predated it, the word *doulos* was softened in its translation to the word *bond-servant* or *servant*.

In an effort to avoid the negative imagery and cruelty bound up in the slave trade throughout Europe and the Americas, translators over the centuries chose to translate *doulos* as the less combustible, slightly more politically sensitive word *servant*.

Frankly, the Greek language has several words that can refer to servants such as household staff, hired help, etc. *Doulos* isn't one of them.[10] Although the duties of bond-servants and slaves often overlapped, there is a key distinction between these two terms . . . a distinction that revealed a world of difference: servants are *hired*—slaves are *owned*.

Servants had a measure of personal rights and freedom in choosing who they worked for and what they did. Slaves had no freedom; they had not one personal right. In the days of Titus—and our own English-speaking world, for centuries—slaves were not people, they were possessions.

Charles Spurgeon, the British pastor of the nineteenth century, identified the shortfall of our English sensitivities and protested:

> Where our Authorized Version softly puts it "servant," it really is "slave." The early saints delighted to count themselves as Christ's absolute property, bought by Him, owned by Him, and wholly at His disposal. Paul even went so far as to rejoice that he had the marks of his Master's brand on him and he cries, "Let no man trouble me: for I bear in my body the marks of the Lord Jesus." That was the end of all debate; he was the Lord's and the marks of the whips, the rods, and the stones were viewed as the branding of Paul's body as the property of Jesus the Lord. Now if the saints of old time gloried in obeying Christ, I pray that you and I will [do the same].[11]

The tragedy of a more politically correct translation is that when we read this opening phrase by Paul in ***Titus 1:1***, we don't suck in our breath and shudder at the gravity of the term. Paul's opening description of *himself* doesn't offend our sensitivities. Worse, it doesn't confront our ridiculous misconceptions of personal autonomy as Christians.

The average Christian thinks he has an *option* to obey Christ, to serve Him, to belong entirely to Him, body and soul. We would rather believe we can negotiate with Him over the terms of His will—protest what He does to our bodies; fuss about the inconveniences of His service; halfheartedly fulfill His clear commands; even dare to complain at the lateness of His blessings or the ill-timing of His burdens.

We think we've been *hired* by God.

No wonder we complain about overtime; long hours of tiresome service; the wages and inconvenience of our station; the one in charge of the benefit package and perks. We've overlooked the fact that we're slaves—owned outright as the personal *possession* of God.

"Have you forgotten," Paul asked the Corinthians . . .

> [D]*o you not know that your body is a temple of the Holy Spirit who is in you, whom you have from God, and that you are not your own? For you have been bought with a price: therefore glorify God in your body* (1 Corinthians 6:19–20).

Paul is redefining our freedom and he's turning it upside down.

This must be, for it is only as a person becomes the slave of the Creator that he can begin to experience true freedom . . . the way of freedom is through slavery to God.[12]

Another author from the 1800s wrote that liberty does not mean doing as you like, it means liking what you ought—and doing it. Such slavery to Christ is the only nobility.[13]

Find the Christian who is arguing with God over the terms of His will and you'll find a Christian bound in frustration or crippled by despair. But find someone who understands his complete ownership by Christ and you will discover someone liberated to serve with contagious joy.

A young lady at a Bible conference stood before her peers and held up a sheet of paper, explaining, "This page represents my life dedicated to Christ; this piece of paper is actually blank—it's been left for Him to fill in as He pleases . . . but I have already signed my name at the bottom of the page."

That's another way of saying, *I am a Christian . . . I am owned by Christ . . . He is my Master and I am His property.*

Paul's Occupation: An Apostle

Paul goes on to say that he is not only a slave of God but **an apostle of Jesus Christ**. Slavery referred to his personal obligation *to* Christ; apostleship referred to his personal occupation *for* Christ.

The word **apostle** (*apostolos*) comes from two words; when combined they mean *to be sent forth*. The term was used more widely to refer to someone authorized to deliver a message from a king.

In this context, the **apostle** then was an ambassador sent on behalf of Christ and the Church with a message to another people.[14]

Paul even used the word ***apostle*** to refer to Timothy and Titus as messengers of the Church, as well as his fellow workers *(2 Corinthians 8:23)*.

But Paul is using the term ***apostle*** here in ***Titus 1:1a*** in the official narrow sense, referring to himself as a member of that select group of men who were personally commissioned by the resurrected Lord.

Titus is going to *need* to speak as a representative of apostolic authority as he appoints elders and instructs the Church on how to conduct itself. Thus, it will need to be clearly understood that when Titus speaks, the Apostle Paul is speaking.

Frankly, Titus is going to be challenged. He will be going into existing churches to bring order and structure, as well as appoint elders/leaders.

Can you imagine some outsider showing up at a church today and after six weeks saying, "All right—here are my appointments for elders and deacons."

That's exactly what Titus is attempting to do. And people are going to respond inevitably, "Who asked you? Do you think you can just waltz onto our island and into our churches and decide who will serve as the leaders in our church? Who are you again?"

"My name is Titus."

"Titus? That's a Latin name—so you're not even a Jew from the Jerusalem church?"

"No."

"You're a Gentile?"

"Yes."

"But surely you were circumcised as a believing proselyte, right?"

"No . . . never was."

"Were you trained in Jerusalem?"

"Nope."

"Did you ever meet Christ personally?"

"Never."

"So you're not technically an apostle?"

"That's right."

"Listen, son, the pillars of this church were saved years ago at Pentecost when they traveled to Jerusalem and heard the Apostle Peter and others preach the Gospel; so who made you their representative? Who sent you here, anyway?"

"Well, let me show you: I have a letter from *Paul . . . an apostle of Jesus Christ.*"

"Yeah, we know him, but does he know you?"

"Yep, just look down at this line: *To Titus, my true child in a common faith*" (Titus 1:4*a*).

"Oh."

In other words, Titus was led to faith by Paul himself. Even more, Titus was discipled by the great apostle personally. And Paul opens this brief letter by giving Titus the credentials, effectively saying that the faith of Titus is the same faith as his own—they share a common bond . . . a common Lord . . . a common faith.

Which would have been remarkable for these pillars of the Church to read here: Paul—a former Pharisee, a devoted Jew, a faithful rabbi, a Hebrew among Hebrews, a man impeccable in his Jewish heritage—is calling an uncircumcised Gentile convert *my son.*[15] In other words, "Titus and I are related; we're in the family of God together . . . and we got in the same way: our *common faith* in Jesus Christ."

Titus probably paused at that point to let it all sink in. Then perhaps he said, "Oh, and while we're reading here, you might notice the next line actually gives *me* an apostolic order to fulfill: *For this reason I left you in Crete, that you would set in order what remains and appoint elders in every city as I directed you* (Titus 1:5).

Case closed.

By the way, Titus was perfect for the job. Earlier Paul had sent him to Corinth to help straighten out the mess—what a church *that* was . . . what division . . . what compromise. And Titus succeeded in not only bringing about unity in the church but strengthening the reputation of Paul in the eyes of the Corinthian believers *(2 Corinthians 7:6–7; 13–16).*

Titus had become Paul's personal troubleshooter.[16] Titus seemed to be the man Paul sent on the toughest assignments.

He even sent Titus earlier to a province known as Illyricum, where a church was struggling to survive in a difficult culture. According to the Roman historian Polybius, "The Illyrians were common enemies of everyone." In other words, those people didn't get along with anybody. Strabo, a contemporary of Titus, wrote that the people of Illyricum were wild and given to their primary occupation: pirates.[17]

How's that for an assignment: "Titus, go start a church among a bunch of pirates." Frankly, it was all strategic preparation for Titus as he arrives to bring spiritual order to the stubborn islanders of Crete—perhaps his toughest assignment yet. You don't just show up on Crete and actually expect to tell the churches who the elders are going to be without major issues.

When I read Titus's job assignment—what he's supposed to accomplish—I can't imagine the confrontation, the hurt feelings, the bruised egos of men passed over in the reordering of the church leadership team.

You just don't do that.

Most church leaders learn early that *change* and *church* don't usually belong in the same sentence. How many pastors have had their heads served up on committee platters for daring to change the color of the carpet, the order of the service, the logo on the church stationary, or anything else that dates back to the Middle Ages?!

I still remember exactly how I felt the first time I decided to attempt a *minor* change in a church. As a college senior, I accepted an assistant role at a church on one of the mountains in Tennessee about an hour away from the Bible college I attended. The pastor was a seminary mate who was a few years older than I was; we'd both been in the church less than six months.

He preached most Sunday mornings to about thirty people, and it was my role to preach on Wednesday nights to about ten. I would drive up Jump Off Mountain in a borrowed car and preach at Jump Off Baptist Church. Those names should have been my first clue.

The church looked old and smelled old. It seated about seventy-five people, with a little one-step platform and a small choir loft that was never used. There was a man in the church who had been there for at least twenty-five years. He taught the only adult Sunday school class and basically ran everything; his wife played the piano.

On the wall behind the pulpit, hanging just above the choir loft, was a banner about six feet long. It had an inspirational statement of some sort on it and I vaguely remember a Bible reference, too. What I still vividly recall was that the banner was faded . . . the edges of the paper had curled, turned brown and brittle. Several places along the edge were torn. Whenever anyone sat in that little chapel and looked at the preacher, that faded banner was unavoidable . . . and it was anything but inspiring. It was obviously time to bury it.

I talked with the seminary student/pastor about an idea I had to create a new logo for the church and a brand-new banner. It was time to give this church some fresh vision and new momentum. I contacted an artist at school, and we finalized the design.

The following Sunday morning, we arrived early enough to replace the fossilized banner with a colorful and creative new one. I was leaning on one of the pews in the choir loft, nailing up one end of the banner, when this pillar of the church walked into the foyer. He took a few steps inside the auditorium and yelled, *"What do you think you are doing?!"*

I knew immediately that I'd done the wrong thing. *I* was the one about to be buried. I quickly explained in an apologetic voice, "We made a new banner and we're putting it up in place of the old one."

His face was beet red. He pointed his finger at me and rattled the windows as he bellowed, "Young man, that banner has been up there for twenty years!" With that, he stormed out of the church and slammed the door behind him; the pastor had to go after him and try to calm him down so he could teach his Sunday school class.

I took down the new banner and nailed the old one back up.

When I read that Paul is asking Titus to go into established churches and *appoint elders*, I've tried to imagine showing up at Jump Off Baptist Church and saying to that man, "I'm appointing elders in this church, and you aren't one of them . . . in fact, you'll never teach a Sunday school class again."

Little wonder that Titus would need an apostolic reference—and a bucketload of encouragement—as he prepared to step into the foyer of that first church on the island of Crete.

Paul's Inspiration: A Blessing

Grace *and* peace *from God the Father and Christ Jesus our Savior* (Titus 1:4*b*).

Here's some encouragement, Titus: *grace* to strengthen you . . . *grace* to pray . . . *grace* to forgive . . . *grace* to serve . . . *grace* to endure . . . *grace* to persevere.[18] *Peace* in the face of doubt . . . *peace* in the midst of struggle . . . *peace* in times of chaos and conflict.

And the source of the *grace* and *peace* that Titus would depend entirely upon, day by day, is **God the Father and Christ Jesus our Savior**.

There's no indication that Titus ever hesitated . . . or doubted . . . or asked for an exit plan or an escape route.

This brief letter is obviously from one slave to another; Titus was also entirely owned by and devoted to His Lord and Savior. And Paul, an old, battle-scarred slave, writes to a younger slave in the faith—and to all of us—as he delivers the wisdom of both truth and experience:

> Titus, when you show up on the island of Crete and take your stand as a *Christian*, you are effectively saying, "I am a slave of God—one of Christ's messengers—delivering a message from the King." And while you're at it, don't forget to draw from the divine reservoir of *grace* and *peace*. God the Father will provide just enough for each and every day . . . one ministry assignment after another . . . one crisis at a time. Underneath your assignment will be the reservoir of *grace* and *peace* from the ultimate battle-scarred Shepherd—the Chief Shepherd of the Church, Jesus Christ.

Get ready . . . and then stay the course.

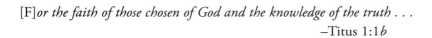

[F]*or the faith of those chosen of God and the knowledge of the truth . . .*

–Titus 1:1b

CHAPTER TWO

PASSION

Titus 1:16

A ZEST FOR LIFE

In the 1720s, there was a board game printed in England that was based on the Christian notion that "life is a voyage in which travelers are buffeted between vice and virtue." The game was created in such a way that *virtues* sped you through each step but *vices* slowed you down.

Parents were encouraged to play the game with their children to teach them this fundamental premise: "Life is a voyage that begins at birth and ends at death. God is at the helm . . . and your reward lies beyond the grave."

Milton Bradley of Springfield, Massachusetts, took up the legacy of that game in 1860 and adapted it to create The Checkered Game of Life. The virtuous path included Honesty and Bravery; the slower path included Idleness, Poverty, Ruin, and Disgrace. Characteristics such as Industry and Perseverance led the game players to win Wealth and Success; of course, landing on Suicide put a player out of the game.

Bradley described his adaption of the game as "a highly moral game that encourages children to lead exemplary lives and entertains both old and young with the spirit of *friendly* competition."

He evidently didn't play games at my house.

The Checkered Game of Life was eventually removed from the market, its Puritan morals considered far too stuffy and outdated for a self-centered culture in hot pursuit of instant gratification.

One hundred years later, the Milton Bradley Company released an anniversary adaptation which they renamed The Game of Life (or, simply, LIFE), which charted fresh territory for board games, with its three-dimensional board and plastic spinner.

To promote the game, the company hired popular radio and television personality Art Linkletter to add an endorsement. The game had been revised to have players earning money to buy furniture and grow a family. Vices and Virtues were no longer part of the game. Players could end up in the Poor Farm or land happily in Millionaire Acres, but everything now simply depended on the luck of the spinner—the Wheel of Fate.

Further revisions would be made to the game:

- 1980s – convertibles were replaced from earlier versions with minivans and Revenge squares were renamed Sue for Damages;
- 1991 – players were rewarded for good behavior, such as recycling trash, helping the homeless, saving endangered species, and solving pollution problems;
- 2010 – players earned money for planting trees, having family picnics, returning lost wallets, joining health clubs and, even, making new friends.

In the newer version, players now have the ability to do whatever they want and get rewarded for it: attend school, travel, start a family, etc. Values are up for grabs; you earn as many points for donating a kidney as you do for going scuba diving. Gambling and Revenge have been outlawed, and players even get extra chances to "Spin again if not in the lead."

All the more telling, the old game's daunting Day of Reckoning has now been replaced with an anticlimactic choice between a government-subsidized retirement community called Countryside Acres or a watered-down Millionaire Estates.

And most interesting, there is no end or final square to the game—you stop any time you want, because [subtle hint here] nobody mentions the *end* of life. In fact, the game's description says, "Do whatever it takes to *retire* in style . . . at the end of the game."[1]

Frankly, I'm surprised the game doesn't come with trophies for every player because everyone's a winner in the end.

What a change in our culture's view of life. The revisions of this game serve as a description of our own cultural regression over the past three hundred years.

In the original game, the successful person was the one who acquired the most virtues and avoided the most vices. And the earliest version made it clear that virtues and vices were determined by God's Word. God was clearly at the helm of a person's journey through The Game of Life.

Of course, when God was dismissed from life in our culture, virtues and vices were dismissed from LIFE, as well. Not only was the winner the person with the most money at game's end, there was no longer any talk of a Day of Reckoning.

The goal of the game shifted from standing before God to moving into a retirement village. You just wanted to play the game well enough to retire with the most toys.

What a difference between today's version of LIFE and the original game which instructed the players that they would be rewarded *after* the grave—after this life—so they should live with eternity in view: the coming Day of Reckoning.

A QUEST FOR LIFE

The loss of moral virtue and the loss of *courage* to list moral vices has deeply impacted our culture. And it isn't a game anymore. In the wake of the London riots of 2011, one religious leader in Great Britain had the boldness to suggest that the rioting was merely a symptom of moral disintegration throughout the western world. *The Wall Street Journal* printed his statement:

There has been a tsunami of wishful thinking that has washed across the West—wishful thinking that you can have sexual relations without the responsibility of marriage; children without the responsibility of parenthood; social order without the responsibility of citizenship; liberty without the responsibility of morality; self-esteem without the responsibility of work. There are large parts of Britain, Europe, and even the United States where religion is a thing of the past and there is no counter-voice to the culture of buy it, spend it, wear it, flaunt it—because you're worth it. The message is that morality is passé, conscience is for wimps, and the single overriding command to follow in life is: "Thou shalt not be found out." [2]

The article then quoted Harvard historian Niall Ferguson, who has a fascinating passage in his recent book *Civilization: The West and the Rest*, in which he asks if the West can maintain its primacy on the world stage or if it is a civilization in decline. Another quote came from a member of the Chinese Academy of Social Sciences, tasked with finding out what gave the West its dominance:

> At first we thought it was your weapons; then we thought it was your democracy; then we said it must be your capitalism. But for the last few decades we have known what gave the West its dominance—it was your religion.[3]

His observations are insightful, but his answer is shortsighted. The solution isn't just *any* religion; in fact, I would argue that the world is, and always has been, *saturated* with religion.

When Paul arrived in Athens, he commented on how religious the city was; there were statues of gods and goddesses everywhere. Actually, the Athenians were so afraid that they might have overlooked a god, they built an altar with this inscription: To an Unknown God *(Acts 17:23)*.

Paul introduced to them that unknown God—the God of the Ages—the Creator who came to earth to redeem mankind, not only from rioting and riotous living but from empty religion.

When Titus began his ministry on the island of Crete, he was surrounded by religion and religious mythologies; he was submerged in a relativistic culture where lying and deceiving were part of the game of life. There were no virtues to win, and vices didn't slow anybody down—it was every man for himself.

The solution certainly wasn't one more religion. The solution was spiritual *reformation*, bound up in the Gospel of Jesus Christ.

That's why, as Paul introduces himself to the churches on Crete through his letter to Titus, he informs both Titus and the churches that he is a very passionate man. In fact, he will describe himself with the kind of passions that change a person's life—his relationships—his work ethic—his entire perspective.

If we, as believers, ever hope to impact our world, his passions must become *our* passions.

A Passion for the Faith

Paul introduced himself to Titus as *a bond-servant* [slave] *of God.*

A slave had no will other than to obey the will of his master. And this wasn't just for the Apostle Paul—God hasn't hired us, either. We have no right to complain about overtime or negotiate for better wages or better living conditions or better health plans or nicer cars or kinder treatment from our world around us.

We haven't been *hired*—we have been *purchased*, Paul wrote, so that we are no longer our own, *for you* [we] *have been bought with a price* (1 Corinthians 6:20).

Paul next described himself as *an apostle of Jesus Christ*—a messenger boy for Jesus. And he was passionate about both the message and his calling as a messenger.

I was behind a van the other day; it had a bunch of ladders strapped onto the roof racks; paint was spattered on the back doors and bumper. The driver was going 40 in a 45 zone.

In my view, that's an unpardonable sin.

I was stuck behind him for several miles; he just wouldn't speed up. I finally got a chance to pass him—legally, in case you're wondering—and I saw he was a young guy, window rolled down . . . just enjoying his afternoon drive.

I couldn't help but laugh to myself as I drove past him because his boss was probably wondering where in the world he was. This guy was obviously getting paid by the hour. He didn't really own anything about his job . . . everything was just fine in slow motion . . . he had nothing to gain or lose by coasting through another workday.

Paul, frankly, lived in a hurry. He viewed himself as not only owned *by* God, but he owned his calling *from* God. And the stakes were high. He recognized that he was both a slave and an apostle *for the* **faith** *of those chosen of God* (Titus 1:1*a*).

The construction of this Greek phrase *kata*, translated *for*, with the accusative points toward the end or the goal [which Paul has in mind].[4]

In other words, Paul is saying, "I am a slave of God and an apostle of Christ *for this goal*—this is my passion: *the* **faith** *of those chosen of God*. This theme is picked up later, where he tells Titus to correct those in the church who are following after fables so that they will be *sound in the* **faith** (Titus 1:13) and *older men are to be . . . sound in* faith (Titus 2:2).

How passionate are we in relaying the soundness of our faith to the next generation of believers—to Christians at large? How important is the faith of those with whom God allows us to join in worship, service, and mission?

D.L. Moody, the famous evangelist of the 1800s who was used by the Lord to establish the school that we now know as Moody Bible Institute and the publishing company Moody Press, preached in crusades throughout England and America. When just a young man, he applied for membership in his home church; an interview with the deacons was required to discern the candidate's understanding of the Gospel. After his interview, Moody was declined for membership based on insufficient knowledge of the Gospel.

But they didn't just leave him there; he was put on a one-year course of study in the Word and then interviewed again. At the end of that interview, they received him into membership, the record shows, *with reservation.*

How many churches would even care today what people truly understand and believe? The average church says, "Just join us . . . *please*! Promise to put something in the plate, volunteer in the nursery every so often, and mind your manners, while you're at it."

Imagine the church today *requiring* a candidate for membership to attain a certain level of understanding of the doctrines of the faith before being allowed to join.

A pastor in a liberal mainline denominational church wrote a book with the title *What's the Least I Can Believe and Still Be a Christian?* It was no surprise that the author would write that biblical inerrancy was actually detrimental to authentic faith.[5]

He also went on to basically affirm homosexuality; argue for evolution; deny the literal, eternal state of hell, as well as suggest that unbelievers will probably make it into heaven, too.

I found it ironic the book was published by John Knox Press—Scottish Reformer John Knox would roll over in his grave.

The question isn't, "What's the *least* I can believe and still be a Christian?" That's like a groom asking, "What's the *least* number of vows I can promise to keep and still get married?" Or an employee asking, "What's the *least* I can do around here and still keep my job?"

The real question is, "What's the *most* I should believe because I am a Christian?" And that was the passion of Paul: establishing the soundness of *the* faith of those who were true believers.

Paul is telling us at the outset of this letter that he is passionate about developing and strengthening the content and substance of the faith of God's elect.

A Passion for the Elect

Paul was passionate about the soundness of the faith *of those* chosen *of God*. Now, that phrase has caused a lot of heartburn over the centuries: *those* chosen *of God*, from the word *eklektos*, from which we get our word *elect*. Perhaps it will be helpful to understand that there are two sides to the coin of redemption.

One side expresses God's perspective (and that will always remain a mystery). The other side presents man's perspective—and we've easily mastered that angle.

Since salvation is described in terms of marriage between Christ and His Bride, think about salvation this way:

1. There is the sovereign proposal by God.

2. There is the willing acceptance by the repentant sinner.

Our earthly marriage arrangement provides an illustration of our heavenly marriage to Christ. Eventually some guy comes to the realization that this woman—this creature of enrapturing delight and infuriating complexity—is not someone he simply wants to live *with* . . . she is someone he cannot live *without*.

He really hasn't fallen in love with her—he is actually *choosing* to love her, and he has made up his mind that she's the one. He proposes. She also came to the same conclusion: he was her choice, too. Their choices, however, did not a marriage make. Somebody had to propose . . . somebody had to accept the proposal.

Now, on the wedding day, if the officiant asked the bride, "Did you choose him?" she could say, "Of course I did." And if the groom were asked, "Did you choose her?" he could answer, "I certainly did." But in the order of events, he proposed and she accepted—which led to a ceremony where marriage vows were publicly exchanged.

Election is the God-initiated proposal of marriage to the Bride whom He has chosen for His Son. It's actually an *arranged* marriage—arranged before time began *(Ephesians 1:4–5)*.

However, no member of the bridal party who hasn't responded to the divine proposal is going to heaven. You have to accept His proposal . . . you have to say yes to Jesus!

> *Whoever will call on the name of the Lord will be saved* (Romans 10:13).

Now you can stay up all night if you want, trying to figure out the mystery of God's initial proposal. I would rather join Paul, the great theologian and, by the way, the greatest evangelist on the planet, in delivering the terms of the wedding contract to anyone who might accept God's proposal. He said in *Romans 10* that the unbeliever *cannot* believe in someone they've never heard about, so they need a messenger. And since *faith comes from hearing, and hearing by the word of Christ* (Romans 10:17), they need to hear the right message.

Unbelievers simply cannot accept the proposal of marriage until they've heard of the Bridegroom, Jesus Christ.

And let me ask this: How do you *know* if you're one of the elect? How do you know if God the Father chose you for His Son before the foundation of the world? There's actually a simple answer. Have you accepted His proposal? Have you said yes to Jesus? Have you accepted the proposal of marriage bound up in the Gospel of Jesus Christ?

If you have, ***those* chosen *of God*** includes you!

But what about all those whom God did *not* choose? Keep in mind, the doctrine of election is a *positive* doctrine intended to dazzle the Bride—He chose *you*!

No woman walks down the aisle and then says to her bridegroom, "I just can't get all those other girls you didn't choose out of my mind. I'm so disturbed about why you didn't choose any of them instead of me."

The point of this doctrine is simply for the amazement and wonder of us all—He chose us to be His Bride. I really don't understand it, but isn't it amazing!

Frankly, I don't *understand* how Jesus Christ could pay 2,000 years ago for a sin I'll commit tomorrow. There are a lot of biblical truths I don't understand, but I believe them because they are in God's Word.

I don't understand how God is going to take the dust of my body in the grave and reconstruct it and glorify it and immortalize it and, in an instant, reunite it with my spirit which has been with Him since the moment of my death. I don't understand any of that, but isn't it all incredibly wonderful!

Charles Spurgeon, the great London pastor of the Metropolitan Tabernacle in the 1800s, wrote:

> Look to Jesus and believe in Him, and you shall make proof of your election directly, for as surely as you believe, you are elect. If you will give yourself wholly up to Christ and trust Him, then you are one of God's chosen ones; but if you stop and say, "I want to know first whether I am elect," you do not know what you are asking. Go to Jesus, as guilty as you are, just as you are. Leave all curious inquiry about election alone. Go straight to Christ and hide in His wounds, and you shall know your election. There will be no doubt about His having chosen *you* when you have chosen *Him*.[6]

Paul effectively says that he is passionate about delivering the truth of the Gospel . . . and those who believe are the elect of God. Frankly, there's nothing more thrilling than watching someone hear the Gospel and believe—to see someone's eyes open with understanding by means of the initiating work of God's grace.

How passionate are we to deliver the saving Gospel of Christ to our world?

Those of us who sat under the teaching ministry of Howard Hendricks are forever grateful for his passion to develop *the faith of those* **chosen** *of* **God**.

Hendricks wrote biographically in his book *Teaching to Change Lives*:

I'm sure I would have died and gone to hell and nobody would have particularly cared. I was born into a broken home, my parents having separated before I was born. The only time I ever saw them together was eighteen years later when I was called to testify in a divorce court. As a boy I lived in a neighborhood in north Philadelphia in which they said an evangelical church could never be planted. But God has a fantastic sense of humor whenever anyone decides what can't be done. The Lord led a small group of Christians to band together, buy a little house, and start a church. One man in the church was named Walt. He had only a sixth-grade education. One day Walt told the Sunday school superintendent he wanted to start a Sunday school class for boys. "That's great, Walt, but we don't have an opening." But Walt insisted, so the superintendent said, "Good. Go out and get a class. Anybody you find is yours to teach."

Walt came into my neighborhood. The first time we met, I was playing marbles out on the concrete sidewalk. "Son," he said, "how would you like to go to Sunday school?" I wasn't interested. Anything with the word "school" in it had to be bad news. So he said, "Well, how about a game of marbles?" That was different. So we shot marbles and had a great time, though he whipped me in every single game. After that I would have followed him anywhere. Walt ended up picking up a total of thirteen boys in that neighborhood for his Sunday school class—all but four of us were from broken homes. Today, eleven of the thirteen boys [went on to serve] in full-time Christian work. So you see, my interest in teaching is much more than professional, it's intensely personal—a passion—because the only reason I have a ministry today is that God brought along my path a committed teacher.[7]

Read Titus story to know that God can use any of us

Paul was that kind of committed teacher—passionate for the establishment and the development of the faith of those who would come to believe in Jesus Christ.

A Passion for the Truth

Paul was also passionate about God's truth; he adds to this phrase the words *for the faith of those chosen of God and the knowledge of the* **truth** *which is according to godliness* (Titus 1:1*b*).

One of our generation's most disliked words now makes an appearance: **truth**. That word conjures up the idea of imposing virtues on someone else—or even more unwelcome, suggesting that something is a vice.

Truth sounds like the potential for right and wrong—it suggests some sort of dogma, doesn't it? No wonder the world doesn't want to traffic in truth. They'd much rather turn truth into an opinion. What's true for you might not be true for me, so keep your opinion to yourself—right?

What did Paul dare to suggest when he said he was committed to leading the believer into *the knowledge of the* **truth**?

The word Paul uses here for *knowledge* is a compound Greek word and a favorite of his; it refers to a full, precise, complete knowledge. Paul often links the word *knowledge* to the word **truth**.[8] Which means that truth can be *known*—we can be *certain*.

We depend on the certainty of truth every day, whether or not we want to deny the existence of absolutes. It isn't a matter of opinion that a spoonful of arsenic will kill you—it's simply *true*. **Truth** can thus hold definitive content and distinction from what is *not* true.

The Bible *is* **truth**. Jesus prayed to His Father, *"Sanctify them in the* **truth***, Your word is* **truth** *"* (John 17:17).

So many of the truths of the Bible are obviously self-authenticating: Israel exists; the Church exists; prophecies have come true by the bucketload. Jesus Christ came, was crucified, and rose from the dead—the course of history itself has been changed by His coming.

The truth will not cease to be the truth if we don't believe it. It will not become false if we ignore it. God lives whether we like it or not.[9]

Imagine traveling down a mountain road and passing a sign that indicates a sharp curve ahead and posts the speed limit as 35 mph; you'll slow down—whether you're paid by the hour or not.

Actually, you can respond to the truth of that sign in three ways:

- You can *obey* it and slow down.
- You can *ignore* and keep going at the same speed.
- You can *defy* it and speed up.

No matter what you decide to do in response to the words on that sign, it *remains* the truth: you will either suffer or be safe, depending on how you respond to its announcement.

Truth matters.

Paul says here that his passion is for the Church to get a grip on these truths—*to grow in knowledgeable precision of these biblical certainties.*

You've noticed that one of the problems in keeping children safe is that they don't understand how precise truth can be applied. For instance, children don't quite get the law of gravity, and they get into all sorts of trouble because of it. The law of gravity is precise . . . and unforgiving.

One afternoon I volunteered to keep an eye on our younger daughter, who at the time was still a toddler. I was sitting in a living room chair reading, and I was thinking to myself, *This is easy . . . What can she do? . . . she doesn't know how to light matches yet . . . she's got on a diaper . . . she'll be fine.* And before I knew it, she had crawled halfway up the stairs. I jumped up, panicked, and did the wrong thing: I yelled, "Charity!" which startled her and made her look back at me. Of course, she lost her balance. As I went up the stairs, she bounced down the stairs toward me. I caught her on the third bounce. It's been my secret ever since.

Paul told Titus that he needed to keep an eye on the churches in Crete. In fact, he will commission Titus to teach the churches and their communities the **truth**—the **truth** about eternal life; the **truth** about sin; the **truth** about relationships; the **truth** about virtues and vices . . . the **truth** that life isn't about getting all the stuff you can before you retire one day in Millionaire Acres.

Titus was going to minister, in a way, by the *old* version of The Game of Life. He would begin teaching them, "Life is a voyage that begins at birth and ends at death. God is at the helm . . . and your reward lies beyond the grave."

[A]nd the knowledge of the truth which is according to godliness, [2]in the hope of eternal life, which God, who cannot lie, promised long ages ago, [3]but at the proper time manifested, even His word, in the proclamation with which I was entrusted according to the commandment of God our Savior.

—Titus 1:1c–3

CHAPTER THREE

ALL OR NOTHING

Titus 1:1c–3

〜✺〜

IT IS . . . *OR IT ISN'T*

In a booklet entitled *Absolute Truth*, the author recounted a story about the customary introduction to a philosophy class taught by Roger Wengert at the University of Illinois. He began his ethics course by asking how many of the students believed that truth was relative—that there was no absolute standard for right and wrong. A show of hands usually revealed that most of the class had bought into moral and ethical relativism. Without pausing, Wengert had his students turn to their class notes and discuss testing dates, paper assignments, and other course requirements. And then He informed the class that they would actually be graded according to their physical height. Every semester at this point, some tall kid usually said, "Yeah!" But then Wengert clarified: "Short students get the best grades."

Inevitably, students spoke in protest, "You can't do that . . . your grading system isn't fair," and he responded matter-of-factly, "I'm the professor and I can grade however I wish." The students always insisted, "But you ought to grade us according to how well we learned the material. You should look at our papers and you should grade us on that basis."

Professor Wengert then replied, "By telling me I *should* do something and that I *can't* do something and that I *ought* to do something, you contradict your belief that truth is relative. If you were true relativists, you would realize there is no external standard to which my grading should conform.

If *my* truth and *my* ethical standard lead me to an alternative grading system that you consider inappropriate, well then, that's life![1]

Relativism isn't original with these students. Travel back to the first century and you'll discover it was the leading philosophy on the island of Crete—a population that had made relativism a way of life.

Little surprise that in the opening words of this letter, you find the Apostle Paul mixing cement around unchangeable, objective truths.

The passions of Paul could be called slave traits: characteristics of someone who is all-or-nothing dedicated to the glory of Christ. Paul says without reservation, "God is my Master and I am His messenger boy."

For Paul, Christianity was, indeed, everything . . . or nothing.

IT IS!

In the previous chapter, we identified three passions that captivated the heart and life of the Apostle Paul:

1. the **faith**—he desired God's people to embrace the genuine nature of their beliefs;
2. the **elect**—he literally gave his life away for the establishment, protection, and development of the Church;
3. the **truth**—he lived to develop the substance of the believer's understanding of the objective truth of God's Word.

And now we can complete the list with three additional passions.

A Passion for God's Glory

Paul, a bond-servant of God and an apostle of Jesus Christ, for the faith of those chosen of God and the knowledge of the truth which is according to godliness (Titus 1:1).

One of the things Paul does in clarifying his statement about **truth** is to send a clear warning to Titus and the churches. They're going to hear a lot of declarations and definitions of spiritual truth—but if it doesn't promote godly living, it isn't a valid message.[2]

If it promotes materialism and self-centeredness, it isn't the **truth**. If it endorses sinful behavior, it isn't the **truth**. If it encourages greed and self-satisfaction, it isn't the **truth**.

Paul is saying that genuine faith leads a person toward god-likeness. He also explains a higher incentive for pursuing **godliness**. In fact, it's easy for us to want to become more like Christ and miss the primary motive. Be warned: we're not passionate about growing in the knowledge of the **truth** just so we can become *smarter*.

This noun translated **godliness** refers to both living out the **truth** in front of others, [but with the added nuance of] reverencing God.[3]

In other words, we want to be godly *because* we want to honor God. We want to be godly *because* we want to build up the reputation of God. We're not trying to grow in our ***knowledge of the* truth** so we can receive an award or get mentioned in the church bulletin. We are passionately attempting to live out our faith so that *God's name* receives greater credibility and esteem.

Someone remarked that it's amazing what God will choose to do through the lives of people who refuse to take the credit.

Hudson Taylor, missionary pioneer to China, was riding in a carriage with a friend later in his life, and the friend said to him, "You must often be conscious of the wonderful way God has prospered you and the China Inland Mission. I doubt if any man living has had a greater honor." Hudson Taylor turned to his friend and said, "You need to know that this is how I think: I believe God was looking for someone small enough and weak enough for Him to use, that all the glory might [rightfully] be His—and He found *me*."[4]

That's the passion of a true slave of Christ. It's not about us—it's about *His* glory and *His* greatness and *His* reputation and *His* honor.

Paul wrote,

> *But may it never be that I would boast, except in the cross of our Lord Jesus Christ* (Galatians 6:14a).

In other words, God forbid that anyone should ever take personal glory away from the person of Jesus Christ. This was the passion of Paul—living out the Gospel in such a way that God was glorified.

Notice the connection in ***Titus 1:1*** between **truth** and **godliness**: ***the knowledge of the* truth *which is according to* godliness**.

That's another way of saying spiritual **truth** that doesn't produce goodness simply isn't spiritually true.

Outward behavior validates the nature of inward belief. In fact, what you *believe* inwardly will eventually show up in how you *behave* outwardly. And how you behave informs everyone of what you *really* believe.

For instance, what you believe about the law of gravity determines how you behave when you're standing on the edge of the Grand Canyon, as we did during our son Seth's wedding to Megan. Gusts of wind kept us alert as we held the marriage ceremony just off the beaten path near the canyon's edge. We behaved a certain way because we believed a certain truth: the objective, unchangeable truth about gravity.

According to this text, *knowing* should influence *living*.

And by the way, knowing the **truth** will not eliminate the battles of life. Knowing one more verse isn't going to get you released from the next spiritual battle with the devil, the world, or your own flesh. That's why **godliness** is something we realistically call a pursuit.

But what exactly is this **godliness** Paul is describing to Titus? Is it a list of do's and don'ts—a standard of living—good table manners? Mind you, I recommend that we use forks instead of fingers, but when it comes to defining **godliness**, you can travel the world over and get different definitions from many different cultures.

For instance, if I were preaching in certain Eastern European countries, I would remove my wedding ring before I arrived at church because, to people there, it would imply materialism and an unnecessary expenditure. I haven't taken my ring off in years. I can't . . . unless I use some butter. I want to keep it on, anyway, because in our culture, it doesn't symbolize materialism—it symbolizes marriage. It tells my world that I belong to someone else.

When I first preached in Santiago, Chile, I asked what I should wear in the pulpit. Who knows? . . . a suit might be a distraction; a long-sleeved shirt and a silk necktie could be symbols of ostentatious wealth.

The problem with defining **godliness** *externally* is that it changes from country to country—even from church to church.

So let's correctly define this word; the proof that it is a *correct* definition is that it will stand the scrutiny of *any* culture. Here it is: **godliness** is acting like God.

One author defined **godliness** as *everyday expressions that demonstrate the character of God.*[5]

- If God is love, **godliness** is loving in word and deed.

- If God is mercy, **godliness** is showing mercy.

- If God is patient and kind, **godliness** is exhibiting patience and kindness.[6]

- If God hates pride and laziness and gluttony, **godliness** dislikes it, stops excusing it, and starts confessing it.

- If God desires sexual purity—both physically and mentally—**godliness** is pursuing purity in every aspect of life.

- **Godliness** is God-likeness.

Frankly, our little list of externals is preferable; it's a lot easier to keep up with our list of the dirty dozen or the sanctified seven than to attempt to *demonstrate the character of God.* It's easier to wear a necktie than imitate the nature of Christ.

Godliness isn't a list—it's a life . . . it is the life of Christ *in* you which then demonstrates *through* you the character of God for the glory of God.

The History Channel aired a program about a man who had recently purchased a piece of property that included a house and a barn, and while inspecting the barn, he opened an old chest and discovered a violin safely tucked inside. As he dusted off the near-perfect instrument, he found the name Stradivarius clearly etched on the violin. His discovery might actually be worth millions of dollars! The experts didn't agree, however. After the violin was appraised, he was told that it wasn't a genuine Stradivarius—the name had been forged. It was an imitation reproduced in the early 1900s, worth around five hundred dollars. The appraiser concluded by telling the crestfallen violin owner, "Remember, just because something has a label doesn't mean it's real."[7]

This is exactly the warning Paul is delivering to the believers on the island of Crete: something labeled spiritual truth or religious truth or biblical truth doesn't necessarily mean it's the real thing.

God's signature has been forged throughout history, and it's still being forged today. Just because His name is attached to something doesn't mean it has anything to do with His nature.

"Be careful," Paul warns Titus, "you're going to have to help the flock grow in the knowledge of the **truth**—the real thing—and the way you know it's genuine is that you will be led along a path of godly living that ultimately brings glory to the character and name of God."

That's living with a passion for God's glory.

A Passion for God's Presence

[I]*n the* **hope** *of eternal life, which God, who cannot lie, promised long ages ago* (Titus 1:2).

Notice the progression between learning and living in Paul's opening statement, as we look for the appearing of Christ. Christ's soon appearing and our presence with Him forever is our great **hope** *of eternal life*.

When we use the word **hope**, we're usually referring to something we're hoping will or won't happen in the future. We say things like:

- I **hope** it doesn't rain at our outdoor wedding.

- I **hope** I get that promotion next week.

- I **hope** our house sells this month.

- I **hope** our dog doesn't have any more puppies.

- I **hope** the New England Patriots lose.

When Paul uses the word **hope**, it has an entirely different quality about it; he uses it as a future [reality] based on the promise of God.[8]

This word for **hope** is consistently used in the New Testament for a confident expectation . . . in this case, of eternal life.[9]

Now keep in mind that the believer *already* possesses eternal life:

> *These things I have written to you who believe in the name of the Son of God, so that you may know that you have* [present tense] *eternal life* (I John 5:13).

But Paul is referring to something future. He's referring to the *final* consummation of eternal life when Christ gathers us to Himself. This is the glorious moment every believer eagerly awaits.[10]

> [W]*e ourselves groan within ourselves, waiting eagerly for our*
> *adoption as sons, the redemption of our body* (Romans 8:23*b*).

And how can we be so certain that our **hope** is not going to be dashed to pieces? How is it that our **hope** is actually grounded in certainty? How can Paul be so sure?!

His answer: **[I]*n the* hope *of eternal life, which God, who cannot lie, promised long ages ago*** (Titus 1:2).

Here's why—God promised!

God, Paul reminds us, is the ***God, who cannot lie***—literally translated, the *cannot-lie* God.[11] This was a startling claim in Paul's generation because the gods of the Greeks, Romans, and Cretans were as adept at lying as anybody else. But not *this* God!

This ***God*** promises a future heaven! This isn't a promise from Paul—or the Apostles—or the Church. Human beings and human institutions can be guilty of making promises that won't be kept. One author wrote that promises are like babies—they are easier to make than to deliver.

Benjamin Franklin wrote, "Our new Constitution is now established and has an appearance that promises permanency; but in this world nothing can be said to be certain except death and taxes."

Paul would disagree and declare what God promises, God delivers.

> *Also the Glory of Israel will not lie* (1 Samuel 15:29*a*); *it is impossible for God to lie* (Hebrews 6:18*a*).

Paul adds an interesting phrase here: ***God . . . promised long ages ago***. The tense is used to refer to an event in the past. This promise of eternal life was made ***long ages ago***. Paul only used this phrase twice in all of his letters. It can be translated "before times eternal" or "before the world was" or "before time began."

In other words, your eternal life and mine is one of the oldest promises that has ever been recorded in Scripture.[12]

Before time began, eternal life was a promise made by God—which means that this promise wasn't first made to us. First and foremost, it was made between the members of the Trinity. They promised *each other*. The Father said to the Son and the Son to the Spirit and the Spirit back to the

Son and the Son back to the Father: "Our promise to each other is that eternal life will be a part of our redemptive plan for creation."

We tend to think that God promised heaven to us as believers (that's true), but God the Father promised it to God the Son *first*. God the Holy Spirit promised it to God the Father, too. This is their promise to each other and they have been working in perfect unity to keep the promises they've made *before time began*.

The plan of redemption for sinners did not come into existence *after* the fall of man but *before* man was ever created.[13]

The atoning work of Christ on the cross was not some emergency plan concocted by God the Father as He attempted to keep one step ahead of sinful mankind. Peter preached that the crucifixion of Christ was part of the plan of God *before* time began:

> [T]*his Man, delivered over by the predetermined plan and foreknowledge of God* (Acts 2:23*a*).

To discover that the promise of **eternal life** was made *before* time between the members of the Godhead makes God all the more mysterious and amazing and infinite and glorious—and we affirm its **truth** because it leads our hearts to want to live *more* for Him and *less* for ourselves; it steadies our feet on the path of genuine and grateful **godliness**.

It makes us long for the fulfillment of the ages and the consummation of the plan of God which brings us into His presence forever . . . when our flawed and failing flesh is put away and we are clothed in immortality and the perfection of holiness *(1 Corinthians 15)*.

Imagine, the Apostle Paul writes here to Titus after having been given a personal tour of heaven and a glimpse of the coming glory *(2 Corinthians 12)*. No wonder he serves as a model slave of God for us all—passionate about the faith—God's people—God's **truth**—God's glory—God's Church—God's presence. Paul has seen the Father's house; his eyes have feasted on the same sights as John; he's witnessed the emotions of final redemption and the glorious worship around God's throne.

Paul is passionate about the presence of God, and he can't wait to be with Him . . . permanently.

A Passion for God's Assignment

[B]*ut at the proper time* **manifested***, even His* **word***, in the* **proclamation** *with which I was entrusted according to the* **commandment** *of God our Savior* (Titus 1:2–3).

Paul refers here to the **manifested Word** of God—His *logos*. Paul often used *logos* to refer to the Gospel itself.[14]

God has **manifested**, or revealed, the one true message about God, the only effective way of finding Him, the only way of pleasing Him, and the only hope of being forever with Him. This He **manifested** in His *logos*—His **Word**.[15]

And Paul emphasizes his own personal **proclamation** of the *logos*. In fact, the word for **proclamation** (*kerugma*) is used of the message of the herald who arrives on behalf of a ruler under whom he serves.[16] The herald merely delivers the message of his superior. He doesn't create the message or adapt it—he just delivers it, on behalf of his king.

Paul relates this analogy to his preacher-sons in the faith. He solemnly charges Timothy in the presence of God to *preach the word* (2 Timothy 4:2). Simply put, "Your job is to deliver the message of your King!"

I remember with fondness the inspiration I felt as a seminary student whenever I saw that large stone pedestal in the center of the campus and the words carved into one side of it that stated, "Preach the word." It reflected the heart of the apostle to his spiritual sons Timothy and Titus.

A herald *is* a preacher, announcing the message of his Master. In our world today, the title *preacher* is virtually disappearing. It's obvious why: it sounds dogmatic; it's too black-and-white; it suggests moral authority in a world of moral relativity. "Don't preach to me," is the popular response to an absolute.

I have watched in recent years as evangelical pastors now prefer to be known as speakers and their sermons known as talks or lectures or, even, conversations.

I read an interview with one popular pastor whose multi-site church includes more than 20,000 weekend attendees; he explained in the interview that forty-two Sundays out of the year, he basically addresses human relationships and human issues and other relevant topics, using a verse or two to buttress his talks. Not surprisingly, he commented that he prefers to be referred to as a communicator.

Paul wrote to Timothy in a way that is sounding more and more anti-quated: *I was appointed a preacher* [*keruxon*] (1 Timothy 2:7).

Why is that particular title so important to Paul? For one thing, he knows that Titus is going to battle false *teachers*. He's going to have to stand up to creative *speakers* who are teaching error and myth and speculation. They will probably be better *communicators* . . . and they'll outnumber him. So Paul reminds Titus ahead of time that he is nothing more or less than an expositor . . . a *preacher*—a herald delivering the message of his Master's Gospel.

Frankly, a *teacher* can teach his own material—he can come up with his own perspective and persuade others to his point of view. A *speaker* can originate his own message. A *communicator* can deliver his own creatively designed content, but not a herald—not an expositor—not a *preacher*. An expositor is simply repeating and explaining what has been previously delivered to him in God's Word.

A further warning needs to be issued to pastors and Bible teachers who use the Bible somewhat randomly—proof-texting their opinions to support whatever they want to say about whatever issue they want to address. What they say may be biblical, but it isn't necessarily the Bible.

Many today are expounding on life and illustrating with Scripture; a true preacher expounds on Scripture and illustrates with life.

If all a pastor/communicator/speaker ever does is effectively present his views on life and the news of the day and the culture and human relation-ships and uses a verse or two to back up his story—if all he does is use the Bible to reinforce what *he* wants to say about what *he* thinks is important—then the church, without realizing it, is actually being *conformed to the mind of the pastor* rather than the mind of God.

That's how you can have a church of thousands of people blindly fol-low their apostate pastor into accepting universalism: everybody's going to heaven after all, and there's no need to fear hell anymore. This former pastor was a skillful communicator, but his gospel was homemade and the cross of Christ redefined.

Take note, Titus . . . Timothy . . . Stephen . . . and every other Bible teacher/preacher/pastor/leader reading this chapter: we are *never* original; we don't create the message. God has delivered His *logos*. We simply read it, translate it, outline it, explain it, illustrate it, apply it, and urge its adherence.

A.W. Tozer's challenge to pastors in the early 1900s needs repeating: "We are not diplomats, we are prophets . . . our message is not a compromise—it is an *ultimatum*."

In 1930, the most popular pastor in America graced the cover of *Time Magazine*. He refused to mention sin, hell, absolutes, and dogma. His name was Harry Emerson Fosdick, and he preached to a packed church built specifically for him by John D. Rockefeller after Fosdick was forced to resign from a Presbyterian church on charges of heresy.

Never mind that . . . the church was full.

His primary message was that the Church needed to be relevant and the message of the Church needed to be positive. The needs of people were the focus of his sermons. In an interview with *Harper's Magazine*, Fosdick said:

> Who seriously supposes that one in a hundred of the congregation *cares* what Moses or Paul *meant* in those verses. The preacher should not end but begin with thinking about the audience's vital needs, and then let the whole sermon be organized around a constructive endeavor to meet those needs. Preachers who pick out texts from the Bible and then proceed to give their historic settings, their logical meaning in the context, their place in the theology of the writer are grossly misusing the Bible. Nobody who speaks to the public assumes that people are interested in the meaning of words spoken 2,000 years ago.[17]

Imagine—he completely scuttled the definition of expository preaching!

Frankly, the loss of health and credibility in the Church today is to be laid directly at the feet of pastors who will not be preachers. They refuse to be heralds, delivering and expounding the troubling, unsettling ultimatums of unchangeable **truth**. The mainline denominational disasters are the result of Fosdick's descendants, who say the Bible doesn't really matter, so why teach its true meaning so carefully.

Is this really an option for God's messenger? Is there really any other message than His? Evidently, Paul doesn't consider the exposition of Scripture to be optional:

> [I]*n the* proclamation *with which I was entrusted according to the* commandment *of God* (Titus 1:3).

In other words, there's not another message and preachers don't have a vote on what they deliver. There are no alternatives to preaching the **Word** to our world. We, as slaves of God, are obeying *the* commandment *of God* to expound the truths of God's **Word**.

When correctly expounded, the end result is a genuine relationship with the living Lord, along with an eternal future that defies our imagination.

Paul ends his opening paragraph with *Grace and peace from God the Father and Christ Jesus our Savior* (Titus 1:4).

When Titus was preaching on the island of Crete and Paul was preaching throughout the Roman Empire, that word translated *Savior* (*soter*) was used to praise the gods Zeus and Apollo; they were referred to as mankind's *savior*. That same word was also given to Caesar who was known as the *savior* of the world.[18]

Paul effectively announces, "I'm going to tell you the truth—and we might as well offend the emperor and all the religious people in the empire while we're at it: Caesar isn't the savior and neither is Zeus or Apollo. The only *Savior* of the world is *Christ Jesus*, who is the true and living God. So preach the **Word**, Titus . . . just as I am preaching the **truth** of God. It isn't going to be popular . . . it might not pack out your churches on the island of Crete, but don't hold back—this **truth** is genuine. Stand up for Christ and deliver *His* **Word**."

Martin Luther the Reformer was given much of the credit for launching the Protestant Reformation, and on one occasion he corrected someone who complimented his efforts. He said these wonderful words as he reflected on earlier years of ministry, "I simply preached and taught the **Word** of God; and the **Word** of God did everything else."

I love that . . . preach the **Word** of God . . . and the **Word** of God will do everything else.

Like Paul, let's be passionate about the faith—about God's elect—about God's **truth**—about God's glory—about God's presence—about God's assignment.

Whatever and wherever, don't deviate from the message or create a new one . . . simply preach the **Word**.

For this reason I left you in Crete, that you would set in order what remains and appoint elders in every city as I directed you.

–Titus 1:5

CHAPTER FOUR

POLITICALLY INCORRECT

Titus 1:5

CREATING THE VOID

If you ever have the idea that we live in a strange, confused world where religious beliefs are more bizarre than believable—if you've come to the conclusion that the Gospel is desperately needed to both liberate and redeem a culture from utter decay—now is that time.

In fact, it has always been *that* time.

Travel back to a flourishing civilization on the Greek island of Crete, where the worship of Dionysius was preferable; where the ruins of his temple are still visible.

According to legend, his father was Zeus, the principal god of the Greek pantheon, ruler of the heavens, and father of other gods and mortal heroes. The birth of Dionysius was anything but normal. While his mother was carrying him, Zeus killed her and snatched from her womb the preborn Dionysius. Just before incinerating her with his fiery wrath, Zeus had the baby sewn into his own thigh until time to be born. The infant god in the thigh of Zeus was to become a world ruler. If that isn't strange enough, just after birth, baby Dionysius was kidnapped by the sons of the earth known as Titans. They didn't want to be ruled by this new god, so they cooked little Dionysius and ate him. However, his heart was rescued just in time by his father, Zeus, who swallowed it and then reconstructed the body of Dionysius. Zeus blasted the Titans with lightning, and from their ashes mankind evolved.

This was the Greeks' theory of origins . . . for *centuries*.

And that wasn't all. Dionysius grew up to create a religion of ecstasy and emotionalism, saturated with drunkenness and sexual immorality. Wine was such a critical part of this religion that Dionysius became known as the god of wine. The Romans picked it up from there and renamed him Bacchus. People participating in this religion engaged in ecstatic orgies of demonic possession and sexual perversion while in a state of drunkenness.

They believed that religion was a transcendent experience and drunkenness allowed a person to achieve communion with the deities by losing any and all inhibitions.

In one excavated temple are the remains of a well dug in the center of a large open area. The colorfully tiled well, designed with grape vines and naked figures, was located there so that worshippers who engaged in their drunken orgies could vomit their food and drink, then gorge again, repeating the process.[1]

Their vomit was literally viewed as an *offering* to Bacchus.

FILLING THE VOID

In the fourth decade of the first century, several Jews had traveled from Crete to Jerusalem to celebrate the feast of Pentecost. On that day they heard a message by a converted fisherman named Peter, and they were born again by faith in Jesus Christ, their Messiah. With incredible passion and perseverance, they returned to the island and began spreading the liberating Gospel of Christ.

Thirty years later the Apostle Paul visited the island, along with a young man named Titus, to review the progress of the Gospel.

More than likely, Paul's visit to Crete came after being released from his first imprisonment in Rome, allowing him to travel and preach for two to three years. He would be imprisoned again after this brief parole and eventually executed in Rome at Nero's order.[2]

We're not told how long Paul stayed on the island of Crete, but we can only imagine the mission field. Their wine industry was famous—and flourishing. Drunkenness was epidemic.[3] Cretans had additionally earned the reputation of deception throughout the civilized world. Their sexually driven religion would certainly pique the interest and devotion of the population far more than the Gospel, which called for repentance and self-restraint and holy living.

But the Gospel had taken root! The Spirit of God had transformed the lives of people who had experienced enough of Dionysius to know that peace and satisfaction weren't found at the bottom of a bottle or vomiting into a well. One orgy after another left them with only more emptiness.

Churches sprang up—assemblies devoted to this new teaching from apostles and messengers had begun flourishing, as well. Spiritual fruit was beginning to show on the vines of transformed believers.

But the Church was in serious jeopardy, with its spiritual health hanging in the balance. False teachers had begun their deceptive work; leaderless congregations were easy prey to myths and speculations.

What the Church on the island of Crete needed was spiritual leadership and mentoring. Paul tells Titus:

> **For this reason I left you in Crete, that you would set in order what remains and appoint elders in every city as I directed you** (Titus 1:5).

The Church in Crete needed the same thing churches need today: men led by God's Spirit, committed to the Scriptures, uncompromising in their Gospel, fearless in their doctrine, blameless in their pattern of living, pure in their personal relationships.

To this day, the Church needs shepherds—men who will wear the mantle of leadership, understanding the gravity of their role, willingly accepting the responsibility of oversight. Men who will feed the sheep and shepherd and protect and nurture the flock of God.

Yes, *men*.

The Church—then and now—needs men. Men who will step up to the plate of duty, swing the bat of integrity, and run the bases of responsibility.

Titus is going to issue a search . . . for men.

I saw a Levi Strauss ad for Dockers© and found it hard to imagine a company willing to be as politically incorrect in our confused culture where sexual identity is blurred, if not completely erased. It was titled "Wear the

Pants," and put forth a *Man*-ifesto (the company's term, with the emphasis on Man). The following is the unedited version:

> Once upon a time, men wore the pants, and wore them well. Women rarely had to open doors, and little old ladies never had to cross the street alone. Men took charge because that's what they did. But somewhere along the way the world decided it no longer needed men. Disco by disco, latte by non-fat latte, men were stripped of their khakis and left stranded on the road between boyhood and androgyny [neither a masculine nor feminine state of being]. But today, there are questions our genderless society has no answers for. The world sits idly by as cities crumble, children misbehave, and those little old ladies remain on one side of the street. For the first time since bad guys, we need heroes. We need grownups. We need men to put down the plastic fork, step away from the salad bar, and untie the world from the tracks of complacency. It's time to get your hands dirty. It's time to answer the call of manhood. It's time to wear the pants.[4]

This tongue-in-cheek piece created quite a firestorm, especially among feminists. I'm surprised somebody didn't sue Levi Strauss & Co. for emotional duress.

Paul will later address what it means to answer the call to manhood in **Titus 2**, where he delivers a radical counterculture definition through Titus to the Church . . . and he'll later do the same thing for women.

But first and foremost, Paul is going to tell Titus to identify men who are willing and qualified to *wear the pants* in the assembly over whom God has given them authority and leadership and care.

Get ready for a politically incorrect message.

SETTING THINGS IN ORDER

Today if you speak about male headship—male leadership—not only in the home but in the Church, you are becoming as politically incorrect *inside* the evangelical church as you are in the world.

If Paul told Titus to implement a unique culture of leadership and responsibility inside the Church which was surrounded by sexual confusion and religious perversion, he certainly expects us to do the same today by the redeeming, life-transforming power of the Holy Spirit.

Now we get the hint that all is not well among the Christians on the island of Crete. Paul tells Titus to *set in order what remains* (Titus 1:5).

This phrase *set in order* comes from the Greek verb *orthow*, which we use in orthopedics.[5] The word was used by the Greeks to speak of setting broken bones or straightening out crooked ones.[6]

The verb *orthow* is also used today in the word orthodontics. My wife and I invested heavily in the practice of one particular orthodontist. I have often told my daughters they have $4,000 smiles . . . so stop frowning. I had braces, too, growing up. In those days, they weren't flexible or plastic, and patients didn't choose colors for spacers. There was only one kind: shiny metal—and you were called Rin Tin Tin for good reason.

I had a really pronounced overbite, and by the time I was in middle school, one of my front teeth stuck out so far my friends joked that I could eat watermelon through a picket fence.

In high school, my younger brothers loved to get my middle school picture and show it to friends who came over. There I was: big ears—which had decided to grow faster than the rest of my body—red hair, freckled face, and crooked teeth.

I was really glad my parents sacrificed dearly to pay for braces. If you had braces—especially back in those days—you know how they hurt, and they required time and effort to clean. They didn't fix my overbite overnight, but the effort and adjustment was worth it all.

And that's the word used Paul uses here—the only place it shows up in the New Testament.[7] He wants Titus to straighten out those things that are crooked and out of place in the churches on the island of Crete—the things that need to be *set in order*.

Paul implies that Titus needs to *set in order what remains* still *out of order*. In other words, Paul wasn't able to finish the job organizing the churches and setting into place proper leadership structures and relationships. There were still broken things to mend and crooked things to straighten out.

It would be painful . . . it would require extra attention . . . it would be emotionally costly—and the problems wouldn't be fixed overnight.

But it would be worth it all.

Can you imagine Titus receiving this as the *introduction* to the letter?

He's going to arrive at an established church, and the people are naturally going to ask him just what he intends to do.

"Well, I'm gonna straighten you out . . . and it's gonna hurt."

"Who said you had the right to do that?"

"I have a letter written to me from the apostle himself; look right here":

> *I left you in Crete that you would set in order what remains and appoint elders in every city as I directed you* (Titus 1:5).

I imagine you could hear a pin drop in every assembly where this was announced. There could be no doubt, Titus had been [authorized and] instructed by a leading apostle to find, select, train, and set apart such men to serve.[8]

APPOINTING THE LEADERS

The term Paul uses here in reference to the men who will lead and serve in each church is *presbuteros* (elder). It was borrowed from the life of the Jewish synagogue, where the common name for a leader was elder. Since the early Church was primarily Jewish, this was perfectly suitable—and immediately recognizable.

Luke writes that *they had appointed elders* (plural) *for them in every church* [singular] (Acts 14:23*a*).

- They would determine church policy *(Acts 15)*.

- They would oversee church affairs *(Acts 20)*.

- They would rule, teach, and preach *(1 Timothy 5)*.

- They would exhort and refute false teaching *(Titus 1:9)*.

- They would act as shepherds, setting an example for all the flock *(1 Peter 5)*.[9]

Throughout the New Testament, we discover three interchangeable terms in reference to this one office of male leadership.

Presbuteros

Presbuteros is one of the words often translated *elder*. From the earliest beginnings of the Church, it was clear that a group of godly men were identified to take responsibility for the development and direction of a church.

The passages that use the term *presbuteros* seem to focus on the character—the *authenticity*—of the man.

Episkopos

Episkopos is usually translated *bishop*. *Episkopos* was to the Greek what *presbuteros* was to the Hebrew. It highlights the delegated *authority* of this office.

Elders aren't under the authority of the flock, the flock is under theirs. Correctly understood, the elder doesn't even speak for the flock; they speak for Christ *to* the flock.

Little wonder that such care would be given to a group of men burdened and blessed with so great a task as shepherding the flock of God.

The term *bishop* would have been immediately understood by Gentile converts as someone who was given responsibility by the emperor to govern newly captured city-states. The bishop was responsible, not to the people, but to the emperor who had delegated to him the right to lead.[10]

Jesus Christ is called the *episkopos* of our souls *(1 Peter 2:25)*; that is, He is the One with the right to rule over our newly conquered lives—He is the govenor of our souls.

So *presbuteros* and *episkopos* were two terms that emerged in early New Testament church life for the men who governed and guided the church, under delegated authority from their Emperor, Jesus Christ.

You can easily see how the Presbyterian and Episcopalian denominations created their names by transliterating these two Greek terms:

- Episkopos = Episcopalian
- Presbuteros = Presbyterian

Perhaps this is why Baptists have been so reluctant to use perfectly biblical titles for this office. Frankly, it's a lot more important to be biblical than

Baptist . . . or Presbyterian . . . or Episcopalian. We need to be committed to the vocabulary of Scripture rather than the vocabulary of denominationalism.

Those who lead the Church will one day give an account for their biblical leadership, not for their ecclesiastical traditions. Every elder will one day experience a stricter judgment *(James 3:1)*, and the question will be whether they fulfilled in the twenty-first century what the Spirit of God commanded the elders to do in the first century.

The culture may have changed over the centuries, but the *role* of shepherd did not. Methods changed but objectives never did. The question will be, "Did the elder wear the mantle of a shepherd well?"

Poimen

The third term for this same leader is from the Greek noun *poimen*. It clearly speaks to the overarching *activity* of the office.

The word appears less often and is translated *pastor* or *shepherd*. The Apostle Peter uses the term when he refers to Jesus Christ as our *Chief Shepherd* (1 Peter 5:4).

Poimen focuses on the feeding of the flock more than anything else. In fact, when Paul wrote to the Ephesians of the gifted men given by Christ to the Church, of the three terms he could have used when referring to the church leader, he chose to categorically specify this office with the title pastor/shepherd—literally, *feeder (Ephesians 4:11)*.

Other texts reinforce this activity of the shepherd:

> *Feed the flock of God which is among you* (1 Peter 5:1–2 KJV).

> *"Simon, son of Jonas, lovest thou me? . . . Feed my sheep"* (John 21:17 KJV).

Jesus wanted Peter to lead them into green pastures, well fed and well taken care of.

That's why it isn't optional that pastors deliver the Word to the flock and expound on it and teach it and apply it and exhort obedience to it . . . anything else is barren ground. The Scriptures are the fertile fields of green pastures for the souls of the flock.

A woman met with a pastor in our community after moving here. She was mature enough spiritually to be concerned about the church she would attend. Her list of questions for the pastor ran thus: Did he hold to the Scriptures? Did he teach the Scriptures verse by verse? Did he believe the Scriptures were applicable to life in the twenty-first century? After a couple of minutes, the pastor interrupted her and said, "Listen, I can tell from your questions what kind of church you're looking for—and let me just tell you we're not into that—but I recommend you visit Colonial. I hear that's what they do over there."

That isn't a compliment to me—it's a condemnation of that false shepherd who either didn't know his true role or had voluntarily abandoned it for something else.

His response to the woman was also a commendation of the entire body of elders in our fellowship who share with me a passion to deliver the Word of God to our flock—and to our generation.

Our country may very well be deserving of the condemnation God delivered to the shepherds of Israel when He said they were feeding *themselves* but not feeding the flock (*Ezekiel 34:2*).

This is our commission as elders/bishops/pastors: preach and teach the Word and lead the flock into the green pastures of God's soul-satisfying truth.

To summarize:

- *elder* refers to the genuine *authenticity* of the shepherd;
- *bishop* refers to the delegated *authority* of the shepherd;
- *pastor* refers to the primary *activity* of the shepherd.

And from these three terms, along with all the passages where these terms appear, emerge the role of the leader.

DEFINING THE ELDERS

There are four principal characteristics of this shepherding role.

Plural in Number

It's very telling that not one explicit reference to a one-pastor/single-elder-led church appears anywhere in the New Testament. In fact, every place where *elder* is used, it is plural except when John and Peter used it to refer to themselves.

This doesn't mean there weren't congregations led by one pastor/elder—no doubt there were new or immature churches that had no more than one man qualified to lead. Further, we can also assume there were churches that had *no one* qualified—or identified—to lead them. Evidently, the churches on the island of Crete fit this category: leaderless . . . or worse—they had unqualified men leading these congregations.

However, to our point, we are never given an example of a flock in the New Testament where one man served alone.

Proponents of a one-elder rule say that there were elders in a city church that was composed of many individual house-churches where a singular elder had oversight; all the house churches in the city got together periodically, and from that you had a plurality of elders. But the fact still remains: the Church was seen as *one* church in that city, and decisions were made by a collective process of elders in reference to the whole Church, not the individual parts. This view effectively supports a plurality of leaders making decisions.[11]

Still others refer to the letters sent by Christ to individual churches in *Revelation 2–3*. They argue that since the letters to the churches were delivered to a singular angel (*angelos*) of the church, that this angel—or messenger—was a reference to a singular elder or singular pastor-teacher.

The problem with that view is that we're simply guessing. In fact, if the angel was indeed a pastor, it would just as easily reinforce the concept of a leader among leaders—a first among equals—in *Revelation 2–3*, since we're not told that this elder didn't represent a group of elders.[12]

In fact, we know that one of the churches that received a letter did, indeed, have more than one elder: Ephesus *(Revelation 2:1–7)*.

The principle of a leader among leaders is illustrated in the church at Jerusalem with the prominence of James, the pastor-teacher who was visibly, observably leading the other leaders, directing the church toward a final decision regarding Gentile converts *(Acts 15:13–21)*. This same text clearly refers to a plurality of elders within the Jerusalem church *(Acts 15:22)*.

We're also told more specifically that some elders are deserving of greater honor. Paul wrote to Timothy in *1 Timothy 5:17–18* that those elders who worked hard at preaching and teaching were worthy of double honor—a word determined in this context to refer to financial remuneration.

This, by the way, also informs us that *all* elders in a local church didn't necessarily spend the majority of their time preaching or teaching. This hints at the emerging role of elders who teamed together in leadership but were responsible for a variety of roles within a local church.

What's important to understand is that there is not one passage that explicitly says one elder has *all* the authority in a church. In fact, that would be characteristic of a cult, not a church.[13]

When taken at face value, the Scriptures indicate that elders (plural) were appointed in every church (singular), and the sharing of responsibilities and authority was the sign of a healthy, vibrant church.

The public, observable role of godly men leading a single church was nothing less than a wonderful testimony of humility, grace, and unity.

A woman visited our church for several weeks before deciding to leave; she sent an email to me in which her chief complaint was simply put: "The problem I have with this church is that there are too many men in leadership."

I wanted to thank her for that observation, but I knew she probably wouldn't appreciate it.

Provide Oversight

While we've touched on the subject of teaching and feeding, this text reinforces the issue once again. There are elders in many churches who love the idea of ruling and leading, authority and power, prestige and prominence. But shepherding and feeding is somewhere lower on the list.

I love the story about the new pastor who wasn't doing a very good job in the pulpit. His message was often confusing as he fumbled for words and thoughts; it was obvious to the flock that he wasn't studying and preparing for his sermons. The other elders finally asked him in a meeting, "When exactly do you prepare your messages?" He responded, "As you know, I live a block away . . . I prepare my sermon as I walk to church on Sunday morning." Their remedy: they moved him a mile from the church.

Walter Kaiser pointed out the anemic state of affairs in the American Church, and he placed the responsibility squarely on the shoulders of shepherds who were doing everything *except* preaching the Word of God:

It is no secret that Christ's Church is not at all in good health. She has been languishing because she has been fed, as the current line has it, "junk food"; all kinds of artificial preservatives and all sorts of unnatural substitutes have been served up to her. As a result, theological and biblical malnutrition has afflicted the very generation that has taken such giant steps to make sure its physical health is never damaged by using food that is harmful to their bodies. At the same time, a spiritual famine has resulted from the absence of any genuine [preaching] of the Word of God.

I would add to that my own observation: church leaders in America have become experts at dissecting life and human experience rather than the Word of life.

In our generation the average church leader today can quote Peter Drucker but not the Apostle Peter. They can give you leadership insights from John Maxwell but not the Apostle John.

There's nothing wrong with principles from other authors, but the pastor-teacher can only give to the congregation what he is studying . . . the Bible seems to be missing from the average church leader's reading list.

My father and I were talking about how pastors are influenced by the material and teachers they've allowed to impact them—and how much this can affect their preaching and philosophy of ministry.

He said something I never forgot because it was so simple and yet so profound: "You know when I was growing up on the farm, we could always tell when our cow Bessie had gotten into the onion grass . . . we could always taste it in her milk."

We feed others what we've been grazing on ourselves.

Let's go back to the Scriptures . . . undiluted, unmixed, untainted truth. The role of the elder is to see that the flock is fed the milk and meat of the Word, cared for and directed by the wisdom that comes from above *(James 3:15–17)*.

The joy of any elder is that which John the Apostle wrote:

> *I have no greater joy than this, to hear of my children walking in the truth* (3 John 4).

That is a true shepherd's joy.

Protect and Guard

The mantle of the shepherd is often stained with blood, sweat, and tears. It is his role also to warn and protect the flock, to refute those who contradict the Gospel. We warn the flock just as fathers warn young men—and warn their daughters . . . of young men!

As a father of daughters, I can appreciate the answer that basketball Hall of Famer Charles Barkley gave to a reporter who once asked him how he was going to handle his young daughter's future boyfriends. He said, "Well, I figure if I shoot the first guy, word will spread."

I'm not recommending violence . . . but I am recommending vigilance. Paul never stopped warning elders:

> *"Be on guard for yourselves and for all the flock, among which the Holy Spirit has made you overseers, to shepherd the church of God which He purchased with His own blood. I know that after my departure savage wolves will come in among you, not sparing the flock . . . therefore be on the alert"* (Acts 20:28–31).

The wolves are coming.

Philip Keller wrote in his wonderful book taken from his many years raising and tending sheep:

> [Paul's warning] reminds me of the behavior of a flock of sheep under attack from dogs, cougars, bears, and wolves. Often, in blind fear, they will stand rooted to the spot, watching their companions being cut to shreds. The predator will pounce upon one, then another of the flock, raking and tearing them with tooth and claw. Meanwhile, the other sheep may even act as if they do not hear or recognize the carnage going on around them. It is as though they are totally oblivious to the peril of their own position.[14]

Sheep are not designed to fight . . . shepherds are.

Charles Jefferson pastored in the late 1800s and wrote:

> The journey from the cradle to the grave is hazardous . . . if every man is surrounded by perils; if the universe is alive with

forces hostile to the soul, then watchfulness becomes one of the most critical of all the pastor's responsibilities. Elders are to be protectors, watchmen, defenders, and guardians of God's people.[15]

Perhaps that's why one national Christian leader answered a reporter the way he did when he was asked, "What is the most important quality for a leader to possess?" His answer: "Courage."

That may be necessary for church leaders, especially in these days:

- to discipline sin;
- to confront internal strife and division;
- to call immorality "sin" in the face of cultural approval;
- to stand against doctrinal error;
- to refute false teaching and false teachers.

Prioritize Leadership

The Church—as counterculture as this may sound, especially to American ears—is *not* a democracy. It isn't even a republic.

Elders are not elected to represent their various constituencies in the church body. They are not representatives of the people to bring their opinions into a boardroom where the largest voting bloc gains the greatest representation. In fact, elders actually are not accountable to the people—they are accountable to God's Word, each other and, ultimately, to their Chief Shepherd as they lead the people for His glory.

The writer of Hebrews weighs in and writes to the same issue with some rather politically incorrect words to the flock:

> *Obey your leaders and submit to them, for they keep watch over your souls as those who give an account. Let them do this with joy and not with grief* (Hebrews 13:17).

Elders do not speak *for* the people as their representatives—they speak *to* the people as representatives of Jesus Christ, the Shepherd of the Church.

ACCEPTING THE CHALLENGE

The Apostle Peter clearly revealed the authority of the elders as well as their accountability to God:

> [S]*hepherd the flock of God among you, exercising oversight not under compulsion, but voluntarily, according to the will of God* (1 Peter 5:2*a*).

Peter continues as he both warns every elder and, at the same time, encourages them:

> [A]*nd not for sordid gain, but with eagerness; nor yet as lording it over those allotted to your charge, but proving to be examples to the flock. And when the Chief Shepherd appears, you* [elders] *will receive the unfading crown of glory* (1 Peter 5:2*b*–4).

In other words, the elders will one day give to Christ an account of exercising their godly authority and oversight. The elder clearly anticipates a unique crown of glory for having provided both an exposition and example of God's truth.

After thirty years of shepherding the same flock, I can say that wearing the mantle of a shepherd has been my great joy. Yes, it can be unbearably heavy at times. Grief and joy take turns, and the penalties of leadership often outnumber prizes. There are innumerable battles along the way and, at times, only the grace of God and the example of Christ's persevering love for His Church will keep one foot moving in front of the other.

Elders are in it for life.

Fighting wolves and feeding sheep isn't optional. In fact, whether or not the flock ever brings joy to the under-shepherd, he has committed his life and ministry to obedience, knowing that in the end, his greatest reward is in bringing *his* Chief Shepherd great joy.

More than any other sound, a true shepherd is always listening for the applause of heaven. He's willing to accept that he will rarely—if ever—hear it on earth.

Besides, sheep bleat . . . they don't clap.

[N]amely, if any man is above reproach, the husband of one wife, having children who believe, not accused of dissipation or rebellion.

–Titus 1:6

CHAPTER FIVE

RAISING THE BAR

Titus 1:6

POSITIONS AVAILABLE . . . APPLY NOW

I n AD 394, a church leader named Jerome wrote a letter to a younger elder in which he bemoaned the lack of qualified leadership in the Church. He included some rather scathing remarks for his own generation of church leaders who seemed more interested in the beauty of cathedrals than the integrity of her leaders. He wrote, "Many build churches nowadays; their walls and pillars of glowing marble, their ceilings glittering with gold, and their altars studded with jewels. Yet to the choice of Christ's ministers in the church, no heed is [given]."[1]

In other words, cathedrals were more important than character. This isn't a new problem. Church offices and seats in the boardroom have often been given to the wealthy, the winsome, and the well-connected. Positions of authority have been granted to the faithfully attending, positively supporting church members—regardless of character or calling.

This is all the more dangerous when you consider the fact that church leaders are the hearts, hands, and feet of the Chief Shepherd. This same Good Shepherd has entrusted His Church into the care of men who *must* be good because they must guard His most costly possession—His Bride for whom He died. Shepherds who lead the Church are literally guiding *His* Bride on her way to the marriage feast.

The more value you place on the Bride of Christ, the more value you will place on those in leadership in the Body of Christ.

Can you imagine any mother or father saying to a random stranger on the street, "Can we hire you to babysit our kids for the afternoon? We don't know much about you and we really don't care what you're gonna be like around our kids . . . we just need a break." That would obviously—and painfully—indicate a low level of value placed on the lives of those children by their parents.

The higher the *value*, the greater the *concern* for those entrusted to care for them. If you had come over to babysit our twin sons when they were a year old—if you actually thought you were up to the challenge—you'd only be there because my wife trusted you and knew quite a bit about you.

Still, when you arrived, you would discover that she had the whole evening mapped out for you: bath time; story time marked in the right book; prayer time instructions (the twins would try to extend this exercise in order to stay up as long as possible). Even their sippy cups would be in the fridge, already mixed with fruit juice and Benadryl—just kidding!

Details included which boy got the white blanket and was tucked in with Barry Beaver; which one got the green blanket and was snuggled next to Michael Monkey . . . you wouldn't want to get this mixed up!

It had taken months to get those boys on a schedule, and my wife wasn't about to let it be ruined by one night of riotous living in some far country.

But there was more to it than a schedule; those boys were our precious children and we weren't going to hand them off to just anybody, to do just anything they good and well pleased.

Does God care any less about His children than we do about ours? Does He not entrust His precious children to those who love the flock, want to guard the flock, feed the flock, and guide the flock . . . who are willing to lay down their lives for the safety and spiritual health of the flock?

In one passage where Christ tells the Church to follow their leaders, an interesting nuance of leadership much like parenting comes to the surface. The writer of Hebrews instructs the believers:

> *Obey your leaders and submit to them, for they keep watch over your souls* (Hebrews 13:17a).

That word translated *keep watch* literally refers to someone going without sleep.[2]

What loving mother or father hasn't lost sleep over the care of their young child or the concern for an older one? Losing sleep is part of being a parent. I don't know about you, but I had a hard time falling asleep while my children were still out at night. Our two daughters were the last to leave the nest, and they knew that Saturday night's curfew was especially important because until they were safely home, I couldn't sleep . . . and I needed to sleep before a long Sunday schedule.

Numberless parents—especially of older children—have stayed awake at night, praying for both their physical and spiritual wellbeing. That's the role of a loving, caring, spiritually minded parent.

Frankly, God says that He wants the same for *His* children. He wants to entrust His children to leaders who are willing to lose sleep over their genuine concern and care for the flock.

So it should come as no surprise that God has revealed a list of more than twenty standards for those men who will lead and guard the Church. And unless someone is adamant about suppressing the obvious, it's pretty clear that God isn't about to entrust the wellbeing of His Church to just anybody . . . to do whatever suits them!

In the previous chapter, we discussed the biblical roles of the elder/pastor/bishop—the three terms used in reference to the same man/office. He guards, protects, feeds, and leads, as well as loves and cares for the flock.

Beyond that, we're not given much more about the role of an elder. In fact, we're told a lot more about *who* an elder is than what an elder *does*.

PERSONAL QUALIFICATIONS

There are two lists in the Bible which give us the qualifications of these shepherds/leaders. The longer list is in *1 Timothy 3* and the shorter list is found here, where Paul writes:

> [A]*ppoint elders in every city as I directed you, namely, if any man is above reproach, the husband of one wife, having children who believe, not accused of dissipation or rebellion. For the overseer must be above reproach as God's steward, not self-willed, not quick-tempered, not addicted to wine, not pugnacious, not fond of sordid gain, but hospitable, loving what is good, sensible, just, devout,*

self-controlled, holding fast the faithful word which is in accordance with the teaching, so that he will be able both to exhort in sound doctrine and to refute those who contradict (Titus 1:5–10).

You get to the end of a list like this and every church leader senses something stirring in his soul that feels a lot like, "I need to resign."

If we compare the list in *1 Timothy* with this list in **Titus**, there are twenty-three standards for an elder. If we include *aspiring* or *desiring the office* from *1 Timothy 3:1*, there are twenty-four qualifications.

Above Reproach

Who can possibly meet these standards? Especially when the first qualification so clearly demands that an elder be **above reproach** (Titus 1:6a). You really don't need to read any further beyond this one phrase alone to wonder how *any* man can step forward and sign up.

It's helpful to understand the word Paul uses here translated **above reproach** does not refer to perfection but to a *pattern*.[3] It refers to a man without any glaring omission, aberration, addiction, perversion, or wrongdoing in his life or character that becomes an obvious hindrance to his credibility.

Above reproach can be translated *without a handle*. In other words, there isn't any obvious baggage by which an elder can be clearly and undeniably indicted.

Keep in mind that an elder, like any other member of the flock, is a fallen sinner . . . and sinners tend to sin. But here's the key difference: the elder, while not having attained godly perfection, is a man devoted to demonstrating a pattern of godly living.

In other words, he doesn't claim flawless *perfection*, but he demonstrates faithful *progression*; a pattern of spiritual progress provided in **Titus 1**.

Above reproach serves as a categorical heading upon which all the following qualifications are hinged, pursuing an **above reproach** pattern of faithful integrity as it relates to his marriage, his children, his character, and his public lifestyle.

And why must he pursue this pattern of holiness? Because his life is a pattern for all who follow him. Leadership is influence. Leadership is endorsement. Leaders are intended by God to be followed—believed, as well as imitated.

Worthy of Imitation

In a Sunday morning sermon I mentioned that I'd enjoyed a delicious meal at a nearby restaurant. The manager contacted me the next day and said I was welcome to come by and get a free meal as a thank-you. He told me that because of my comment, the line of customers that Sunday afternoon had stretched out the door and down the sidewalk.

Whether we want to admit it or not, the very nature of leadership *invites* imitation. The New Testament not only acknowledges this fact, it unashamedly *encourages* it. Paul wrote to the believers in Philippi:

> *Brethren, join in following my example, and observe those who walk according to the pattern you have in us* (Philippians 3:17).

Another text encourages the believer to:

> *Remember those who led you, who spoke the word of God to you; and considering the result of their conduct, imitate their faith* (Hebrews 13:7).

Peter tells the elders to *be examples* [*tupos*—literally, a pattern] *to the flock* (1 Peter 5:3), and Paul wrote to the Corinthian believers, *Be imitators of me, just as I also am of Christ* (1 Corinthians 11:1).

Paul didn't tell them to imitate him just because he was their leader— Paul clearly said to imitate him *as* he imitated Christ. People can't see Christ, but they can certainly see His representatives. Because of that, **Titus 1** is effectively the pattern of the character of *Jesus Christ* put into print.

A leader must pursue this pattern of living because he is setting the standard for all those who follow him, patterning after him their own lives and conduct. He *must* lead the flock to mimic the character of Christ.

We are, by nature, copycats. Madison Avenue depends on it; there's a billion dollar clothing industry built on the fact that we basically want to be like each other.

A mall in Orlando advertised a new design of Nike athletic shoes—a limited edition, going on sale at the moment the NBA All-Star game started in that city. When the supply of shoes was gone, the sale would be over. Public interest quickly grew. After all, those shoes were the style worn by the athletes people looked up to, and because their heroes wore them, they wanted to wear them, too. Before the sale even began, riot police had to be called out to maintain order while the crowd gathered . . . waiting for the moment the game began.

There's nothing wrong with human beings wanting to look like people they admire, but there's a dangerous downside: celebrities might not be worth admiring, much less imitating.

No wonder James the Apostle said:

> *Let not many of you become teachers, my brethren, knowing that as such we will incur a stricter judgment* (James 3:1).

Why? Because a teacher's life is multiplied many times over in the lives of those who follow him. For that very reason, Paul begins with the particular qualification that an elder must be ***above reproach***.

One author wrote that this phrase refers to a general assessment of a man's maturity and reputation.[4]

It's actually a compound Greek word; the first part means *up* and the second means *to call*, which taken together means *to call up*.[5]

An elder, then, is one who's been called up—he's received a calling to a higher standard of living. What comes to mind is the phrase *raising the bar*—after a pole vaulter clears the hurdle, it's raised to a higher level.

To call up can refer simply to raising the standard. In a world where the pattern for good character has reached an all-time low, it has never been more desperately needed.

Eugene Peterson exposes the loss of integrity today:

> There is little to admire and less to imitate in the people who are prominent in our culture. We have celebrities but not saints. If we look around for what it means to be a mature, whole, blessed person, we don't find much. These people are around, but they aren't easy to pick out. No journalist interviews them. No talk show features them. They do not set trends. There is no cash value in them. No Oscars are given for integrity. At year's end [when the lists of the ten best-dressed or the ten best-looking are compiled], no one compiles a list of the ten best-lived lives. Our society today is devoid of models. Neither the adventure of goodness nor the pursuit of righteousness gets headlines [anymore].[6]

The question isn't, "Where are the perfect people?" but, "Is there a pattern—a person—for people to follow?"

According to Paul, pastors were to provide the pattern. In fact, *every* Christian is to set an example—even the younger believers are implicitly challenged by Paul as he wrote to young Timothy:

> [I]*n speech, conduct, love, faith and purity, show yourself an example of those who believe* (I Timothy 4:12).

To Titus, Paul will write later that young men are to **show** [themselves] **to be an example of good deeds** (Titus 2:7*a*).

If the elders are to be godly because they are being imitated, then those who are following have the same goal—and the same high calling from God to live their lives with the uppermost standards of purity and holiness.

That's why the Apostle Peter could write:

> *Now for this very reason also, applying all diligence, in your faith supply moral excellence, and in your moral excellence, knowledge, and in your knowledge, self-control, and in your self-control, perseverance, and in your perseverance, godliness, and in your godliness, brotherly kindness, and in your brotherly kindness, love. For if these qualities are yours and are increasing, they render you neither useless nor unfruitful* (2 Peter 1:5–8).

Frankly, it's time for the entire Church to raise the bar.

Husband of One Wife

[I]*f any man is above reproach, the husband of one wife* (Titus 1:6*a*).

You could understand this to mean that the elder is to provide a pattern for living as it relates to the commitment he's demonstrating to his wife. He is **the husband of one wife**. Paul isn't prohibiting a single man or a widower from becoming an elder. He's simply setting the standard for the man who *is* married.

In fact, the substance of Paul's statement isn't upon the fact that an elder has to *have* a wife—Paul simply stresses that he is to be openly devoted to **one wife**.[7]

Literally translated, he is to be a *one-woman man*. Sounds like a country and western song, doesn't it? But not many people in the first century were singing this particular tune, because infidelity was acceptable among married men. In the Roman Empire, men kept a legal wife for inheritance purposes and the bearing of children but were unapologetically involved with mistresses, slaves, and temple prostitutes.[8]

Divorce was also rampant. One man who lived in the first century left documents revealing he had been legally married and divorced twenty-seven times. Roman women were said to have dated the years by the names of their husbands and to have been married so many times they wore out their bridal veils.

Paul is certainly not intending to communicate that an elder can be married to one woman *at a time*, so long as he seems to be committed to his current wife. The particular language he chose refers to a public awareness that an elder is clearly devoted to his wife. In other words, he's not on the prowl for another woman—or two—on the side. He's a one-woman man.

By the way, this idea would have been as radical to the first-century world as it has become in this twenty-first century world.

We live in a culture where twenty-four million Americans will have been involved with someone other than their spouse this past week alone. In fact, one particular website was designed for people willing "to kick their vows to the curb." A cell phone version of the site was recently released so no one would leave a trail of evidence on their computer at home or work. In just one month, 679,000 men and women used this website to begin an extramarital affair. The CEO of the site shrugged off any criticism during an interview, saying, "We're just a platform. People cheat because their lives aren't working for them." And then he made this chilling comment that I have actually heard twice in the last few months, "Humans aren't meant to be monogamous."[9]

Monogamy, one woman said in an interview, is *unnatural*. And in a twisted sort of way she's right. Committed, faithful, covenant love to one person goes against our *sinful* nature. It is indeed unnatural to our natural selfishness and pride.

Faithful commitment to loving our spouse requires dying to self . . . and self does not naturally lie down and die.

When Paul wrote to the Ephesians for husbands to love their wives as Christ loved the Church, he left no potential for *natural* inclinations.

Love your wife as Christ loves the Church? Are you kidding?

- He died for the Church.

- He sacrificed His personal comfort for the Church.

- He suffered humiliation for the Church.

- He intercedes persistently for the Church.

- He loves the Church regardless of any lack of affection in return.

- He longs to be in the presence of the Church.

- He desires the final glory of the Church in His coming kingdom.

So, then, this would mean that elders—and imitators—are to demonstrate that they are pursuing this high calling to:

- die for their spouses;

- sacrifice their comforts for them;

- suffer any humiliation alongside them;

- take on their suffering and help bear it;

- maintain intercession for their benefit;

- remain faithful regardless of any lack of affection in return;

- long for their final glory in the coming kingdom of Christ.

If that isn't convicting enough, here's the amazing thing about Christ's love for the Church: *in that while we were yet sinners, Christ died for us* (Romans 5:8).

You want to raise the bar? Loving your spouse is not loving them as a saint, but loving them as a sinner—which is exactly how Jesus loves us.[10] And yes, that's just not *natural*.

The elder should be leading the way in this regard; it's one of the qualifications—in fact, it's listed first in both **Titus** and *1 Timothy*.

Perhaps this is why the marriage of the pastor/elder is such a target of the Enemy. If you survey the divorce rates in the United States, you'll discover that pastors have the third highest divorce rate, exceeded only by that of medical doctors and policeman.[11] So more than ever, a man clearly committed to sexual and marital fidelity is becoming harder to find. It was certainly difficult on the island of Crete and throughout the entire empire of Rome.

Keep in mind that the Apostle Paul is not *forbidding* a divorced man from occupying the role of elder or, for that matter, a man who in the past was unfaithful to his wife. Paul is certainly not excusing failure. Instead, Paul is specifically addressing the fact that an elder has earned a reputation in his church and community as a faithful husband.

In fact, because of the public ministry of an elder, Paul is demanding that an elder candidate be viewed by those inside *and outside* the church as a man committed to his wife. In his list of qualifications written to Timothy, Paul required that elder candidates must *have a good reputation with those outside the church* (1 Timothy 3:7).

Again, Paul's language specifically addresses the current, public demonstration of marital commitment and a lifestyle of discretion where the Church—and public—can inspect and trust the commitment he has to his wife.

It doesn't mean the elder doesn't have a good reputation or that he hasn't failed. It *does* mean that he is demonstrating purity in his actions toward other women and loving faithfulness in his actions toward his wife.

There are at least two practical reasons why the Church should pause at this qualification and demand the highest standards of purity and fidelity: First, because an elder's sexual and marital history, as well as his current marriage, will be a matter of public scrutiny like none other. Secondly, and equally important, an elder's loving commitment to his wife must be worthy of imitation—a living illustration of Christ's love for the Church.

God has called the shepherds of the Church to demonstrate in flesh and blood the spiritual, mysterious union of Christ and His Church *(Ephesians 5:25–32)*. And the best way to demonstrate the union of Christ with His Church is for elders to publically and faithfully demonstrate their marital vows, to love their wives, for better or for worse, in sickness and in health, for richer or for poorer, to love and to cherish, till death they do part.

Those in the flock who've experienced the betrayal of an unfaithful spouse or the agony of abandonment and divorce will know how and why their leaders must raise the bar in purity and fidelity.

This is not the time for the bar to be lowered; a pattern of sexual purity and marital priority must be demonstrated—modeled for this generation—by those who lead the Church.

Today, more than ever, the issue of marriage has become all the more confusing within the Church at large. Mainline denominations are ignoring a rather troubling implication of what Paul requires of an elder; that he must be ***the husband of one wife***.

Since homosexuality was an acceptable and predominate feature in Paul's world, we can understand him to include in this standard a heterosexual marriage. In other words, an elder is to be a *one*-woman man, not a *one*-man man.

Even *Time Magazine* caught on to the irony of the current debate within the Church when it reported, "Denominations that once would not tolerate divorced ministers now debate whether or not to accept lesbian [ministers]."[12]

How did the Church change so drastically? By lowering the bar—one notch at a time.

More than ever, it's time to raise the bar in the Church. We can do that one marriage at a time; one self-sacrificing husband at a time; one praying wife at a time; one committed-to-the-Word husband and wife at a time; one couple at a time, dedicated to loving and serving one another as a living demonstration of Christ's love and service to the Church.

Men, especially, it's time for us to reinvest in marriage, to raise the bar in every aspect possible as we pattern our life after the character of Christ.

In Kent Hughes's book *The Disciplines of a Godly Man*, he encourages men to begin spending time with their wives—not to take them for granted—to never stop courting them. He provided, tongue in cheek, the following illustration;

> Years ago in the Midwest, a farmer and his wife were lying in bed during a storm when the funnel of a tornado suddenly lifted the roof right off the house and sucked their bed away with them still in it . . . they just sort of floated around in a big circle. The wife began to cry, and the farmer called out to her that this was no time to cry. She called back that she

couldn't help it—she was just so happy—it was the first time in years they'd gone out together.[13]

Father of Obedient Children

[H]*aving children who believe, not accused of dissipation or rebellion* (Titus 1:6*b*).

Again, Paul isn't requiring that an elder have children; but if he does, this was the standard. First, this phrase **having children** implies that the children are under the authority of their elder/pastor/father. In every culture the conditions of this parental authority may change; during Paul's day in Rome, a father's authority could last a lifetime.

For most of our Western world today, the father's authority typically ends when a child leaves home for college or a career, where they begin to exercise their independence and personal autonomy.

The further description of these children **who believe** has created centuries of interpretive debate, as you can well imagine. Does this mean that every elder must have children who become Christians? And at what age?

The challenge in understanding this qualification is the fact that this adjective *pista* can be translated actively as *believe* or passively as *faithful*.[14] And it's used both ways in the Pastoral Epistles.

The word can certainly refer to a genuine believer/Christian. In fact, Paul uses it this way for masters who are *believers (1 Timothy 6:2)*. But Paul also uses the same word to refer to *faithful* men *(2 Timothy 2:2)*.

The Gospel of Matthew uses it this way, as well, to refer to an *obedient* servant who carries out the request of his master *(Matthew 24:45)*.[15]

So which is it? Is Paul saying that an elder's children have to be Christians or that they have to be obedient to the authority of their father?

Frankly, the only way to determine the meaning of this adjective as either passive or active is the context. And I believe the context here is clearly one of *submission*, not salvation.

Consider the fact that if salvation is the issue, all of the qualifications are under the power of the elder candidate to achieve, except this one. Clearly, the salvation of an elder's children is not a guarantee, nor is their conversion the result of their father's authority to achieve it. Even though every godly elder in the Church desperately longs for and prays for the salvation of his own children, that decision ultimately rests in the sovereign grace of God.

Like godly Samuel in the Old Testament, whose children never adopted his faith in God, an elder in the New Testament cannot *make* his children become Christians . . . either by command or by example.

So the issue at stake here as it relates to an elder's qualification cannot be the *belief* of his children but their *behavior*—and that fits perfectly with *1 Timothy 3:4*, where the elder *must be one who manages his household well, keeping his children under control with all dignity.* Simply put, his children behave.

Further, if this qualification demanded that an elder's children become Christians—if that was the requirement Paul had in mind—the following explanatory clause would be unnecessary: ***not accused of dissipation or rebellion*** (Titus 1:6*b*).

Dissipation was a word used of drunken revelry at pagan festivals.[16]

So if Paul means to say here that an elder's children have to become Christians, then that's all he needs to say. He can put a period after ***believe***. It would be unecessary to add they can't be guilty of pagan, ritualistic drunkenness. That would be like saying, "Your children must be nice to other students in school, and they can't be cannibals." If they're nice, they won't *need* to be told not to kill and eat any of their classmates.

That clarifying phrase at the end of the verse further explains that Paul has their *conduct* in mind, not their *conversion*. Whether or not they are saved will not erase the father's responsibility to maintain order in the home: he simply cannot allow them to stoop to the level of perpetual drunkenness and idolatry.

This text also implies these children are old enough to go to a drunken festival. In other words, they are old enough to resist their father's authority and discredit his reputation. Paul would be insisting that these young men and women, while under their father's authority (aka roof), can't be guilty of this kind of public ***dissipation***.

So let's not lower the bar and say it doesn't matter. It does. Pastors' children can discredit their parents and it needs to be taken seriously.

Paul further adds that these children must not be accused of ***rebellion***. The word Paul uses for ***rebellion*** in this verse is used for someone entirely unable to be ruled.[17] This isn't a momentary temper tantrum. This isn't even referring to intermittent rebellion. This word is used of someone who persistently refuses to submit to the law of God.

Paul doesn't have in mind a child going through a period of rebellion or a child who refuses to pick up his toys or a teenager who sins. He is referring here to a child who is old enough to openly and persistently rebel against the standards of morality and civility represented by his father, to the point where his father's reputation is publically scandalized and discredited.

Again, the context is pointing to a father's *authority* being rejected in the home while the child misbehaves under his roof and rule. The context also implies that this has become the young person's *pattern* of behavior. It also may very well indict the elder candidate's pattern of parenting; a *pattern* that increases suspicion that he lacks genuine concern over his son's or daughter's rebellion—rebellion which has digressed to include drunkenness and paganism.

Paul has in mind here a young person's public carousing which has cemented into obvious and public disdain for his father's authority to the point where the father, having effectively lost control of his household, is now disqualified from leading an assembly of households—the local church.

This standard presented by the apostle is that the elder must maintain dignified control over the children in his care and under his authority. For some children, godly authority is easily received. For others, persistent ungodly behavior will demand eighteen to twenty years of difficult parenting and ongoing discipline in the elder's home.

When this text in Titus is combined with Paul's words to Timothy, the most critical issue isn't actually the behavior of the child but the behavior of the elder candidate in view of his child's rebellion. Does the elder discipline the rebel or excuse him? Does he exercise his authority or ignore her offense? *His* response will determine his qualification to serve as a leader.

Even after his children leave the home, a true shepherd/elder proves his credibility to lead the church by his grief and concern over his adult child's sinful lifestyle. An elder's children may never believe the Gospel and they may choose to follow the world without reservation when they leave the home, but a genuine shepherd's concern, prayer, exhortation, and challenge will never cease on their behalf.

I served part time in a church, leading the choir and working with the youth group, during my senior year in college. Not long after assuming the role, I learned that one of the young women in the choir was sexually involved with an older married man in the community. To make matters worse, she was the daughter of one of the deacons in the church. She lived on her own, but her father's response to the revelation of her sin led to his own disqualification to lead. When he was eventually told about his daughter's immorality, he not only refused to challenge her but, instead, attacked the other leaders for exposing the issue.

This man was discredited and disqualified for leadership—not so much because of his daughter's immorality but because he refused to demonstrate a godly response. Instead of lovingly challenging her sinful lifestyle, he demanded that the church leaders ignore the issue. In fact, he was infuriated that anyone suggest she should step down from serving in the choir. His refusal to confront her actions effectively condoned her actions; in so doing, this man failed to demonstrate the pattern of leadership for those who followed him.

Tragically, he lowered the bar for that entire church.

SUBMIT RESUMÉ

Paul is passionate for Titus to find men who will raise the bar as high as possible; men who recognize that it is time for the Church to represent the pursuit of *holy* living in the midst of a world equally passionate about *unholy* living.

In our marriages and in our homes, let's resist the natural undertow of our flesh and our culture. Let's raise the bar and pursue our high calling in Christ Jesus . . . He is deserving of nothing less:

Love so amazing, so divine,
Demands my soul, my life, my all.[18]

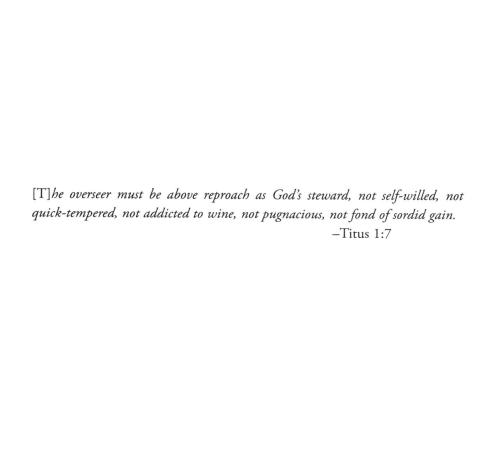

[T]*he overseer must be above reproach as God's steward, not self-willed, not quick-tempered, not addicted to wine, not pugnacious, not fond of sordid gain.*

—Titus 1:7

CHAPTER SIX

TWENTY-FIRST CENTURY STEWARDS

Titus 1:7

AN AGE-OLD DILEMMA

S ir Arthur Conan Doyle was a medical student with a yearning for adventure when he first began writing stories for magazines. After graduating, he began the practice of medicine and continued to pursue writing. In the late 1880s, the characters Sherlock Holmes and his sidekick, Dr. Watson, appeared; the series in which the great detective solved mysteries was born.

On one occasion, Doyle decided to play a practical joke on a dozen close friends and prominent business associates. He sent them all the same telegram anonymously, which simply announced, "All is discovered!" Without ever intending to, he created quite a scandal: within forty-eight hours, half of the recipients of his telegram had mysteriously left the country . . . without a word!

Evidently those men had secrets.

Diogenes, the fourth-century BC cynic and philosopher, was known to walk around Athens with a lantern burning brightly. When asked why, he answered that he was looking for an honest man and having a hard time finding one.

Warren W. Wiersbe, former pastor of Moody Church and a prolific author, wrote in *The Integrity Crisis*:

> The Church has grown accustomed to hearing people question the Gospel simply because the message seems foolish; but today the situation is embarrassingly reversed, for now the *messenger* is suspect.[1]

In other words, where have all the honest church leaders gone?

The reason this matters to the Church is fairly obvious. A cynical world today is basically looking for the same thing. And they're asking the same questions: "Why should we listen to the Church leaders? How do we know you're telling the truth? Do you really believe that stuff yourself? And if you do, are there some secrets you're hoping never get uncovered?"

WHO'S MINDING THE STORE?

Paul the Apostle will reveal that integrity begins with the Church asking some questions of her own: Who's leading the Church and what *exactly* qualifies them to lead?

In his commentary on Titus, Chuck Swindoll writes that Paul demanded leaders to be men of character, regardless of their age, their wealth, their experience, their power, or their position. Leaders must demonstrate proven Christian maturity.[2]

A leading Christian statesman came to Colonial several years ago; he was a pastor so well known that if I told you much more, you might figure out who he was. He's with the Lord now and I don't want to disparage him in any way.

On one occasion when he was visiting, I was showing him around my hometown; our church was young and we were looking for land and needed money to erect our first building. He said rather matter-of-factly, "What you need to do is put well-known, wealthy men on your board. Their influence and financial resources will provide for you to do what you need to do."

While I thanked him for his advice, I remembered thinking to myself, *Business connections and financial portfolios aren't in the biblical list of qualifications for a church leader.*

Several years later, long after this man had resigned from ministry, a scandal arrested the attention of the city where he had pastored. The chairman of his church board for decades—a prestigious banker and landowner—and his wife were involved in a car accident and killed. I learned that their funeral was well-attended and very elaborate; their deaths impacted thousands of people.

But the news that came out shortly afterward strongly affected that city in an entirely different way. When the man's will was probated by the court, a young woman in her twenties arrived, claiming to be the deceased man's illegitimate daughter. She had proof that he had been secretly providing for her all those years—in the very same town.

The family, the church, the ministries and, most importantly, the name and cause of Christ was sullied as the news spread throughout the community. What's more, all the major decisions the man had made over the past few decades were now in question.

That doesn't mean a banker can't be an elder or that a wealthy or well-connected businessman is disqualified to be a servant-leader. It doesn't mean that wealth is evil or that someone influential in the community has a secret or two he's hiding. The point is, choosing leaders according to business acumen or success isn't the standard provided by God. How much a man owns doesn't qualify him for spiritual oversight.

Paul reminds Titus that qualifying for the role of elder has nothing to do with a financial portfolio—it has everything to do with a spiritual portfolio.

QUALIFICATIONS FOR THE JOB

For the overseer must be above reproach as God's **steward** (Titus 1:7*a*).

Paul now changes the term from what is found in ***Titus 1:5***; he shifts from *presbuteros* (*elder*) to *episkopos* (*bishop*): ***For the overseer*** [bishop] ***must be above reproach***.

Why this shift in terminology from elder to bishop? The Catholic commentaries would maintain that a bishop is simply higher up on the ecclesiastical food chain than an elder, and thus Paul is now going to give different qualifications for a higher office: bishop.

That's convenient. It separates those of the bishop from the qualifications of an elder, where he must be a faithful husband and father, obviously allowed to be *married* and have children.

Catholic dogma maintains that Paul gives us one list for married elders in the Church and a new list for the office of celibate bishops *(Titus 1:7–9)*, where there's no reference to a wife or children. And then, of course, you're off and running up the celibate food chain to, eventually, cardinals and, finally, the pope.

The problem with all that tradition and hierarchy is the verse itself. The *text* actually ruins all of that. It begins with the little Greek word γαρ translated *for*: **For the overseer must be above reproach** (Titus 1:7). In other words, Paul is effectively continuing his thoughts without taking a grammatical breath . . . he isn't changing the subject.

In fact, grammatically, there's no break in the flow of characteristics.[3]

He's simply giving additional requirements for the same office, along with a further explanation of what kind of elder/bishop/pastor should hold the office of leadership in the Church.

The Apostle Peter, ironically, is the biblical writer who uses the terms elder, bishop, and pastor in the *same* text for the *same* man and the *same* office *(1 Peter 5:2)*.

And Peter was a married man. How inconvenient. At least that would be the obvious assumption, since Jesus healed Peter's mother-in-law *(Matthew 8:14)*. I don't know many men who would be willing to have a mother-in-law without the benefit of a wife.

Paul re-emphasizes the categorical characteristic of blamelessness: **For a bishop must be blameless** (Titus 1:7 KJV). Remember from our previous chapter that this doesn't mean a church leader is flawless; no one could then apply. But, while he isn't flawless, he must be faithful in the *private life* of his marriage and home and be worthy of imitation in his *public life* and character. That's the shift Paul has in mind here—from private life to public life.

In fact, Paul adds an interesting word in this opening phrase: **as God's steward**.

The word **steward** comes from *oikonomos* (*oikos*: house; *nemo*: arranger).[4] A steward is the arranger—the keeper—of the house.

A steward in Paul's day was most often a slave who had risen through the ranks as someone capable, honest, and who could be trusted to manage his master's estate. The steward didn't own the house, he just managed it.

Much like a stewardess—now referred to as a flight attendant—on an airliner. She manages everything inside the plane on behalf of her employer. She doesn't own the plane or the peanuts, but she makes all the arrangements so that the flight, along with that miniscule bag of peanuts, is carried out properly.

The term **steward** in our English language came from an old Anglo-Saxon word *stig-ward* (literally, *keeper of the sty*), which meant he was the keeper of the pigs. That doesn't sound very flattering, but back in the Middle Ages, this was a critical position of management because the survival of the estate depended upon honest and faithful management of their primary meat supply.[5]

The most famous **steward** in the Bible is Joseph *(Genesis 39)*, who was sold into slavery and belonged for a time to Potiphar. He became such a trusted man that Potiphar placed him in the position of manager—**steward**—of his estate.

This is the idea as Paul writes to Titus: the elder arranges and manages the household of God.

Earlier, Paul told Timothy, an elder:

> *But in case I am delayed, I write so that you may know how one ought to conduct himself in the household God, which is the church of the living God* (1 Timothy 3:15a).

In other words, the Church is God's household, and elders/bishops/pastors are God's stewards in that household—which is a reminder that the Church belongs to *God*. It also reminds us that God has given human oversight to elders, who manage the Church; they steward His Church on His behalf, accountable to Him as they fulfill His will in feeding, leading, training, counseling, disciplining, guarding, discipling, encouraging, and equiping the household of God.[6]

THE "NOTS" OF TITUS 1:7

If you've ever left your house in the care of someone while you were away, you probably found yourself telling them several things *not* to do before you got around to telling them what to do.

You might start with the negatives simply because you want their full attention—as in, *this is critical*—before you get around to a list of positives.

That's exactly what Paul does here in **Titus 1:7**; he gives us five negatives before giving us the positives in the next verse.

Not Blinded by Arrogance

God's steward, not self-willed. The reason this is first in the list is because it's the exact opposite *attitude* of a steward. A steward does the will of the master, not his own. The household is on loan to him for a while for him to manage it.

You wouldn't expect to come home and find that the babysitter had worn your clothes, painted the living room lime green, and gotten rid of the dog—unless you told her that she could. She'd probably not be hired again. Those aren't her clothes, it's not her house, and she can't get rid of the dog. She was never brought into your home to do *her* will.

Let me add that the word **self-willed** comes across to us English readers a little milder than Paul intended. He's actually referring to someone so given over to arrogance and self-serving that he has an attitude of *entitlement*. His perspective is that the Church exists for his benefit instead of his existence serving the Church.

And in the analogy of a babysitter, this would be that she had actually put all your clothes on the front porch, changed the locks, and switched the name on the mailbox to her own.

This is the **self-willed** arrogance of a man who is not only unqualified to lead the Church but is a *danger* to the Church. He doesn't walk, he struts. He's enthralled with his own importance . . . he's blinded by his own reflection.

This was the downfall of Satan, who was given great responsibility as the highest of the created angels—his stewardship and management responsibilities must have been enormous. And what did he do? He became blinded in his self-serving arrogance:

> *"'I will ascend to heaven; I will raise my throne above the stars of God, and I will sit on the mount of assembly . . . I will ascend above the heights of the clouds; I will make myself like the Most High'"* (Isaiah 14:13–14).

I will . . . I will . . . I will . . . I will . . . I will. Satan had great authority—he just forgot whose authority mattered most.

One author wrote,

> An elder never says, "This is *mine!*" All that he has comes from God. His time, possessions, ambitions, and talents are all loaned to him by the Lord and he must be faithful to use them to honor God and build the Church of God.[7]

Paul says, "Titus, make sure you grant power only to those who are not in love with it . . . or infatuated with themselves."

Not Controlled by Anger

God's steward . . . not quick-tempered. It's important to understand that Paul is referring to a way of life—a habit. In fact, there are two primary Greek words for anger. One word is *thumos*, and this word pertains to anger that quickly blazes up and just as rapidly subsides. Throwing straw on a fire and causing an immediate, temporary blaze is one example of *thumos*.

The second word is *orgilos*, which is an anger that a man actually nurses to keep warm.[8] This is the word Paul chooses. He isn't referring then to someone who has an occasional burst of anger but to those who have a propensity toward anger.[9]

In other words, they are *known* as angry men. They have an internal inclination toward anger more than any other emotion, and they are easily provoked to respond in combustible outbursts . . . revealing an inner anger that has been there all along, staying warm on the stove.

This is so critical to detect simply because working with the flock will provide innumerable opportunities to become irritated and angry.

People who've taught in a classroom, led a Bible study, volunteered on a ministry trip, coached a team in the sports ministry, headed up a committee or department—they have been surrounded with many opportunities to lose their cool.

And if responding in anger is their default setting and predisposition, everyone loses. The ripples of their anger will touch the edges of ministry long after their angry words and reactions fall into the pond of church life.

The qualified elder must guard against a spirit of hostility, resentment, and anger—even when everything in the church seems to be going in the wrong direction and people are critical or indifferent.[10]

That reminds me of another author's tongue-in-cheek words, and every leader can identify with this: being a leader is like running a cemetery . . . there are a lot of people under you, but no one is listening.

So what are we going to do about it . . . how should we respond?

Can you imagine spending three years with Simon Peter, Thomas, and Judas in the same class? Even after three years they're debating who's going to be the greatest in the kingdom.

Jesus answers with gracious patience and love by getting up from supper and washing their feet, including the feet of Judas *(John 13:5)*. He didn't pinch their toes or use scalding hot water to teach them a lesson; he knelt and humbly served them with a towel and a basin of water. They would never forget it.

Hours later He taught them how to reply to the worst offenses by praying as He died on the cross, *"Father, forgive them; for they do not know what they are doing"* (Luke 23:34).

It's as if Paul is saying this is exactly the kind of pattern he wants modeled in the Church by her shepherds . . . modeled perfectly by our Chief Shepherd.

Not Influenced by Alcohol

God's steward . . . not given to wine. The word used here carries the idea of being continually alongside wine. Wine isn't to be his companion.[11]

If you study the biblical instruction regarding alcoholic drinks (as we call them), you'll soon discover that abstinence is never mandated. There isn't a verse that states that Christians should abstain from all wine at all times. What you do find are forceful exhortations against *strong* drink and *much* **wine**.[12]

This qualification simply describes an elder as someone who isn't perceived to be controlled by or under the influence of **wine**. In fact, what's most often overlooked in this issue is an understanding of what wine was like in Paul's day. Most people never stop to consider that the wine of the New Testament days was remarkably different from the wine in our local grocery store.

We know from history that wine was basically purified water. Pliny, the first-century historian, referred to wine as eight parts water and one part wine.

We have enough data from the first century to know that the average mixture was about three to four parts water to one part wine.[13]

The fermenting process effectively purified their drinking water, which explains why Paul had to tell Timothy to *use a little* **wine** *for the sake of your stomach and your frequent ailments* (1 Timothy 5:23).

Evidently, Timothy was so concerned as a young elder about his reputation—that he not be viewed in any way as addicted to wine or under its influence—that he swore off all of it and began drinking unpurified water, which obviously wasn't a safe thing to do.

I've been to countries where water isn't safe, and I've only drunk bottled water. I brushed my teeth with bottled water; when I took a shower, I closed my eyes and shut my mouth so tightly my lips hurt. One drop could change everything.

Paul recommended to Timothy that he needed fermented wine—water which was basically cleansed from contamination.

One Bible scholar who studied the making of wine in the first century commented that the average first-century person would need to drink twelve eight-ounce glasses of wine to get the same amount of alcohol one could get today from one martini.[14]

Most of our culture's wines today are comparable to the *strong* drink of the early centuries, which the Bible clearly forbids. Why? Because it so quickly can bring people under its influence and impair their judgment.

Centuries ago, Solomon warned those in positions of leadership:

> It is not for kings to drink **wine**, or for rulers to desire beer [NIV translation for "strong drink"] for they will drink and forget what is decreed, and pervert the rights of all the afflicted (Proverbs 31:4–5).

Solomon was obviously referring to strong drink.

What I find personally tragic in this age is when any elder would rather defend drinking alcoholic beverages instead of modeling a pattern that stays as far away from it as possible.

We now *know* that:

- half of the murders, suicides, and accidental deaths in America are related to alcohol;

- one in four families has some kind of problem with substance abuse;

- alcohol is one of the largest health problems in America;

- consumption of alcohol reduces life expectancy, breaks up families, destroys people financially, etc.

Another point that seems lost in this debate where liberty tends to trump common sense is the fact that Paul and Timothy and Titus had virtually *nothing* from which they could choose to drink. We have *hundreds* of choices which will never impair our judgment or hinder our testimony or, perhaps, tacitly endorse something that might cause a younger believer to become confused or compromised:

> *For through your knowledge he who is weak is ruined, the brother for whose sake Christ died* (1 Corinthians 8:11).

Timothy was on to something . . . there's your model. It isn't how *much* you can drink without offending someone else or needing a ride home . . . it's how far away from it you choose to stay.

Paul writes here **not given to** **wine**; literally, he's referring to a man who isn't always drinking—which would imply he can't be the kind of man who's going to drink twelve eight-ounce glasses and more so he can get a buzz.

I am frankly amazed—and I've watched it happen in recent years—how pastors and elders are now bragging about their own breweries in their basements . . . making their own brew. This is the new pastoral claim to relevance and liberty.

A man came to Colonial from another church in our community for one reason: the men's Bible study in his church typically included drinking beer—the pastor included—and that man was a recovering alcoholic. He found it far too tempting to engage in what they viewed as their personal badge of Christian liberty.

Sometimes liberty strangles common sense.

If anything, Paul would encourage men not to have a reputation of being near wine—even though that was the common drink of the day. The elder wasn't always after his wine bag.

For no other reason than that of influencing others toward holy living, elders are asked to model not how much they can handle but how clean a life they can possibly live.

And it isn't just this issue; there's gluttony, media choices—certainly pornographic material, sensuality in movies and music—the use of drugs, and more.

Sheep might want to excuse things and shove most of it into *Romans 14* and say, "It's my prerogative and my right to eat or drink, so don't bother me about your hang-ups and rules."

A Shepherd *doesn't* think like that. He's always considering what would be best for the flock . . . what would keep them away from the precipice and what would best protect them.

Every father and mother needs to take note as well: what you allow on television becomes the standard that will be stretched by your children. What you listen to endorses whatever world it comes from. What you have in your refrigerator becomes the starting point for them . . . and they'll take it farther than you ever dreamed.

Paul is simply prohibiting the elder from participating in a manner of life where something is allowed to cloud his mind or captivate his senses.

Not Recognized As Abusive

God's steward . . . not **pugnacious.**

This is a word that refers to a *striker*. In the Apostolic Canons, we find this interesting prohibition: "We order that the bishop who strikes an erring believer should be dismissed."[15] Evidently, anyone who was out of order in the fellowship got slapped—literally!

The word came to refer to violence not only in action but in speech. It meant a browbeater—someone who berated and verbally abused others. This characteristic would become so critically important simply because elders handle highly emotional conflicts; they are involved in deeply felt doctrinal disagreements. An elder will often be in the middle of tense situations as a referee, and sometimes the crowd turns on whom? The referee!

What Paul is saying here is that if the elder is given to responding to abuse with matching abuse, if he is reviled and becomes a reviler himself, if he shouts his way through one disagreement after another, if he berates and belittles others into submission—then he isn't qualified because, as a pattern of life, he doesn't model Christ's response to reviling and abuse and mistreatment.

In the past, I have witnessed the damage a verbally **pugnacious** elder can bring into the flock as well as into the boardroom . . . damage impossible to repair unless the elder is held accountable to this particular qualification.

One author wrote if an elder will treat the sheep roughly and hurt them, if he will in his frustration respond to the sheep with verbal assaults, he cannot be one of Christ's under-shepherds.[16]

It's as simple as that.

Not Driven by Affluence

God's steward . . . not fond of sordid gain.

Paul is referring to an elder whose life is all about money, no matter *how* he makes it. An elder can't be a man driven by money . . . the business deal . . . the profit margin. When money dictates his character—drives his ambitions—is the subject of most of his conversations—everyone knows that making money is really his chief love in life. I've served in the past with pastors like that, where making money became more important than making disciples.

Perhaps this characteristic made the list because the Cretans had a reputation for greed.[17] It's as if Paul is warning Titus to make sure these Cretan Christians have the Cretan squeezed out of them first before they serve as elders.

For the elder driven by perks and profit, his ministry will favor the wealthy. He'll be easily bought. He'll make best friends with those who own things . . . give things. And ultimately, he'll make decisions based on money and not ministry.

His hidden motive for serving in ministry is to fleece the flock instead of feed the flock. That is the opposite of the nature of an elder's ministry; he is to give . . . to be generous . . . to manage funds for the benefit of *others*.

In fact, in our next chapter we deal with **Titus 1:8**, a direct contrast to greed: **hospitable**—generosity of spirit. Generosity and giving should be the hallmark of a shepherd's heart. Is there anyone more generous than Christ, our Chief Shepherd? Does He not daily lavish us with His grace?

READY TO SERVE

God's steward—His under-shepherd—must not be stingy, greedy, unethical, or angry, but generous and greathearted and giving and patient. Frankly, every believer should shun these prohibitions and strive to model these attributes so that Christ is seen in us all.

Paul's challenge for us who would model our Master is to remember these negatives and strive toward His example:

- not to be recognized as arrogant;
- not to be controlled by anger;
- not to be influenced by alcohol;
- not to be viewed as abusive;
- not to be motivated by affluence.

Those who reflect the characteristics that Christ exhibited for us are to be the twenty-first century stewards of God's house.

[Be] *hospitable, loving what is good, sensible, just, devout, self-controlled.*

—Titus 1:8

CHAPTER SEVEN

THE NEW NORMAL

Titus 1:8

ELIMINATE THE NEGATIVE

I was invited to speak to the student body at a Christian college and seminary for their annual Bible Conference. It would be my first visit to that campus, and I took time to pack just the right suit, necktie, and shoes to wear—the standard Chapel uniform. I arrived, but my luggage did *not*.

The president of the graduate school loaned me some of his clothes: a sport coat four sizes larger than I wore; a necktie I would never have bought for myself; a pair of his dress shoes, size 13. I wear a 10½. I can still remember clomping across the stage to the podium. I told the students that morning what had happened—mainly because I didn't want them to think I chose to dress like that.

My luggage arrived the next day.

Showing up to speak somewhere for the first time is a lot like showing up for an interview—you want everything to be right. You want to put your best foot forward. You might not bring a suitcase, but you do polish your resumé. Every good thing you've ever done, every project you've accomplished, every title you've earned, and every award you've been given are somewhere on that resumé.

A prospective boss is going to want somebody with experience . . . executive management skills . . . personal charisma . . . good taste in clothes . . . the right educational background . . . all the best connections.

Besides, you can only imagine that every other candidate is intelligent, attractive, intimidating, oozing prestige and popularity—and just the right amount of confidence to prove they're better suited for the position than everyone else.

Nobody lands a job because they're humble . . . or holy. And by all means, keep your religion to yourself and play along with just enough compromise to get by . . . without agreeing to do anything illegal.

That kind of thinking has a way of spilling over into the Church.

Titus arrives on the island of Crete in the first century, and his apostolically commissioned job is to find shepherds who are qualified to wear the mantle of leadership in the Church *(Titus 1:5)*.

He might have been tempted to fill the office with the wrong kind of men—those with charm or personality, intellect, and the right taste in togas.

Instead, Paul provides a list of resumé qualifications, directing his quest. There were five negatives to avoid in his search to appoint men to the office of elder.

Paul implies that there are going to be plenty of candidates who can't wait to be in charge—like Diotrephes, who wanted to be out front: he just loved being the first guy in line and then telling everybody how to line up behind him *(3 John 1:9)*.

Samuel in the Old Testament searched for a king among Jesse's sons, assuming that the tallest, best-dressed, oldest, and strongest would certainly be God's candidate for King of Israel. The LORD said to him:

> *"Do not look at his appearance . . . for God sees not as man sees,*
> *for man looks at the outward appearance, but the LORD looks at*
> *the heart"* (I Samuel 16:7).

As you survey the resumé of an elder in *Titus 1*, you don't find anything listed about speaking ability, leadership skill sets, business accomplishments, or physical attributes. In fact, the list has almost *nothing* to do with what the man has done . . . it has everything to do with who the man *is*.

Paul clearly reveals that what was normal on the island of Crete can't be normal in the Church. Cultural norms aren't the believer's norms. In fact, the elder is actually tasked to *change* the norm. By his own character and lifestyle, he is going to model a new pattern for the church and lead the congregation into a *new normal*, as well.

ACCENTUATE THE POSITIVE

[H]*ospitable, loving what is good, sensible, just, devout,*
self-controlled (Titus 1:8).

Can you imagine a job interview where the questions related to the candidate's chance of getting the job are connected to *Titus 1:8*? Questions such as:

- Are you are a good person?
- Do you have common sense?
- Are you fair?
- Are you personally devout?
- Can you give me a personal example of self-control?

Are you kidding? The average candidate being interviewed would respond by saying, "That's none of your business!"

But this *is* the business of the Church; this is the new normal—not just for elders, either, but for the entire flock they will lead and influence toward godly lifestyles.

You'll find every one of these qualifications encouraged throughout the New Testament in the lives of *every* maturing believer. Many of these qualities listed in *Titus 1* are given in *Galatians 5* as the fruit of the Spirit-controlled life.

Elders are simply men who are progressing under the influence of the Holy Spirit as they lead the flock by way of example, providing the flock a pattern they can actually *see*. The elder is, in many ways, nothing more than a living demonstration of the new normal. And the flock pursues that goal as they are led to submit to the Holy Spirit.

Remember this distinction: while the congregation *may* progress in these characteristics, the elder *must* progress in these qualities.

Paul spells out the new normal for us by giving seven virtues to embrace for those who will be qualified to shepherd the flock of God. We will accentuate four of these positives in this chapter.

Personal Concern for Others

Hospitable: disposed to treat guests with warmth and generosity. This word in the New Testament is made up of *philos* (love or strong affection) and *zenos* (stranger).[1] Hospitality is a love for strangers . . . literally translated *stranger-loving*.[2]

Paul is not necessarily saying we are to love people who are *strange* —we're not setting a new standard for who your daughter can date—he's referring to people who are *strangers*. This is rather unexpected because you'd think that the first thing out of the gate in these seven virtues would be how the shepherd loves the *flock*.

Perhaps Paul implies that love for the flock would be a little too easy—a little too rewarding, too self-congratulating—and many men might qualify. They love the church and never miss an activity or a service, perhaps because it adds to their personal reputation. But Titus is told to look for men who show care and concern for people when there's no such church obligation, no family connection, no kudos or badges of honor, no public affirmation.

The true test of hospitality is not what we do for those whom we like to be around or those who are likely to repay us in some way, but in what we do for others out of sincere concern for their welfare.[3]

And this certainly extended to the Church at large. The Apostle Peter commanded the Church to *be* **hospitable** *to one another without complaint* (1 Peter 4:9).

In fact, during Paul's day, traveling was especially hazardous if you didn't have anywhere to stay for the night. Inns were not only expensive but were notoriously evil. Travelers could expect to be robbed and even beaten.[4] Plato referred to an innkeeper as a pirate who held his guests for ransom. Inns were equally infamous for their immorality, often serving as the village brothel. It would be the *last* place you would want to stay if you were traveling.

Because of all these issues and dangers, the world of the apostles had created a system called *Guest Friendships*. Over generations, families made arrangements with other families to give each other accommodation and hospitality. Members of families were unknown by sight, so a method was devised for recognition: a coin or placard of metal or wood was cut in half. Over the years, when a member of the family traveled to a distant city and needed lodging, he carried with him half of what was called a tallie. The host family had the other half; when the two halves were fitted together, the host knew the traveler was a legitimate member of the family with whom they had guaranteed hospitality.[5]

That's why this first characteristic from the Apostle Paul would have been so counterculture. Paul is saying that the basis for biblical hospitality is not family agreements or tallies or connections but a *love for strangers*—love and care for those in genuine need.

Here's the new normal: open your doors to people in need, whether or not you know them; whether or not your family had established a *Guest Friendship* with them in the past.

This same Greek word used by Paul for **hospitable** is found in our English words hospice and hospital . . . for good reason.

Even the Greeks with their god of medicine did not build hospitals or offer free care for the sick. A correct understanding of history will show that those who came into the temple of Aesculapia (*askulepia*), the Greek god of healing, came not for medical treatment but to sleep in the temple or shrine, hoping that the god would appear to them in their dreams and reveal to them the treatment which they ought to follow.[6]

Both the Romans and the Greeks had some type of hospital or infirmary reserved for their soldiers; they offered nothing to the general population.[7] What we knew as charity hospitals in the past became the forerunners of the hospitals that exist today (they no longer operate by charity); these were created by the Christian community. They grew out of the Gospel and became a method of delivering the Gospel to those in need.

One historian noted, "There is simply no evidence of any medical institution supported by voluntary contributions until we come to Christianity . . . Christian hospitals revolutionized the treatment of the poor, the sick, and the dying."[8]

The Greeks and Romans built their statues and temples, their coliseums and arenas, their aqueducts and highways—but they *never* built a hospital. Why? Because the norm of Paul's day, summed up by historian Philip Schaff, was, "The old Roman world was a world without charity."[9]

There was simply no reason to love the sick and dying, especially those not related to you. You would never volunteer to take care of a sick person you didn't know—and you certainly would never invite a person like that into your *home*.

Obviously, Paul is promoting a radically different culture; he's telling Titus that it's time to find men who will lead the Church into a new normal. And who are these men? Those who show genuine love and an open door to people they don't know and who will probably never be able to repay them.

Personal Conviction for Good

Loving what is good: a lover of [all that is] good. Again, Paul uses a compound word *philos* (love or strong affection) with *agathos* (that which is good). The Greek term could be rendered "lover of good things." In other words, an elder not only loves strangers, but he loves whatever is **good**.

One ancient manuscript used this same word for a man who loved virtue;[10] he loved what was intrinsically good. An elder then is a man who loves anything that reminds him of God because, as Jesus told the rich young ruler who came to visit him, *"[T]here is none good but one, that is, God"* (Matthew 19:17 KJV).

If you want to know if someone is truly walking after God, ask if he loves the things that God would love. It doesn't mean a lover of good is sequestered from all that is bad, but it does mean he doesn't love what's bad; he gravitates to those things intrinsically pleasing to God.

Paul put it this way to the Philippians:

> *Finally, brethren, whatever is true, whatever is honorable, whatever is right, whatever is pure, whatever is lovely, whatever is of good repute, if there is any excellence and if anything worthy of praise, dwell on these things* (Philippians 4:8).

In other words, meditate on, dwell with, accompany, ruminate on, and devote your time to these things.

Warren Wiersbe wrote that this would include good books, good people, good music, good causes, and the like that are excellent, that are pure, that will not in any way violate or offend the intrinsic glory and goodness of God.[11]

Now why is this kind of characteristic—**loving what is good**—difficult to find? Because the world is filled with so many people who actually love what is bad.[12] Paul wrote to Timothy in *2 Timothy 3:3* that as society continued to grow more and more corrupt, one of the signs would be that it would become *haters of good*. This is the same word here. People are actually going to *hate* what is *good* and *love* what is sinful.

Proverbs 2:14 says that men *delight in doing evil and rejoice in the perversity of evil*, and that *doing wickedness is like sport to a fool* (Proverbs 10:23).

In other words, sin is just another indoor sport. It's just another thing to do. Men of the world lose the ability to distinguish what's bad from what's good as they spiral away from the innate goodness of the God whom they've rejected. This is why the world is more openly delighted with sinful people, evil activities, bad language, and corrupt ideas. Culture then digresses to the point of approval: "You Christians are just too uptight . . . this activity isn't really bad—it's good":

[T]*hey not only do the same, but also give hearty approval to those who practice them* (Romans 1:32*b*).

Paul tells Titus to go find men to serve as elders who will straighten out the definitions—men who will form their personal convictions after the inherent nature of God's goodness and then be able to turn around to the flock they lead and say, "This is actually what is *good*, and this is what is bad."

Paul implies that Titus will be able to spot a potential leader as the man who not only tells people what's good but actually loves **what is good**. What an elder loves is revealing; what he wants to linger over and talk about and read and listen to and look forward to and be in the company of sends a strong message.

Paul is asking, "Are they good things?"

Here's the challenge for us all: Can you write "Good" over the titles of books, magazines, internet sites, movies, television programs, and music that you partake of? Are they in any way offensive to or in violation of the intrinsic nature of God?

That doesn't restrict the definition of "good" to those activities you'll only allow in church to the exclusion of those activities you can enjoy after church. For instance, I go home and take a nap on Sunday afternoons. And when I get up, I might even say to Marsha, "That was a *good* nap." It wasn't a spiritual discipline; it wasn't something I'd do in church—although some in my flock are skilled at it—but it was, indeed, good.

That nap or, perhaps, that novel or that walk in the park or that painting canvass or that drive or that ball game doesn't violate the intrinsic nature of God's goodness—it isn't offensive to His character. There are multiple things we can call "good."

Titus is to be on the lookout for men who **love what is good** . . . those whose lives embrace personal convictions that mirror the goodness of God.

Personal Common Sense

Sensible: having or showing good sense or judgment. This compound word gives us *sophos* (wise) with *phroneo* (to set the mind). The combined idea refers to a *wise mindset*. Keep in mind that wisdom is putting into practice the things you know.

One Bible scholar wrote that this word means "to think soundly; to use common sense."[13] I can't help but immediately think of what someone once said: "The problem with common sense is that it isn't so *common* anymore."

The word Paul uses here as an elder qualification has the nuance of practical sensibility . . . you could paraphrase this word to refer to literally keeping one's head about him.

Paul is demanding, one author wrote, that an elder must not be a man given to wild and foolish ideas. Yes, he must be a man who believes that God is the God of the impossible. But he must mix such a faith with a good dose of common sense. For God who gave us our hearts is the same God who gave us our heads."[14]

The Church needs leaders who use both their hearts and their heads. Elders should have a wise perspective simply because they're going to be involved with people and problems and conundrums and decisions, and there will be a great need for both faith and practical discernment and a good deal of practical wisdom, too.[15]

The concept of common sense includes a nuance of *courage to think differently* . . . to think unlike the majority. Maybe this is why Paul, later in this letter, will encourage others in the Church to model this same attribute. They're going to need to think differently if they expect to create a brand-new culture—a new normal.

Their thinking should no longer be influenced by the crowd but by Christ. A growing believer's opinions will not change according to the latest polls or news reports.

One former president of the United States wrote years ago:

> I can't help but wonder what Jesus Christ would have preached if He'd taken a poll in Israel. I wonder how far Moses would have gone if he'd taken a poll in Egypt. Where would the Reformation have been if Martin Luther had taken a poll in Germany? It isn't the polls or public opinions of the moment that count. It is what's right and what's wrong. That is what makes good leadership—men with courage, honesty, and a belief in what's right. That's what makes epochs in the history of the world.

I would not only agree but add that this mindset is exactly what makes for godly leadership in the Church.

Personal Consistency in Integrity

Just: honorable and fair in one's dealings and actions. You could translate this word *upright*. In fact, these last three characteristics all have to do with right relationships:

- **Just** deals with an elder's right relationship with people.

- **Devout** refers to an elder's right relationship with God.

- **Self-controlled** defines an elder's right relationship with oneself—that is, his own appetites and attitudes.[16]

Just is the idea that fair play and a handshake matter. That's how you have just relationships with others. You show up and follow through.

The Greeks defined a just man as someone who gave to men whatever was due.[17] **Just** relates to a man's efforts to walk the talk—to make sure his walk is consistent with his words—to practice what he preaches. And that's important because a shepherd's life is to be patterned to reflect the honest character of the Chief Shepherd.

People are watching! Much like our children watch us—more than we know . . . more than we imagine . . . more than we desire. So much so that they end up walking like us and talking like us . . . accent and all. Frightening, isn't it? May that reality drive us to our knees more often to claim the grace of God over all our lives.

I was working as a youth pastor many years ago, and I dealt with a teenager who constantly lied; it was nearly impossible to get a straight answer out of him about anything. I simply couldn't tell if he was telling me the truth. I discovered years later that his father had lost his job . . . for dishonesty.

Now, don't misunderstand—I'm not implying that every dishonest child has a dishonest parent. I know, because I was a dishonest child and I had honest parents. The trouble comes when the parent refuses to be honest and abandons the model of integrity. The child hears Mom or Dad call in sick and knows they're going golfing or fishing or shopping. He gets a mixed message when he answers the phone and his parents tell him to tell the boss that they're out in the yard and can't take the call . . . or they're not home at all.

That type of dishonesty becomes their inherited norm.

A California mother was observed going through the grocery store tapping various items. Behind her came her two little children who would pocket the items she tapped. That mother didn't realize it then, but one day, tragically, her kids will probably steal from her.

The *Boston Globe* ran an article about the annual convention of the American Heart Association. More than 30,000 doctors and nurses and researchers are members of the AHA. At that year's convention, the focus was on the fast food industry and the perils of cheeseburgers, fries, quarter pounders—you know, all the good stuff. When one cardiologist who had been observed eating a fast food hamburger during lunch break was interviewed and asked about whether he was being inconsistent, he replied, "No, I don't think so; I made sure I took off my name tag before I went in."[18]

I guess that makes everything okay!

In a way, Paul is telling the elders that they never get to take off their name tag—and that goes for every Christian. Your name tag is permanent.

The word Paul uses here, translated **just**, means that you are a man or woman of your word, and you live with the sense that the name tag "Christian" is visible for everyone to see. The stakes are even higher if you're not only a Christian but a Christian elder/shepherd/leader.

That name tag goes with you *everywhere*.

One day I was golfing alone and was paired with a group of three guys. I really didn't want to be with anybody . . . if you saw the way I played, you'd understand.

But here was this threesome . . . swearing like sailors . . . telling off-color jokes as we worked our way down the course. I purposefully hung back and kept to myself. Finally on the fifth tee, one of them looked at me and said, "Hey, we're sorry we've been leaving you out; what do *you* do for a living?" When I replied that I was a pastor, their faces blanched, and they began to apologize for their French . . . *it wasn't French*. They were obviously embarrassed and tried to amend their ways. They even started calling me *Father*. Of course, from that moment on, I also had to watch *my* attitude; when I hit a ball that sliced into the woods, I couldn't slam my club in the bag and mutter under by breath. I now had a visible name tag . . . and there was no way it was coming off for the rest of that round.

Frankly, accountability is a good thing. A rare example of integrity that won international respect and became part of the living legend of PGA champion Tom Watson occurred as he was making a run for another trophy:

> The pressure was incredible and the attention on this new-comer was relentless. On one of the greens, as he moved up to get ready to putt, he placed his putter behind the ball and, to his dismay, the ball moved ever so slightly. The other players were busy with their own game at the moment. No one saw his ball move—but he did. He walked over to an official and said, "My ball moved." Everything just sort of froze; Tom Watson, without anyone seeing it happen, had just admitted what might cost him more than a stroke—it could cost him the match. But he told the truth. That action cost him a stroke and he lost the hole, but he came back to win the match.[19]

THERE IS NO IN-BETWEEN

If you love what is **good** and **sensible** and **just** and **devout**, you will govern yourself in a manner where there is no doubt about your standing in the Christian community. What matters in life, especially for the believer— and even more for the elder who not only has to declare what's right but live it—is to pursue these traits listed in *Titus 1:8*:

- personal concern for those in need;
- personal conviction for everything that's good;
- personal common sense in making wise decisions;
- personal consistency of uprightness and integrity.

Charles Wesley wanted to have a conscience that was sensitive to the Lord's leading, to do the right things to please his Lord and Master. He wrote many hymn texts that were published and sung during his ministry in the 1700s, but this lesser-known text is worth mentioning:

> *I want a principle within, of watchful, godly fear,*
> *A sensibility of sin, a pain to feel it near.*

I want the first approach to feel of pride or wrong desire,
To catch the wandering of my will and quench the kindling fire.

From Thee that I no more may stray, no more Thy goodness grieve.
Grant me the filial awe, I pray, the tender conscience give.
Quick as the apple of an eye, O God, my conscience make;
Awake my soul when sin is nigh, and keep it still awake.

Almighty God of truth and love, to me Thy power impart;
The mountain from my soul remove, the hardness from my heart.
O may the least omission pain my reawakened soul,
And drive me to that blood again,
Which makes the wounded whole.[20]

[8][J]*ust, devout, self-controlled,* [9]*holding fast the faithful word which is in accordance with the teaching, so that he will be able both to exhort in sound doctrine and to refute those who contradict.*

–Titus 1:8*b*–9

CHAPTER EIGHT

CHOCOLATE CHRISTIANS

Titus 1:8b–9

WANTED: A FEW GOOD MEN

I have a devotional book written by a Chinese evangelist and missionary leader of a strategic mission enterprise. The Chinese believers involved in this movement daily risk their lives to take the Gospel to Muslims and Hindus as they go to countries where Christianity is forbidden.

This particular leader has been imprisoned several times, often hunted with a reward on his head—beaten many times, and even tortured for his insistence on preaching the Gospel. At one point in a Chinese prison, both legs were broken; he had to lie on his back and prop his legs on the cell wall to try to ease the pain. He admitted to struggling with the will of God there in the solitude of his suffering. Who wouldn't?

In his devotional writings, I learned that many believers in China teach five things that every disciple needs to be ready to do at any time:

1. **pray**, regardless of circumstance;

2. **speak** the Gospel;

3. **suffer** for the name of Christ;

4. **die** for Jesus Christ;

5. **escape**, if possible, to continue preaching the Gospel.

The fifth directive—to escape—is their application of Christ's command:

> *"But whenever they persecute you in one city, flee to the next"*
> (Matthew 10:23*a*).

They have to be ready to pray, speak, suffer, die, or escape.[1]

C.T. Studd, a fearless nineteenth-century British missionary who pioneered the Gospel in China as well as in India and Africa, endured incredible deprivation and hardship in ministry. To give you an idea of the kind of dedicated missionary he was, Studd once wrote a little two-line poem:

> *Some want to live within the sound of Church or Chapel bell;*
> *I want to run a Rescue Shop within a yard of hell.*

Studd also delivered a written challenge that called for perseverance and courage:

> A chocolate Christian dissolves in water and melts at the smell of fire. Living their lives in a glass dish or in a cardboard box, each clad in his soft clothing, a little frilled white paper to preserve his dear little constitution . . . God never was a chocolate manufacturer and never will be.[2]

In other words, God wants Christians who will not melt or dissolve in the face of peer pressure or opposition or suffering. Sounds a lot like Paul the Apostle who challenged Timothy to endure hard times like a good soldier of Jesus Christ *(2 Timothy 2:3)*. Paul further exhorted his son in the faith to train himself for the purpose of growing in godliness *(1 Timothy 4:7)*.

I have little doubt that there are fewer men qualified—or even willing—to serve as leaders in the Church today because of its penalties: greater demands and pressure, discipline and study, potential suffering, and lonely isolation.

Chocolate Christians cannot wear the mantle of a shepherd. There's too much danger lying in wait; too much incoming fire to deal with. They might be tempted to run . . . to melt down under all the pressure.

The Apostle Paul gave Titus a task that has been ongoing in the Church since the first century: find elders who will not melt in the heat of battle.

Many men will *look* the part, but when the pressure's on, they won't be willing or able; they can't guard and feed, encourage and challenge, discipline and love, and lead the flock of God over whom they have been appointed.

Titus would naturally have asked what kind of resumé Paul could give him to avoid choosing the wrong shepherds and point him in the direction of those qualified for the position. So Paul gives Titus this list—one that has stood the test for twenty centuries; it's simply outlined as The Qualifications of Elders.

He began with the elder's relationship to his wife and children; then he named five vices the candidates could not be known to habitually pursue, and finished by laying out seven virtues that the men should exemplify as a *pattern* of life.

In our last chapter, we covered the first four virtues; now we'll address the final three:

> **[D]***evout, self-controlled, holding fast* (Titus 1:8*b*–9*a*).

And I remind the reader—these qualities are to be the passionate pursuit of *every* believer. None of us is to be molded in chocolate. We are all fighting a battle, and to make matters more difficult:

> [O]*ur struggle is not against flesh and blood, but against the rulers, against the powers, against the world forces of this darkness, against the spiritual forces of wickedness in the heavenly places* (Ephesians 6:12).

The Church needs men who will lead the charge and provide a model for the flock by their own daily battles with the world, the flesh, and the devil.

FRAUDS NEED NOT APPLY

Little wonder that Paul asks Titus to pry into the *private lives* of these elder candidates. They must be confirmed as having private disciplines of godliness.

Personal Strength of Holiness

Devout: displaying reverence or piety. The word comes from *hosios*, which refers to holy piety. It is used by Paul in *I Timothy 2:8*, where he encourages *the men in every place to pray, lifting up holy hands*—hands that are genuinely clean and genuinely holy in private before God . . . and, thus, they will be the same in public.

The idea that whatever a man does in private doesn't affect what he does in public is nonsense. In fact, it's dangerous. According to the Apostle Paul, whatever a man does in private *qualifies* whatever he hopes to do in public. If he can't be trusted in private to care about the will and character and nature of God, he can't be trusted in public to care about any of that, either.

One author said that when Paul uses this word for **devout**, he is referring to an elder/overseer who is fully dedicated to the glory of God.[3] If he isn't dedicated to the glory of God in his private life where the pressure is *off*, he'll never live up to pursuing the glory of God when the pressure's *on*. When the heat's turned up, he will melt.

An elder candidate must be personally devoted to God, and that quality of devotion will be evident both privately and publically.

Personal Strength of Character

Self-controlled: control of one's emotions, desires, or actions by one's own will. This is a compound word made up of *in* and *power*. It describes a person who is in control of, in power over—and in this case here—one's self.[4]

I dreaded the end of the grading period when I was in elementary school. The report card was divided in half: one side had the subjects, and the other side had character qualities—courtesy and helpfulness and **self-control**.

I always scored well on spelling and reading but rather poorly in arithmetic. But those grades didn't mean a hill of beans to my parents; they were more interested in that other section—issues of character and **self-control** . . . their priorities were obviously messed up!

From what I remember, "Self-Control" typically received a low grade, and the spaces next to the grade allowed my teacher to do nothing more than tattle on me. She was such a gossip.

Let's admit that a mark of *immaturity* is the *lack* of **self-control**. And every child has to grow up in that regard—some children, faster than others.

Your child wants to run and jump when he feels the urge—and you teach him to sit still. He wants to eat—and you tell him to wait; he really wants dessert—and you tell him not until he's eaten his vegetables. Growing up means saying no to the wrong things at the right time, and also saying wait to the right things if it's the wrong time.

A mark of maturity is controlling urges . . . emotions . . . choosing the right action or response, even if it's hard or doesn't taste good or is unpopular or painful or time-consuming or unrewarding.

Paul tells Titus that one way you can discern whether an elder candidate is likely to melt is whether he's able to control his emotions and impulses. One author wrote these perceptive words:

> An [elder] who does not continually monitor his own life, submitting his sin to the Lord's cleansing and keeping a clear conscience, is not fit to lead God's people, no matter how outwardly righteous his life may appear to be. If he acts right only when others are looking, he is doing just that—*acting*.[5]

The Pharisees had it down to a science. They gave their money, they fasted, and they prayed in public, Jesus revealed—to be seen by men. *To be seen* is the Greek word *thainomai*, which gives us our word *theatre*.

These religious leaders were putting on a spiritual show. And they were good at it. But when the pressure was on, the spiritual leaders of Israel caved in to peer pressure and greed and jealousy—all those corrupt inner urges ran free, and they ultimately led the chant and the charge to crucify the Messiah.

Keep in mind that this virtue of **self-control** is among the fruit of the Spirit in *Galatians 5:23*. Paul isn't telling Titus to find men who are moral and emotional captains of their own ship . . . amazing men who have an unusual ability to control their mouth and heart and mind and hands.[6] No, **self-control** is actually the result of willingly surrendering to the Spirit's control. **Self-control**, along with every virtue, is a daily decision and a daily battle and a daily discipline ultimately developed and demonstrated by submission to the Holy Spirit.

Elders are men who must be, as a pattern, under the controlling influence of the Holy Spirit. These are the private battles which become public patterns: being **devout** and **self-controlled**.

Personal Strength of Dedication

Holding fast: "sticking to firmly." This is the last and most developed of all the virtues and means Paul moves from private exercises to public exposition. In fact, you could say that he makes the shift from what an elder *is* to what an elder *does*:

Holding fast *the faithful word which is in accordance with the teaching* (Titus 1:9*a*).

In other words, a faithful shepherd isn't going to abandon ***the faithful word***—he's going to revere it and read it and study it and memorize it and obey it and believe it and teach it . . . he's literally going to love the faithful Word of God.

And he's going to set the example for the flock in relation to it:

- being *constantly nourished on the words of the faith and of the sound doctrine* (1 Timothy 4:6);

- longing for *the pure milk of the Word* (I Peter 2:2);

- commending [them] *to God and to the word of His grace, which is able to build* [them] *up and to give* [them] *the inheritance among all those who are sanctified* (Acts 20:32).

A pastor/elder preaches and teaches the Word of God because he is fully convinced that the Bible is alive and uniquely designed to bring about a reformation of soul and heart and character. He clings to that conviction like he clings to God's revelation.

He's committed to the Scriptures because he knows the Word alone reveals:

- the character of God;
- the will and purpose of God;
- the promises of God;
- the plan of redemption from God;
- the dangers of the enemies of God;
- the way to walk with God and serve God and commune with God and confess before God and love God.

Paul wrote:

All Scripture is inspired by God and profitable for teaching, for reproof, for correction, for training in righteousness so that [so that!] *the man of God may be adequate, equipped for every good work* (2 Timothy 3:16–17).

The pastor/elder who recognizes that Scripture alone is inerrant—inspired (literally, *God breathed*)—also recognizes that Scripture is the only sufficient authority for faith and life and practice, and he fully understands why Paul would tell Timothy to *preach the word* (2 Timothy 4:2); *to fully carry out the preaching of the word of God* (Colossians 1:25) to the flock of God.[7]

Anything less is inadequate . . . anything else is parched ground, not green pastures.

A firm grip on the Word of God allows an elder to get his arms around the *work* of God.[8]

If the preaching of the Word slips, the work will slip. If the elder strays from the Word of Christ, he will soon enough stray from the work of Christ. If he isn't all that interested in the true word of God, he won't be completely interested in the true work of God; his ministry will be nothing more than an appendage of his own petty fascinations, self-centered desires, and self-promoting reflection.

That church will simply join the majority in their quest for relevancy, tying the ministry to passing fads, superficial and self-focused. As they let go of *the faithful word*, their highest goal will shift to the enjoyment of the spectator rather than the pleasure of God, and a fulfilled life will trump a transformed life . . . a life that develops into the holy image of Christ and the glorious character of God.

Apart from the clear commitment and exposition of Scripture, the Church becomes driven by entertainers and storytellers, which John Piper, in his book *The Supremacy of God in Preaching*, describes simply as the slapstick of evangelical worship.[9]

The evangelical Church at large is now set up to melt down. The first fires of persecution will be devastating . . . and revealing.

Paul emphasizes an elder must cling to *the faithful word which is in accordance with the teaching* (Titus 1:9a). In other words, his teaching tracks back to and is in agreement with the apostolic doctrine—to the body of teaching by the apostles upon which the New Testament Church was formed *(Acts 2:42).*

Essentially, any teaching that wasn't in correlation with the inspired record of apostolic truth and preaching and doctrine was considered spurious and dangerous and, even, devilish *(Galatians 1:8–9).*

There is only one apostolic doctrinal body of truth: the Bible. There is only one Lord . . . one baptism . . . one Church . . . one faith . . . one Spirit . . . one hope . . . one God *(Ephesians 4:4–5).*

There are not *many* gods—there is only *one* true and living God. There are not *many* faiths—there is only *one* true and genuine faith . . . every other belief is both deadly and eternally damning.

If a group of people believed that 2+2=4 and another group believed that 2+2=5, none of us would say, "Isn't that nice, we have two answers. We have two different viewpoints. And what matters most is whatever the answer means to each of them."

My algebra teacher never gave me that kind of latitude: it was either right or wrong. She didn't care what $x + y = z$ meant to me *personally*; I don't think she even cared about me personally. And she certainly didn't give any points for getting *close* to the answer.

Anything apart from the truth of this God-breathed Word is simply wrong. Are you ready to take that stand? Are you ready for that kind of heat? Are you willing to communicate that kind of conviction to a world saturated in pluralism? If not, you shouldn't become an elder/shepherd.

G.E. Lessing, an eighteenth-century German critic, played an instrumental role in popularizing pluralism: the view that there are many ways to God—a view that has now taken root in American thinking and mainline Protestant churches. In his biography, he said the house of God, *if there is a God*, has many doorways. He often used a story he created to promote his viewpoint:

> A father had a magic ring which he was bound to give to one of his three sons when he died. Not wanting to be accused of favoritism, he had two imitation rings made. Each son thought his ring was the real one, and an argument broke out among them as to who was the owner of the genuine ring. The three troubled sons agreed to go to Nathan the Wise and explain what happened. After hearing their tale, Nathan the Wise responded that each of them was to think that his own

ring was the true one and not try to persuade anyone differently.[10]

That sounds nice, doesn't it? It's certainly non-confrontational; however, it isn't the truth. At the end of the day, there really was only one ring, and the others were imitations.

There is only one Gospel, and all others are fake. There is no magic in the others, either—no supernatural power, no cleansing, no redemption, no hope, no heaven to be found by those who are deceived.

So, Paul cautions Titus to make sure he finds men who will cling to the apostolic faith, unswerving in their defense of its narrow truths.

Times will change, but the message won't. Titus is to find men who will refuse to let go of the Gospel—men convinced of their position. Men willing to take on the mantle of a shepherd, knowing that as soon as they do, the heat will be turned up like never before; the pressure will be enormous for them to soften the edges of repentance and doctrine and discipleship and to compromise the exclusive claims of faith in Christ alone.

Anybody made out of chocolate just isn't going to survive.

THE CHALLENGE

Paul moves on to give Titus two statements about what the elders actually accomplish through the exposition of God's Word.

Preaching Sound Doctrine

Exhort: to urge by strong, often stirring argument, admonition. This implies urging the listener to respond—to receive and apply the truth. It's more than transferring information from the notes on the pulpit to the note-takers in the pew. Exhortation is verdict-oriented:

> [S]*o that he will be able both to* **exhort** *in sound doctrine* (Titus 1:9*b*).

To **exhort** means to seek by God's Spirit to influence the heart and the conscience and the will of the listener.[11]

The word Paul uses here is from *parakaleo*, which refers to the Holy Spirit (the *parakletos*), who encourages and convicts and reforms us.

A modern equivalent would be a reference to a good coach who knows what his players need, even though they might disagree.[12] I don't know about you, but out on the practice field, I never heard my high school soccer coach say, "Guys, the real reason we're out here today is for you to feel good about yourselves; give the guy next to you a big hug. And I want you to be comfortable in your new cleats, so if you want to run some laps, that'll be just fine with me . . . I mean, I'd like you to be in shape, but you go ahead and figure out what that means to you personally—I just want this season to be filled with happy thoughts for all of us."

Hardly. My soccer coach used to run us until we collapsed. We prayed for the rapture. But he also knew just how to encourage us—and motivate us—and stretch us. He talked strategy and teamwork and let us know about the teams we were going to go up against. And after we were dead tired, he'd tell us why it mattered—but we already knew . . . and it paid off.

He was an exhorter.

True biblical exposition is **exhortation**: it actually joins the truth of the Word of God with the Spirit of God in bringing about transformation to the child of God so that truth becomes a way of *life*.

Notice Paul's wording: he describes this doctrine as *sound*. It comes from the Greek word *hugaino*, which gives us our English word *hygiene*.

It literally means *healthy*. In past times, doctors referred to someone as "sound of wind and limb"—in other words, they were healthy.[13] So *sound doctrine* produces healthy Christians, and doctrinally healthy Christians make up a healthy church.

Behind it all is a commitment to sound biblical exposition. Titus was to find men who love the Word enough to study it and deliver it so that the body will be spiritually healthy.

Confronting False Doctrine

Refute: to prove to be false or erroneous; overthrow by argument or proof. The elder's ministry is both constructive and confrontative—both positive *and* negative:

[T]o refute those who contradict (Titus 1:9c).

John Calvin the Reformer wrote that a pastor needs two voices: one for gathering the sheep and the other for driving away the wolves and thieves.[14]

Paul is going to spend several verses detailing what that kind of confrontation looks like, and we'll come to that portion later in *Titus 2*.

But for now, this word translated **refute** means to literally show people their sins and summon them to repentance.[15] Paul knew that Titus needed men who would be willing to both deliver the truth and expose the error; something every generation needs, especially today.

In our day, to call something sinful or to say that someone is in need of salvation is to be considered unloving or judgmental . . . or even divisive. "What right do you have to judge me . . . to call what I'm doing sinful?"

Calling cyanide a form of poison is not being judgmental. Telling your child that the neighbor's dog will bite him isn't being unkind to animals. Telling someone they need to be saved and that they are following a false prophet or false god or false messiah is not being unloving—it is actually a loving thing to warn someone of hell and teach them the way to heaven.

Our culture is like an airplane which has flown into thick clouds; you can't see out the window. You might think you're okay, but you're actually heading for the side of a mountain; you think you're ascending but you are descending. A tragic end is just ahead.

Titus has the list of all the qualifications, and he's to find men who know how to read the instrument panel . . . men who will stand up and accept both the positive and negative aspects of Bible exposition . . . men who will tell the truth in spite of congregations who believe everything is safe.

I remember my first rumblings of both sadness and anger as I listened to a false teacher deliver a message to his church:

> When I was a freshman in Bible college, several buildings downtown were used for classes and dormitories (a campus was yet to be built). As I walked to class, I passed a beautiful church of stone with stained glass windows and an immaculate lawn. The name of the church was generic to me; it said Universalist Church on the sign. I knew nothing about its doctrine but decided to find out. On Easter Sunday, I slipped into that beautiful stone chapel—slate floor, hand-cut pews, soft cushions. People around me were well-dressed and held

neatly printed bulletins in their hands. We stood to sing a hymn as the service began. It sounded religious enough, although I'd never heard it before and it contained nothing of Christ—certainly nothing about His resurrection for this Easter service. Then Dr. So-and-So, in his robe and stole, rose to speak. He rambled on and on, and as I sat there listening, I was horrified that he was delivering to this congregation—on Easter Sunday—reasons why Jesus Christ did *not* rise from the dead. Jesus was still in the grave! He explained that the Church was more than Christ, and it didn't matter if Jesus were dead or alive.

I can still feel today what I felt in that pew: righteous anger at that man made out of chocolate who stood for nothing; a man who had melted down years earlier—and then great pity for the people sitting there who, instead of rejoicing in the resurrection of the Savior, were being led to believe He was still dead.

That moment marked me. Even though I was planning at the time on becoming a history teacher after college, that event uniquely stirred me to realize that people needed to hear the genuine Gospel of Christ.

THE CALLING

Now, almost forty years later, it remains my great duty and delight to wear the mantle of a shepherd, to both battle the wolves as well as exhort and encourage the flock along a saving path of sound doctrine.

Chuck Swindoll, the Chancellor of Dallas Seminary, wrote some commentary on this text in Titus—words that I hope will reassure the flock but also impress all who wear the mantle of a shepherd:

> If God is pulling His people toward their [spiritual] destiny, I suppose that makes the spiritual leader God's rope. Though the tension gets almost unbearable and sometimes I fear my rope is coming unraveled, no one should pity me. While one end drags the church through each difficulty, the other feels the firm, reassuring grip of an ever-faithful God. And, for

reasons not even I can explain, there's no place I'd rather be. Maybe that's why this is not a job; this is a calling.[16]

That's the heart of a true shepherd.

According to Paul's own perspective to Titus, Jesus Christ will not be pleased with anyone else. The Church deserves nothing less.

This is a calling, then, for men—either vocationally or voluntarily—to stand diligently on the Word of God . . . driven by the pleasure of God . . . dedicated to the people of God.

Paul urges Titus to find this kind of men who can withstand the heat; men who will refuse to melt.

[10]For there are many rebellious men, empty talkers and deceivers, especially those of the circumcision, [11]who must be silenced because they are upsetting whole families, teaching things they should not teach for the sake of sordid gain.

– Titus 1:10–11

CHAPTER NINE

CHRISTIAN CON ARTISTS

Titus 1:10–11

SCAMMED BY PROS

Do a little research on con artists and scams and you'll uncover more information than you have time to read:

- **Irish Sweepstakes** – the Irish don't sell sweepstakes in the United States, so that's your first clue!

- **Going-Out-of-Business sales** – recently opened businesses often announce GOING OUT OF BUSINESS! sales, run by professionals who may be offloading stolen goods or inferior brands.

- **Counterfeit goods** – everything from designer purses to high-end watches are pawned off on those who can't believe the low price.

- **Rental properties and vacant lots** – a scammer's delight to pose as an owner renting or leasing property, sticking around just long enough to get the down payment or first month's deposit before they disappear.

- **Natural disasters** – a con artist's opportunity to raise money door-to-door, by internet or phone, pretending to assist those affected by the disaster but, in reality, keeping the money.

The definition of a *con artist* is a person who intentionally misleads another person for the sake of personal financial gain.

Italian immigrant Charles Ponzi became a household word as one of the most famous con men in American history. Today, a crooked investment offering unrealistic returns is tagged with his last name.

You may have heard of another man who fabricated different professions:

> During his criminal life, Frank Abagnale passed off bad checks worth more than two million dollars in twenty-six different countries. He posed as a Pan Am pilot, abusing airline courtesy which allowed pilots to travel free of charge. After he was nearly caught leaving a plane, he changed his profession to doctor, working as a medical supervisor. He also worked as a lawyer and a teacher. He was eventually arrested but escaped from prison impersonating an undercover officer. Caught and imprisoned again, he served only five years before being offered his freedom in return for helping the government develop systems to counter fraud and scam artists. Today he has his own financial fraud consulting firm, is a millionaire and an author.[1]

Who said crime doesn't pay?!

One con artist from the early 1900s built and sold a device to produce the perfect counterfeit hundred dollar bill. He was able to convince people to buy it for $30,000 but warned that the device would only print one bill every six hours His printing press contained two genuine hundred dollar bills, but once the machine emitted them, it produced only gray paper. By the time the buyer discovered the scam, the con artist had used those twelve hours to put hundreds of miles between him and his latest victim.

Ever heard the quip, "If you believe that, then I've got a bridge to sell you"? One man's exploits have passed into pop culture, giving rise to that expression as a way of referring to someone as extremely gullible:

> George Parker was one of the most audacious con men in American history. He made his living selling New York's public landmarks to unwary tourists. On several occasions he sold Grant's Tomb, posing as the general's grandson. Other sales included the original Madison Square Garden, the Metropolitan Museum of Art, and the Statue of Liberty. He

set up an office to handle his real estate scams, producing impressive forged documents to prove that he was the legal owner of whatever property he was selling. But His favorite object was the Brooklyn Bridge, which he sold several times, convincing his gullible victims that they would be able to make a fortune by controlling access to the bridge. On more than one occasion, police had to remove the unsuspecting new owners when they tried to put up toll barriers so they could start charging drivers on their morning commute. On his third conviction of fraud, he was sentenced to a life term in Sing Sing, where he spent eight years until his death.[2]

The internet is constantly touting one scam after another; as soon as you send your deposit or downpayment, you're left holding a bag of empty promises.

One current claim promised: "Earn a college degree at home; no tests; no grades." I wish that had been around thirty years ago. Of course, it's a diploma mill and the degree is worthless, but you can hang it on the wall and impress your friends.

Another banner flashes:

BAD CREDIT? NO CREDIT? NO PROBLEM—YOU'RE PRE-APPROVED!

One online pop-up offers a laptop and printer for only $39.99, direct from the factory . . . *just click here.*

Another promises: Earn $5,000 a week working from home, part-time. Send money for the instruction kit to tell you how.

All I can say is if you believe these ads . . . well, there's a bridge in Brooklyn you can buy.

Obviously, scam artists proliferated in all cultures. Travel back to the Old Testament and listen to Micah the prophet warn:

> *They dream up crimes while lying in bed and as soon as its morning light, they take off, full of energy to put their schemes into practice.* (Micah 2:1 paraphrase).

It's one thing for a scam artist to cause people to lose their money—it's quite another when a *religious* scam artist causes people to lose both their money and their spiritual equilibrium, potentially losing their souls as they are led into deception.

SPIRITUAL COUNTERFEITS

The Apostle Paul instructs Titus how to put the Church in good effective working order; it was paramount to appoint trustworthy men who would wear the mantle of the shepherd so that people would be led honestly and biblically.

It's little wonder that after giving the qualifications of an elder, Paul immediately reminds Titus and all the churches of Crete that there are dangers on the island . . . and the primary danger is nothing less than con artists who were intent on scamming the Church by teaching a mixture of truth and error.

Wherever the seeds of truth are sown, the seeds of deception will be germinating, as well. There's no such thing as a lawn or garden without weeds. Those who serve as shepherds must not only sow the seeds of doctrine but pull the weeds of deception—what Paul called *doctrines of demons* (1 Timothy 4:1) . . . doctrines that seem orthodox and correct but actually mislead, taking followers through the gates of religion into the grasp of hell.

Satan happens to be *the* master at deception. He's incredibly and patiently skillful. He's had several thousand years to practice on people, and from the Garden of Eden at the beginning of human history to the twenty-first century, he has honed his craft.

Satan is the ultimate con artist.

His favorite scam—where many have been distracted and divided and, even, destroyed—has been, as one author put it, to drape his lies in the beautiful robes of truth.[3]

He hides his deceptions behind stained-glass smiles and pious promises. Paul effectively writes, "Titus . . . you've got to be able to spot the lie and expose the liars. And for that you need to select men who can do the same—men with spiritual discernment, courage, and insight."

Chuck Swindoll writes of this task given to Titus who was surrounded by spiritual deceivers:

> And how convincing these false teachers are. Keeping their true nature carefully concealed—even from themselves [remember they will one day stand and say, "Did we not prophesy in Your name and cast out demons in Your name and perform miracles in Your name?" and the Lord Jesus will say, "I never knew you."]—yet they deftly move among the elect, up through the ranks of authority, and into positions of

power. Lacking [biblical] truth, they win friends and influence people by means of a charisma that's difficult to resist, even for those who despise falsehood. Nevertheless a trained eye can spot them.[4]

How do you spot a con artist?

Paul writes, as he sets the stage for the defensive role of a shepherd:

> **[S]***o that he* [the elder/bishop/pastor] ***will be able both to exhort in sound doctrine and to refute those who contradict*** (Titus 1:9*b*).

How do you spot them? Paul provides three descriptive characteristics of these decievers who lead the Church astray. At least one or more of these will be evident to those trained in the Word and given the role of guarding the flock—and certainly the Church at large should be trained, as well.

Untrustworthy Personalities

For there are many* rebellious *men (Titus 1:10*a*).

The word here translated **rebellious** is the same word found in ***Titus 1:6*** for an elder candidate's child whose lifestyle is uncontrollable disobedience (someone who sets himself up as the authority, having no regard for the authority of his father); the child discredits his father from serving as an elder. Paul uses the word here to describe those who contradict the truth.

Under the guise of serving as a spiritual leader and teacher, this is the man who claims to be the *ultimate* authority in spiritual matters. His favorite phrases will explicitly state or subtly imply, "God doesn't speak to you like He speaks to *me*; God told *me* what I'm telling you . . . if you wanna argue with God, that's your problem." In other words, he becomes the spiritual authority and he alone is the true *source* of spiritual insight.

The Bible will be a *resource* for what he teaches—it will not be the *source* of what he teaches. And his favorite verse will probably be often quoted,

> *"Do not touch My* [God's] *anointed ones, and do My prophets no harm"* (I Chronicles 16:22).

That verse becomes his shield . . . he sets himself off limits to scrutiny; he's above and beyond anyone's jurisdiction. Besides, no one else is as smart as he is or as close to God as he is or as anointed as he is—so whatever he says must be from God and you just need to keep your hands off.

He's God's anointed.

Someone sent me a video link to a church service some time ago:

> Several thousand people stood and cheered as a visiting evan-
> gelist brought onto the stage a huge scroll of the Torah—the
> first five books of the Old Testament. The evangelist claimed
> that he would perform a ceremony in which the pastor would
> receive a special anointing from God. Part of the scroll was
> unrolled and the pastor stood there on stage, while part of it
> was wrapped around his body until he was hidden from sight.
> Then, after making all sorts of declarations that sounded
> slightly biblical but mostly mystical—actually, heretical—the
> scroll was unwrapped and, as the pastor stepped forward, he
> was proclaimed as one uniquely anointed to speak with the
> *same* inspiration from God as the Torah was inspired by God.
> This inspired pastor was then seated in his pastoral chair and
> several men lifted him up over their heads and paraded him
> around the stage as the evangelist proclaimed that he was now
> a prophet and a king. And everyone cheered.[5]

I sat there watching the video with my mouth open. How does that kind of blasphemy go unchecked? How do any man's thoughts and words become inspired *equally* with the text of Scripture?

Frankly, one of the protective benefits of a plurality of spiritual shepherds is that no man remains unaccountable to inspection . . . even the Apostle Peter was rebuked for errant thinking *(Galatians 2:11)*; Paul was willing to defer to the counsel of other leaders in the church at Jerusalem *(Galatians 2:2)*.

What makes spiritual deceivers all the more dangerous is the implication here in **Titus 1:10**: they are rising from *within* the body. These are professing believers, not unbelievers.

We can piece together from Paul's warning here that their deceptive teaching seems to have the endorsement of the Church. In other words, they aren't being shouted down, they're being cheered on.

Empty Promises

For there are many rebellious men, empty talkers (Titus 1:10*b*).

Paul goes further here by describing these false teachers as **empty talkers**. This is the only time this adjective is used in the entire New Testament. It refers to someone who speaks with worthless words—someone who uses impressive language with little or no solid content of truth.[6]

They are fluent but shallow.[7]

They are great at making speeches, but when you evaluate the content, they are biblically shallow at best and deceptively misleading at worst.

One author said, "You can always spot those who don't teach the truth by the way they so beautifully say absolutely *nothing*."[8]

They're slick . . . they're smooth . . . they're persuasive . . . they're pleasing . . . they're captivating. Just try to pin them down on a matter of biblical truth and they'll always wriggle out of it.

I watched as one false teacher who pastors a church with thousands of followers was asked straight forward black-and-white questions about what the Bible says on a variety of issues. Rather than provide clear biblical answers that would have been, no doubt, offensive, he dodged the issues time and again by responding, "Well, I don't know . . . I just can't say . . . I'm leaving that up to God."

It's one thing if the world never asks us what the Bible says about a particular matter—but when it does, there must be leaders within the Church who will tell the world the truth, no matter how unpopular. And the truth is God has actually *left it up to us* to inform our world of whatever He's already said.

But there's a greater danger bound up in this characteristic of a false teacher. Paul says that he's an **empty talker**. What he says has no lasting spiritual value. He delivers smooth words without spiritual life.

In his powerful exposé on contemporary Christianity, Michael Horton entitled his book *Christless Christianity*. He explains that Christless Christianity doesn't mean that false religion or false spirituality refuses to use the names of Jesus, Lord, or Savior.[9] The trouble is, those names are simply removed from their biblical contexts of sin, rebellion, divine rescue, heaven, and hell. He adds that Jesus becomes a therapist or a buddy, a significant other, a political messiah. The Gospel might be tacked on at the end of a sermon, but in reality, the Gospel is only window dressing.

Horton extensively evaluated the content of messages preached by popular speakers and authors Joel Osteen, Joyce Meyer, T.D. Jakes, and Kenneth Copeland. They may wrap up their sermons by asking people to accept Jesus as their Lord and Savior, which makes them sound all the more biblical, but a Savior from *what*? That question remains unanswered unless you understand that these false teachers, and others, are merely referring to being saved from an unfulfilling job or oppression or sickness or low self esteem or, worst of all, poverty.

The Bible is a resource for their teaching and advice but not the *source* of their teaching.

Horton goes on to write that when he and his wife were raising their triplets, they wanted all the advice they could get from everybody. And they didn't necessarily get it from Christians. Some of their best advice came from his barber and his wife.

He makes the point that you don't have to read the Bible in order to know that your children need regular sleep patterns; that the secret of a good marriage is talking to each other; that divorce is devastating for children; that if you don't rule your credit cards, they will rule you. Of course the Bible gives us a lot more wisdom than this, but there are plenty of non-Christians who actually do a better job at doing the right thing than some Christians.[10]

Michael makes this point: the truth is, someone can lose weight, stop smoking, improve his marriage, and become a nicer person *without* Jesus.[11]

In other words, if Christianity is nothing more than ethical advice—ways to become a better person and live the best life possible—who are we to say that our religion is the only true religion? There are other religions that have similar doctrines of morality . . . and other people can become *better* people because of it, as well.

If religion is basically ethics—if you reduce Christianity to good advice—it blends in perfectly with the culture of [religion]. Our teaching might seem especially relevant, but it actually gets lost in the marketplace of moralistic therapies.[12]

So who are we to say that Christianity is the only *true* religion—especially when the kind of Christianity now peddled by so many false teachers is nothing more than good advice, moral platitudes, and marriage pointers?

Here's the point: what distinguishes Christianity at its heart is not necessarily its moral code but its [truth] about a Creator who, although rejected by those He created in His image, stooped to reconcile them to Himself through His Son.[13]

In other words, Christianity at its *heart* is the Gospel—the Good News that God has reconciled us to Himself in Christ. *That's* the distinguishing mark of Christianity. And everything flows out of the context of who we are as redeemed, reconciled, clothed-in-the-righteousness-of-Christ children of God . . . by faith alone in Christ alone. We have *that* kind of Savior and *that* kind of Lord and *that* kind of salvation.

But what does the false teacher focus on?

- How to get heaven here and now.
- How to get some of that gold pavement up there down here.
- How to get healthier and stay healthy.
- How to learn the secrets of a good self image and a positive way of thinking for today.
- How to pull out of yourself those seeds of greatness for successful living now.

Other religions teach these empty words, as well. Everything is taught *except* the Gospel, which is sin and redemption and Jesus Christ as the crucified atoning Lamb for sinners slain and, even now, the soon-coming King before Whom we will fall and worship.

That's the *good* news.

The good news goes way beyond bank accounts and health checkups. Think about it: if money made people happy, then the richest people on the planet would be the happiest and the poorest would be the most miserable.

And we know that isn't true.

If good health made you secure and satisfied, then sick people would have no joy and personal trainers and body builders would be the truly happy people.

We know that isn't true, either.

A con artist gives you what you think you want, but in the end all you have is empty promises.

If an angel were to give us all one wish, I wonder how many would ask for wisdom, like Solomon—the only man ever to have been given a one-wish opportunity from God—who asked for something most meaningful and profound.

An angel came to a married couple in their mid-sixties and said, "I am allowed to grant each of you one wish—ladies first." The woman said, "Oh,

I've always wanted to go on a Caribbean cruise and I'd love tickets for my husband and me to go first class." The angel said, "Sure," and *poof!*—she was holding two first-class tickets. The angel looked at the husband and said, "Okay, your turn." He looked at his wife, grinned, and said, "Well, I'd like to go on that cruise with a woman thirty years younger than me." The angel said, "Sure," and *poof!*—he was ninety-six years old. Serves him right.

One of the reasons there will *always* be a market for spiritual con artists is because our hearts pander for whatever they happen to be peddling: heaven now . . . health now . . . money now . . . greatness now . . . no problems now . . . the *false* gospel is all about *me, me, me.*

Frankly, if people got everything these empty talkers promised, why would anyone ever want to go to heaven? Heaven would be anticlimactic!

These false teachers promise what they cannot deliver . . . and in the end, the Gospel is missing from the conversation—and that's the only thing that will ultimately deliver anybody.

In an issue of *The Christian Post*, an article ran entitled "Why Muslims Convert to Christianity." And among the leading reasons were these: as they read the Bible, they were convicted by its truth; they were attracted by the concept of God's unconditional love [through Christ]; they could never be certain of their forgiveness and salvation as Christians can.[14] Their religion simply wasn't the same; it wasn't good news . . . even their great prophet Mohammed wasn't certain of his own forgiveness.

Christianity is more than the empty promises of the world's religions.

Deceptive Promoters

For there are many rebellious men, empty talkers and deceivers, *especially those of the circumcision* (Titus 1:10c).

Notice Paul writes, literally, they are *out of **the circumcision**.* In other words, there were converts from among the Jewish people who had entered the Church without being willing to fully embrace the new covenant.

Much of the Book of Acts attempts to deal with the issue of Jewish and Gentile believers reaching consensus based on the Gospel and this brand-new organism called the Church—something no one had any idea of prior to Pentecost and the coming of the Holy Spirit.

The largely Jewish early Church wanted Gentiles to become Jews in order to become Christians. They demanded that Gentiles be circumcised, adhere to the Sabbath, abstain from eating non-kosher meat, keep the Mosaic Law, and bow to rabbinical teachings. Basically, these false teachers wanted to turn Christianity into another Jewish sect.[15]

Paul spent most of his life battling these Judaizers, as they were called. They dogged his footsteps, subverted his converts, attacked his apostleship, challenged his authority, undermined his teaching, and distorted the Gospel.[16]

To put it simply:

- They were teaching that the Gospel wasn't sufficient for faith.
- They were teaching that grace wasn't the standard for life.
- They were teaching that Jesus isn't enough and you've gotta keep our national rules if you ever hope to get into heaven.

Paul wasn't going to take it sitting down. He tells Titus in very strong words: ***They've got to be silenced!*** (Titus 1:11*a* paraphrase).

The word for ***silenced*** literally means *to muzzle*—to cover over their mouths.[17] The present tense points to continuous action, which lets you know that an elder/shepherd is never off duty in watching for, being alert to, and addressing false teachers.

Paul urged Titus to catch these con artists and bring them out into the open . . . expose them . . . silence them—not by literally gagging them but by responding with the truth which effectively shut their mouths.

This takes us back to an earlier qualification of an elder:

> **[T]*hat he will be able both to exhort in sound doctrine and to refute those who contradict*** (Titus 1:9*b*).

And notice what these false teachers are doing to the flock.

SCANDALOUS CONSEQUENCES

[T]*hey are* upsetting *whole families* (Titus 1:11*a*).

Upsetting is the same word used of Christ *turning over* the tables of the moneychangers in the temple *(Matthew 21:12)*.

Families Were Being Turned Upside Down

Everything was literally turned upside down. You can only imagine the conflict and emotion, pain and confusion, anger and despair over the false teaching in these churches on the island of Crete; their unity was now dangerously at risk.

I went to a city in Africa to preach in several churches not long after a self-proclaimed Christian "prophet" held crusades in that city, announcing to his stadium audience that Jesus had told him that He would be making a brief appearance on stage one night of the meetings. On a particular night, he suddenly looked in one direction and began to get excited . . . he put on quite a show, as if he were seeing Jesus on the stage. He then asked that huge crowd, "Did you see Him . . . did you see Him?" People fainted and cried as pandemonium broke out.

I was having lunch with two church leaders in Kenya—men who served as secretaries of two evangelical denominations in that region—and they both informed me that so many of their churches were now confused and divided over who believed Jesus had appeared and who believed that He really hadn't.

That false teacher who claimed to have direct communication with Jesus was now turning everything upside down, dividing the African believers into factions of anger, frustration, and confusion.

False Teachers Were Raking in the Dough

[T]*hey are teaching things they shouldn't teach,* for the sake of sordid gain (Titus 1:11*b*).

The prepositional phrase **for the sake of** indicates that this was the goal of their activity. This was the heart of their motivation for teaching things that were unbiblical.

By the way, **sordid gain** can certainly mean money, but Paul uses it elsewhere for non-financial motivation—social leverage, power, and prestige. In other words, these teachers were more interested in what they could get *out* of people than what they could invest *in* people. No doubt, financial gain often accompanied the popularity of these false teachers.

As they do today, the fraudulent con artists on the island of Crete might have to defend their opulent lifestyles, saying that since they preached prosperity they, above all others, should live prosperously.

It is tragically amazing what false teachers are able to get out of the Bible and what their followers let them get away with. Some of these false teachers today—many with television programs—don't even attempt to hide their wealth: they're dripping with designer clothing and jewelry . . . and always asking for more.

If you eliminated everything from their programs having to do with health, wealth, and prosperity, all you'd end up with is the opening music and the closing credits.

False teachers aren't driven to build up believers, they are driven to fill up their own pockets.[18] They are skillful con artists running organized scams.

STEADFAST COMMITMENT

Paul reminds Titus that the flock is in constant danger of being misled, abused, and fleeced, so when they appoint elders in the Church, make sure they protect the flock by unmasking the fraud and speaking up for the truth in order to keep the flock on the path.

After spending Thanksgiving with family in Seattle, James and Kati, along with their daughters Penelope and Sabine (ages four and seven months), began their long journey back to San Francisco. They traveled until late in the evening, intending to exit and spend the night in a lodge, but they missed their turn. Instead of backtracking, they followed a map that seemed to show a shortcut; after encountering snow drifts too high to drive through, they turned off onto a spur road. They struggled along that unpaved road until their vehicle became stuck in the drifting snow. The family remained with the car for one week, hoping for rescue, running the car intermittently for heat and rationing their small amount of food. When the car ran out of gas, they burned magazines, wood, and the car tires to keep warm. James decided to hike back for help but never made it. A search party found his body one-half mile from where he started; had he walked the other direction, he was only a mile and a half from a fully stocked fishing lodge. His wife and children were eventually rescued.[19]

The flock of God is on a path leading home—heaven isn't here and now, but it's coming soon. False teachers stand by the roadside, selling counterfeit maps and promising short cuts to the coast. "Why struggle" they urge, "through deep valleys and cold mountain tops? Our way is easier, happier, healthier, faster, and you can have all your wishes come true along the way."

Don't be conned by those who come "in the name of Jesus." Repeating our Savior's name is simply part of their game . . . it cleverly disguises their scam. What they offer is empty, shallow, temporary promises, and road maps that never quite match up with God's Word.

Paul is telling Titus to warn the flock to be careful . . . stay the course . . . ignore all the advertisements—and be willing to take the long way home.

¹¹[T]*eaching things they should not teach for the sake of sordid gain* ¹²*One of themselves, a prophet of their own, said, "Cretans are always liars, evil beasts, lazy gluttons."* ¹³*This testimony is true. For this reason reprove them severely so that they may be sound in the faith,* ¹⁴*not paying attention to Jewish myths and commandments of men who turn away from the truth.* ¹⁵*To the pure, all things are pure; but to those who are defiled and unbelieving, nothing is pure, but both their mind and their conscience are defiled.* ¹⁶*They profess to know God, but by their deeds they deny Him, being detestable and disobedient and worthless for any good deed.*

– Titus 1:11–16

CHAPTER TEN

UNMASKED

Titus 1:11–16

THE FAÇADE

Have you ever noticed that those who commit crimes cover their faces—and sometimes their heads and bodies—before comitting their crimes? We see images of foreign fighters on the news with their faces and heads swathed in cloth and photos of thieves and vandals disguised by masks. The reasons are obvious.

The Apostle Paul is committed to unmasking the deceivers and false teachers, sounding a warning that every generation should heed.

In his commentary on the Book of Titus, Warren Wiersbe writes:

> It did not take long for false teachers to arise in the early church. Wherever God sows the truth, Satan quickly shows up to sow lies. False doctrine is like [cancer]; it enters secretly, it grows quickly, and it permeates completely unless it is attacked before it has a chance to spread.[1]

This was a serious problem on the island of Crete. False teaching—false religion—false teachers—deceived flocks—twisted Scripture—additions to Scripture—distortions of Scripture . . . all done by seemingly religious men whose motives are *actually* self-serving.

Paul won't completely stamp out the problem, nor will Titus. It has continued spreading to this day and its viral symptoms have already reached your town and mine.

In **Titus 1:14** we notice immediately that the infectious plague of false teaching was easily discernible; it was mixed with myths and fables, along with *extra* commandments made up by misleading men.

In fact, it was simply *manmade*—make-believe—things that sounded biblical but weren't actually *in* the Bible. The result was epidemic; Paul will refer to their religious mythologies and extra commandments taught as a way to seduce the flock for their benefit rather than shepherd the flock for its benefit. These self-proclaimed prophets were ripping the churches apart on Crete.

Paul knows that the critical need is for the Church to be well-led and well-fed. He leaves Titus to appoint shepherds/feeders in every church who would courageously expose these teachers—false teachers who were supposedly revealing *deeper* truths . . . explaining *wiser* principles for living . . . uncovering *newer* secrets about God and the way to heaven.

For the sake of the Gospel and the protection of the flock, Paul tells Titus (and every elder since) to unmask the pretenders—dismantle the façade—allow the Church to see them for who they really are.

UNMASKING THEIR MOTIVES: MONEY & FAME

[T]*eaching things they should not teach for the sake of* sordid gain (Titus 1:11*b*).

Paul simply dives in and calls it like it is—it's all about money and fame. In fact, the word translated **gain** can be understood to be either money or fame . . . or both, and in this case, Paul is probably referring to both.

When Paul was writing this letter to Titus, the ancient world spoke of three evil C's: the Cilicians, the Cappadocians, and the Cretans.[2]

By the time of Titus's ministry on the island, the Greek historian Polybius had already written that the Cretans were given to self-promotion and gain; they lived in a perpetual state of private quarrel and public feud and civil strife—tricky, deceptive characters. He writes:

Money is so highly valued among them that its possession [provides instant credibility]; greed is so native to the soil in Crete that they are the only people in the world among whom no stigma is attached to any sort of *gain* whatever.[3]

In other words, to the Cretan it didn't matter *how* you got what you had, so long as you had it. In our modern vernacular we might call **sordid gain** drug money or laundered money or hush money—you're rich and you got it the wrong way, but who cares?

The Cretans didn't!

If you had money, nothing more mattered . . . and nothing mattered more. Money talked . . . and fame was everything. This was the culture of Crete.

Now what Paul says next is surprising. He appeals to common knowledge in his ancient world by quoting someone who was highly respected and revered as a prophet . . . a man who centuries earlier had pulled the mask off the Cretans and left them barefaced:

> **One of themselves, a prophet of their own, said, "Cretans are always liars, evil beasts, lazy gluttons." This testimony is true** (Titus 1:12–13*a*).

What makes this so intriguing is that the guy pulling off the masks of Cretan deceivers is a Cretan himself, evidently experiencing a brief moment of honest reflection.

Paul is bolstering his argument—which is going to be hard to swallow on the island of Crete—when he writes this. So he effectively says, "Listen, a Cretan even admits that Cretans are lazy liars; he's not just *any* Cretan—he's one of your own revered prophets."

Paul is quoting Epimenides, a native-born man from the island of Crete. Plato placed his life around 500 years before the birth of Christ.[4]

And notice the first thing their beloved prophet had to say about his own people, as a general rule: *"Cretans are always liars."*

And Paul adds, *This testimony is true*!

In other words, this is the rule of thumb: the civilization of Crete is literally given over to lying.

Can you imagine a culture so saturated with deception? Do Cretans seem like someone *you* know?

USA Today ran the results of a survey where 7,000 resumés were investigated. The results showed:

- 48% exaggerated their former compensation;
- 52% turned partial college or graduate work into earned degrees;
- 60% exaggerated the number of people under their former supervision;
- 64% exaggerated their former accomplishments;
- 71% lied about the number of years they spent at their former job.[5]

Another survey found people admitting to:

- calling in sick at work when they weren't;
- taking office supplies from their company for personal use;
- shifting blame to a co-worker for something they did;
- receiving too much change from a cashier without telling them;
- downloading music without paying for it;
- cheating on their income tax;
- switching price tags to get a lower price;
- lying to friends and family over multiple things.

Sounds a lot like Cretans to me.

This text isn't given to Titus or to us so the Church can sit around and say, "Look at all those terrible Cretans." It was designed for evaluation. Has the tide of lying and deception flooded our island, too?

In raising children, we discover that these sinful problems didn't originate on the island of Crete—they appeared when the first humans lied in the Garden of Eden. This is why you never have to teach your children *how* to lie. By age five, they're pretty good at it.

We're like that little guy who got his Bible memory verse mixed up and said a mouthful when he quoted, "Lying is an abomination unto the Lord, but a very present help in time of trouble."[6]

Frankly, lying can pay off in the short run . . . fifty percent of those resumés indicated that people were banking on it. But it can easily entangle you and catch up to you over time. Sir Walter Scott famously wrote, "Oh, what a tangled web we weave, when first we practice to deceive."

My father often said to us four boys as we were growing up, "Boys, tell-ing the truth is actually a lot easier on you than lying because when you tell the truth, you never have to remember what you said."

There is an implicit warning from Paul in this text: don't buy into the culture of your island.

Paul quotes further in this verse that Cretans were also ***evil beasts***. This term refers to someone who was untamable and uncontrollable—they liter-ally had no respect for authority and could not be reined in.

In fact, during the days of Titus, people were already joking that there were no wild animals on the island of Crete because the people were so wild.[7]

Going further, Paul called them ***lazy gluttons***. This can be translated *idle stomachs*, referring to those who were given over to luxurious feasting and refused to work [an honest job].[8] In other words, they wanted to do nothing more than deceive people into supporting their work while they grew figuratively and literally fat by means of their opulent lifestyle. They were living off their deceptive ways, always on the lookout for new ways to pull off another scam.

Paul responds to this characterization by Epimenides by adding his own exclamation point: ***This testimony is true.***

There was no need to deny it. The congregations on this island and especially the elders/shepherds need to face the facts: this is true![9]

The game of religion had already begun . . . false teachers who were nothing more than greedy hucksters were selling their message for the sake of sordid gain. Religion was their way to cheat people out of money and affec-tion—and it continues to be a most profitable scam today!

Paul warns Titus, "Listen, this is what you and the men you appoint as elders are up against. The role of a shepherd is to warn the flock and protect them—and while you're at it, unmask the motives of false teachers; behind their masks of pious and religious language are men who only care about building their own portfolio and popularity."

Paul isn't offering suggestions, either—he literally commands the elders into action:

> ***For this reason* reprove them severely *so that they may be sound in the faith*** (Titus 1:13*b*).

The Greek root word translated **sound** (*hugaino*) gives us our English word *hygiene*.[10]

In other words, these false teachers were spiritually diseased and needed to be made sound—healthy in the faith. And the command is to **reprove them**—stand up to them—expose their error—**reprove them severely**.

That adverb can be rendered *abruptly* or *sharply*.[11] It implies the swift and skillful cutting of the surgeon's knife, excising that which isn't healthy so there can be healing.

I am an illustration of that procedure; when the doctor diagnosed my broken knee—again—he said this time there would have to be surgery. I couldn't excuse myself from the severity of the injury. I couldn't settle for ice on my knee to take away the swelling. I couldn't ask for one of those SpongeBob SquarePants Band-Aids© I saw on the counter or start taking some really strong medication to take away the pain.

I could have used all three, but they would never have brought healing. It had to be dealt with *severely* . . . invasively . . . in order for me to be restored to good health.

Paul says for Titus to **reprove them severely**. And that, by the way, is in the present tense, implying that this invasive procedure and its effects are going to be felt for a long time.[12] In other words, the problem isn't going to be fixed overnight.

Titus and the other elders need to be in this for the long haul; Paul isn't suggesting a Sunday series to address false teaching—this is an ongoing obligation for those who wear the mantle of a true shepherd.

UNMASKING THEIR TEACHING: MYTHS & FABLES

[N]*ot paying attention to Jewish* myths *and* commandments of men *who turn away from the truth* (Titus 1:14).

Paul continues to reference these false teachers who are putting forth concepts that are manmade. They *are* teaching—don't miss this—they've got outlines, study notes, handbooks, and best-selling hardbacks. They're holding seminars and weekend conferences. And they are good enough at speaking and teaching that, from what Paul implies, many people are buying into everything they say.

But if you take the time to inspect the issue, they might quote the Bible but don't really care about it. To this day, many will use the Bible as a resource but not as the primary source; this exposes the flock to all sorts of error and spiritual danger.

For instance, in Titus's generation *The Book of Jubilees* was a best-seller, supposedly revealing extra information on the biographies of the patriarchs; it led to all sorts of superstitions and speculations.

In addition to this, by the end of the first century, many rabbis had given mystical or numerical meaning to letters of the Hebrew alphabet, which they applied to the Old Testament Scriptures, coming up with all sorts of bizarre interpretations.

Then in the succeeding early centuries other writings were composed, claiming to be from God: Bel and the Dragon; The History of Susanna; the writings of Tobit and Judith—pure fiction, filled with historical errors and questionable morality.[13]

The Gospel of Thomas, written in the third century, claimed to contain one hundred twenty secret words of the living Jesus; it's a book that doesn't resemble the true Gospel but includes sheer myth.[14]

The Apocrypha, the Talmud, and the Cabbala are also early writings outside of inspired Scripture that have promoted some kind of moral lesson, at best, and having redefined Gospel truth, at worst.

Then there are twenty-first century authors who put traditions, legends, and gnostic gospels together—along with a bucketload of historical speculations—and you have intriguing books of fiction which, unfortunately, millions of people believe as fact.

Dig deeper into these ancient Gnostic texts and you'll discover that Jesus never was crucified at all; he married Mary Magdalene, moved to the south of France, and raised a family.

And people aren't finished treating the Bible like some sort of secret code book, either. There are currently some twenty million pages on the web devoted to the Bible Code, with the belief that secret messages are embedded in the text and all you have to do is lay out the letters and then skip every third letter and every seventh line, and the words that are formed are secret messages from God.

Never mind that the Bible Code predicted presidential assassinations that never occurred and that a more recent American leader would subsidize the Antichrist and launch global persecution. That never happened either. So, do the Bible Code people apologize for getting their secrets from God all wrong and walk away from such nonsense? Hardly. They simply search for more coded messages. And the credibility of Christianity is kicked to the curb.

By the way, the Bible Code also revealed: the South *won* the Civil War, Germany won World War II, and the moon is literally made out of Swiss cheese.

Secret codes, myths, and missing words from Christ are terrible distractions at best—spiritually destructive at worst. One thing remains, all of it is without an ounce of spiritual nourishment for the growing believer.

Evidently, the false teachers were preying on the fears of people by giving them secret messages from the mythical past of their forefathers, with all sorts of new applications and principles from hidden biographies.

Paul adds a warning about *not paying attention to Jewish* **myths** *and the* **commandments** *of men* because they will not only distract you, but *turn* [you] *away from the truth*—the truth of the Gospel of Jesus Christ.

But that's not all.

By the time Titus was appointing elders in the churches of Crete, these Jewish false teachers were promoting their centuries-old view that God had actually given the nation of Israel *two* sets of laws at Mount Sinai: one was the written law—the Torah, the first five Books of the Old Testament; the other was the oral law, which was made up of ever-growing writings, opinions, rulings, interpretations, discussion, and traditions.[15]

So you end up with the Bible (the Old Testament) *plus* something else that was granted equal authority. Think how many religions and cults around the world have the Bible *plus* something else. Think how many religions and cults out there continue to get new *updates* from God!

The uniqueness of Christianity is that God *has* spoken. We're not waiting for Him to say, "Uh . . . there's one more thing you need to know in order to live your life correctly . . . or to go to heaven."

No, true Christianity hasn't added anything to the Old Testament for thousands of years and nothing has been added or taken away from the New Testament for nearly 2,000 years.

But in Crete, teachers were gaining an audience within the Church, promising, "We've got something new from God . . . a coded message from heaven . . . wait'll you hear this one." And instead of relieving the spiritual burden of their followers, they *increased* it.

For instance, the Jews had the simple commandment to keep the Sabbath day holy—don't make it a day of work or labor. For centuries they added interpretation upon interpretation, law upon law, nuance upon nuance, so that by the time of Titus, they had decided that eating your soup was not a violation of the Sabbath law if—and I mean *if*—it didn't weigh more than one fig. I don't know how much a fig weighs, but I'm sure I've put bites of chocolate cake into my mouth that weighed much more.

It was debated whether or not you could carry your baby on the Sabbath. They assumed that taking a journey on the Sabbath would be work, so it was decided that you couldn't walk more than 200 feet past your front door. But that wasn't very accommodating, so some taught that God would allow them to tie a rope that was 200 feet long to their front door and then walk 200 feet farther.

So many regulations . . . so many rules . . . so many burdens.

All of these **myths** and **commandments** were distorting the clarity and simplicity of the Gospel. They were damaging the purity of the Gospel of faith in Christ's work alone.

Damaged doctrine damages people.[16]

Acceptance with God isn't found in manmade rules, minding your p's and q's, or washing behind your ears. All of these additional **myths** and **commandments** lead people—and the Church—into one of two errors: personal despair because you can't keep the lists of man; personal pride because your list is actually longer than others.[17]

The Gospel reveals that we are accepted in the beloved not because we've kept a list but because we've come to life . . . in Christ *(Ephesians 1:4–6)*.

There is value in convictions and sensitivities and standards and cautions and disciplines; *Romans 14* makes that very clear. Frankly, the Church today isn't struggling with being too sensitive or disciplined or careful. However, if we think that by exercising one more discipline or caution or standard or by doing everything more consistently will bring us into the favor and love of God, we will be led into *despair* for failing . . . or into *pride* for succeeding.

We live under the constant flow of Christ's cleansing blood on our behalf, for He continuously *cleanses us from all sin* (I John 1:7*b*) and because of Christ's perfect work, we imperfect people are *already* clothed in His righteousness and nothing *will be able to separate us from the love of God, which is in Christ Jesus our Lord* (Romans 8:39).

Titus and the other elders needed to make sure they were on the alert for false teaching. Paul cautioned them not to have any patience with the myths and fads of their generation or the legalistic commandments that kidnap a believer from the very truth that he is safely within the love and favor of God through Christ alone.

Paul adds this principle:

> **To the pure, all things are pure; but to those who are defiled and unbelieving, nothing is pure, but both their mind and their conscience are defiled** (Titus 1:15).

The word for **pure** means *clean*. It's the Greek word *katharos* from which we get our word *catharsis*. Taken in the context of this paragraph, Paul is saying that if you've believed the Gospel, then nothing can ever place you outside the realm of that clean estate.

That doesn't mean we can't sin—we can—but we must daily ask forgiveness so that our fellowship with the Lord is unhindered. But we don't confess in order to become a Christian all over again; we are *not* confessing for the sake of sonship—we are confessing daily sin for the sake of *fellowship*.

Paul is also conveying that those who are **pure** [clean] look at everything with the purest of intentions, desiring to be clean—they're not looking for the dirt and smut in life.

In contrast, those who are not cleansed by Christ (note the opposite word) *are* **defiled** *and* **unbelieving**. Those who don't believe the Gospel are still in their sins—their state of unbelief. And in that estate, there is nothing they can do to make themselves pure or clean. Only Christ can cleanse someone and make them whole.

Paul describes the unbeliever here as a **defiled** person whose ***mind*** and ***conscience*** can only embrace the dirty, tainted things in life.

One commentator wrote it this way:

> We change whatever we touch into our own nature; the man with a dirty mind soils every thought; his imagination turns to lust every picture which it forms . . . he can take the loveliest things and cover them with smut.[18]

It's a matter of their nature: one redeemed and cleansed; the other unredeemed and defiled. It's like the little girl who brought her pets into the farmhouse, putting both the pig and the lamb into the bathtub and scrubbing them until they were squeaky clean. Then she dried and brushed them and tied a pink ribbon around their necks. When she took them outside to play, they each ran in different directions: the lamb toward the green lawn and the pig back into the mud.

It was a matter of their nature; the pig longed for mud and the lamb longed for green pasture. Paul is expressing the same thing here: the **defiled and unbelieving** long to sin, while the forgiven believer longs to live a **pure** and clean life out of gratitude for the amazing grace of God.

UNMASKING THEIR FUTURE: MISERY & FRUITLESSNESS

They profess to **know** *God, but by their deeds they deny Him, being detestable and disobedient and worthless for any good deed* (Titus 1:16).

They profess to **know** God! The word Paul uses here for knowledge of God isn't *ginosko*, a word that stresses the experiential, relational knowledge, but *oida*, meaning intellectual knowledge gained by information.[19]

These false teachers look the part—they know the vocabulary—they know facts about God . . . but they don't **know** God.

One man related:

> During my physical, my doctor asked me about my daily activity level. I told him that I spent all yesterday morning outside, wading along the edge of a lake; at one point I had to jump away from an aggressive rattlesnake. I walked up and down some rocky hills, ran from some wild dogs, and stood in a patch of poison ivy. The doctor replied that I must really love the outdoors, but I don't—I'm just a lousy golfer. I look the part—I know the language—I've got the equipment . . . but that's about it.

There are only about eight inches between heaven and hell for us; *knowing* about God in our head or *believing* in God with our heart.

Is that too simplistic for you?

Having shepherded a flock for three decades, I've talked with many people who knew the facts about God without having a personal relationship with God, which would have been evident in their repentant hearts and lives.

They knew the vocabulary . . . but they didn't know His voice.

Dietrich Bonhoeffer was a defiant German pastor who was hanged at Flossenbürg by the direct order of Adolph Hitler only days before the American liberation of the POW camp at the end of World War II. The last words of this courageous and controversial thirty-nine-year-old opponent of Nazism were, "This is the end—but for me, the *beginning* of life."

Now that I've read the 624-page biography of Bonhoeffer, I can honestly say that I know quite a bit *about* him. I can even quote a line or two *by* him—but I don't **know** him . . . I've never met him.

Maybe you've read the Book written by God about God . . . maybe you can even quote a line or two out of it. Maybe you've never even denied the truth regarding what you know about Him from childhood. You know the facts *about* God . . . but have you given your heart and life *to* Him?

SHIELDING THE FLOCK & SPARING FALSE TEACHERS

The Apostle Paul warned of the consequences of having these imposters in the Church's midst:

[T]*hey* [the false teachers] *are upsetting whole families, teaching things they should not teach* (Titus 1:11).

Saving the Church Family from Harm

His primary reason for writing to Titus the passage we are studying *(Titus 1:11–16)* was to protect believers from the aberrant teaching of the day. Wolves in sheep's clothing were mingling with the flock, disseminating their false teaching and tearing families—and the larger Church family—apart.

It had to stop.

He enjoined Titus to wear the mantle of a shepherd and protect the flock from harm.

Saving the False Teachers from Hell

Paul had a second reason for issuing the warning . . . a stunning one:

> ***For this reason reprove them*** [the false teachers] ***severely so that they may be sound in the faith*** (Titus 1:13).

He wanted Titus to know that the Gospel he delivers is not only for the purpose of warning the flock but winning *false teachers* and those who follow them to saving faith in Christ.

What a surprise! You would expect Paul to get to the end of this warning and say, "These false teachers and their followers are utterly hopeless!" Didn't he describe them in this manner?

> ***They profess to know God, but by their deeds they deny Him, being detestable and disobedient and worthless for any good deed*** (Titus 1:16).

That word for ***worthless*** is *adokimos*. If a builder found a stone that had a flaw in it, he'd mark it with a capital A for *adokimos*—it was useless and unfit for the building.[20]

In other words, these false teachers, like their Cretan contemporaries, are gluttonous, constantly lying, defiled, detestable, unfruitful, and unable-to-accomplish-even-one-good-thing people.

And now you'd expect Paul to get to the end of his description and say, "Titus, these are such wicked people and everybody knows it, so leave them alone—they are *beyond* redemption."[21] Instead, Paul says, "Go after them! Give them the Gospel, too . . . they are *not* beyond redemption."

False teachers can be saved, too![22]

Yes, they are after our hearts, but we are just as passionately after *theirs*. And the reason they can't have ours is because we've already given our hearts away—and we now urge them to give their hearts away to Jesus Christ, as well.

Our evangelism training program at Colonial sends out teams weekly to share the Gospel with others. One team had a young lady who was fluent in Spanish. She wasn't a regular member of the team but felt a desire to come that particular night and join the others. Her team visited an apartment complex and found a man very interested in the Gospel. He invited the team into his apartment, where there were two guests, neither of whom spoke English. This young lady was able to present the Gospel to them in Spanish, and they both accepted the claims of Jesus Christ as their personal Lord and Savior that night.

A coincidence? No—just a passionate witness for Christ, willing to expose the error of the unbeliever and present the truth of the Gospel.

There are no mysteries to our Gospel, either . . . no long lists to compile and keep along with secret, deeper codes to learn. No, only the clear Gospel of Jesus Christ.

Paul wants Titus to find shepherds who will live under the conviction that:

- life is short,
- death is sure,
- sin is the culprit,
- Christ is the cure.[23]

Titus, go find men who really believe this; men who will not add to the Gospel—who won't compromise it—who will defend it and bravely unmask those who twist it.

Go find men who will guard and protect and teach and love the flock, even to the point of giving their lives to the pressures and penalties, the delights and duties of the office of elder.

Find men who will live for the advancement of the Gospel and the equipping of the saints and the building up of the Church until Jesus Christ says the time has come . . . the Church is now complete.

Titus, find men who will live for *that* day; and when you find them— and you *will*—place upon their shoulders and around their hearts the mantle of a genuine, Gospel-loving, Christ-exalting shepherd.

But as for you, speak the things which are fitting for sound doctrine. [2]Older men are to be temperate, dignified, sensible, sound in faith, in love, in perseverance.

–Titus 2:1–2

CHAPTER ELEVEN

THE TREASURE OF OLD MEN

Titus 2:1–2

ACT YOUR AGE!

Old age gets the better of us all. Three sisters had lived together for a number of years; their ages were 92, 94, and 97. The 97-year-old drew her bath and was halfway in the tub when she yelled out, "Was I getting *in* or was I getting *out*?" The 94-year-old downstairs hollered up, "Wait a minute and I'll come up and help." She left the kitchen and started up the stairs; halfway up she stopped, stood there for a moment, and then called out, "Was I going *up* or coming *down*?" The youngest sister (92 years old) was sitting at the kitchen table having a cup of tea, listening to her sisters—one now stuck in the tub and one on the stairs. With a smirk on her face, she shook her head, *Goodness I hope my memory never gets as bad as theirs . . . knock on wood.* She yelled out, "I'll come up and help you both as soon as I find out who's knocking at the front door."[1]

That's where we're all heading . . . every day a little closer. There are definitely a lot of things about growing old that nobody likes. If you've ever walked into a room looking for your glasses, only to realize later when looking in the mirror that you had them on your head, you know what I mean.

We are surrounded by a culture that is in desperate denial of the aging process and is paying a fortune to keep up appearances—to look young, sound young, dress young, act young. The anti-aging industry with products related to reversing or stopping the process is now a hundred billion dollar industry each year in this country alone.

The cultural mantra is simple: whatever you do as you age, never look older, sound older, or *act* older.

In direct contrast, the Scriptures view old age as a fruitful time where someone can give back to their generation the knowledge, wisdom, discernment, and balance they've gleaned from a long and faithful life. David writes:

> *They will still yield fruit in old age* (Psalm 92:14*a*), [and having grown old enough to say with authority] *I have been young and now I am old, yet I have not seen the righteous forsaken or his descendants begging bread* (Psalm 37:25).

For a culture that is terrified of getting older, it's time to rethink not only the opportunities but the *obligations* that come with age. The Bible never suggests that we avoid old age or even resist it—it welcomes us to it and then demands that we take advantage of it. Scripture venerates gray hair: it considers old age tantamount to wisdom. Solomon wrote that for those who walk with God, their gray head is a crown of glory *(Proverbs 16:31).*

At the same time, the Bible challenges those who are aging to maximize their wisdom and experience and trial-tested faith for the glory of God and the good of the Church. In a culture that refuses to grow old, Paul is about to command us all to act our age.

FAMILY TALK

Paul's solution to false teaching and false teachers on the island of Crete was not only to send Titus to the churches to put qualified shepherds into leadership roles but to put the rest of the church family on special assignment . . . one that was directly related to their age and station in life.

In the New Testament Epistles—most of which were written by the Apostle Paul—Paul will often speak to particular groups of people.[2] Sometimes he speaks directly to men, sometimes to women—or to husbands, wives, fathers and, even, to children. These are family talks, so to speak.

Paul effectively launches into such a *family talk* as he teaches the congregations on the island of Crete through Titus; we quickly discover that Titus is charged to first and foremost challenge the **older men.**

When Paul wrote this letter, there were no chapter divisions or verse numbers—they were added about four hundred years ago to help Bible students locate the text more quickly. Most of the time it's been helpful but sometimes it interrupts the flow. In order to capture the force of Paul's next statement as **Titus 2** begins, we actually need to back up one verse earlier:

> **They** [these false teachers] **profess to know God, but by their deeds they deny Him** [they don't act like they really know God], **being detestable and disobedient and worthless for any good deed . . . But as for you** (Titus 1:16–2:1a).

You is emphatic—literally, *But you.*[3] The older men in the second chapter are in direct contrast with the false teachers of the previous chapter. Paul emphasizes the contrast as he begins his family talk and urges, "*This* is what the false teachers are teaching and *this* is how the false teachers are living, **but as for you**, Titus—speak **the things which are fitting for** sound doctrine" (Titus 2:1).

Titus is to teach the people in these island churches **sound doctrine**. There's that word **sound** again: *hugaino*, which gives us our word *hygiene*.[4] In other words, Titus is to deliver to them (not just to the men) things related to spiritually healthy teaching; pure teaching; *hygienic doctrine*—wholesome and clean teaching.

And the present imperative makes this verb **speak** (*teach*) a command that Titus is to do *continually*. The congregation was to receive from their shepherd regular and careful pastoral instruction about practical Christian living and the godly attitudes and actions that should result from believing and obeying sound, wholesome doctrine.[5]

Now what's surprising here is that you might think Paul will immediately launch into an exposé of what **sound doctrine** is—what to *believe*. Instead, he embarks upon teaching how each member of the family should *behave*.

> **But as for you, speak the things which are fitting for sound doctrine** (Titus 2:1).

He's telling Titus to call a family meeting of the Church and spell out the **things** [kind of lifestyle] **which are fitting** [that which is appropriate—that which matches] **sound doctrine** . . . that which goes hand in glove with genuine Christianity.

Titus 2 isn't about *belief*—it's all about *behavior.*

Paul has already exposed the character and lifestyle of the *Cretan* as he effectively cleaned their clocks; now he moves on to describe the character and lifestyle of the *Christian.*

And he will be just as blunt and to the point with the Christian as he was with the Cretan. In this family talk, he will address issues of anger, immorality, immaturity, gossip, substance abuse, laziness, priorities, dishonesty, disobedience, back talk, innuendo, and stealing.[6]

Here's Paul's point: if they want to be perceived by the Cretans as Christians, these are the kinds of attitudes and actions that match up with **sound doctrine** . . . authentic Christianity.

IT'S ABOUT GODLY CHARACTER

Paul begins his family talk by addressing the **older men**. He will deliver six characteristics of what it means to be a godly older man.

Temperate

Older men are to be temperate (Titus 2:2*a*).

By the way, don't miss the implication in the first part of this phrase: **older men are to be**. In other words, it's possible to be an older Christian man and *not* be these things.

An older Christian isn't automatically a godly Christian. Old age doesn't make a Christian man more faithful, more satisfied, or more effective in service to God.[7]

You might be wondering who qualifies as an *older* man in the mind of Paul? Who is he addressing as this family talk begins? While he doesn't reveal anyone's birthdate, we know from Greek literature that during the first century, the word used here for **older men** was used for those who had reached the age of fifty.

If you're fifty . . . or you're borderline . . . or you crossed the border years ago, Paul places *you* in the category of an old man.

I've read that you know you're getting old when:

- the candles cost more than the cake;
- you recognize the music in the elevator and can sing along;

- you've owned clothes so long they've come back in style;
- everything hurts, and what doesn't hurt doesn't work.

In the mind of Paul, who wrote this long before the invention of elevators, if you're fifty, you qualify.

Frankly, you might assume that Paul wouldn't need to tell old men to be anything—surely, by now, they *are*! But the fact that they are not only included in this family talk but referenced *first* implies the critical importance that these men—above all other family members—grow up and mature in these following areas.

First, Paul challenges them to be **temperate**, which literally means *unmixed with wine* or, more woodenly, *wineless*. It came to refer to people who were sober, discreet, in control of their words and actions.[8]

The word later came to be used for a man who resisted being overindulgent, careless, given to passions and emotions that flare up and just as quickly die down.

One commentator added that this word also came to describe a man who is free from excess—free from addictions to destructive things, like pornography or illegal drugs.[9]

Paul has already described the Cretans as dirty old men: ***both their mind and their conscience are defiled*** (Titus 1:15*b*); now he's saying, "Let's do something about it—you men used to be Cretans, too. Now let's show them what it means to be spiritually healthy, mentally wholesome, and emotionally controlled. Let's show this island what a godly old man looks like."

Dignified

***Older men are to be temperate,* dignified** (Titus 2:2*b*).

This word from *semnos* means to be worthy of respect. It's the idea of being serious-minded. This doesn't mean that he's a killjoy who won't laugh out loud or ever have any good, clean fun—far from it. But it does refer to a dignity that refuses to laugh at the wrong thing: an innuendo; an off-color joke; the suffering of another person.

Dignified means that a man isn't superficial or shallow—he has depth. There is *weightiness* about his character.[10] It's the description of a man who has truly grown up.

The Cretan men were just the opposite. They were adolescent and immature. And what defines an adolescent? Someone who lives for himself and his own pleasures; someone who views people as pawns to be moved about for their own purposes; someone who must have their own way . . . or else.

Adolescents throw temper tantrums. Cretans, like adolescents, didn't want to work. Paul early on called them **lazy** (Titus 1:12). They wanted to be paid, have the latest luxuries and toys, and have all their needs met on demand. If they *didn't* get what they wanted when they wanted it, tempers flared and everyone around them was likely to get burned.

The men on the island of Crete would rather tell a lie than go to work; they refused any difficult responsibilities and work ethic that demanded sacrificing their own comfort, which brings us back to the word adolescent.

It's a frightening thought, but Paul clearly implies that it is possible for an old man to act like a little boy. No wonder he begins his family talk by describing what it means for older men to act their age. If *they* won't, why would anyone else on the island even try?

To this day, an adolescent male is all about his shallow reflection: "Look at my clothes, look at my muscles, look at my money, look at my women, look at my condo, look at my car, look at my job . . . look at *me!*" In other words, "Respect me because of what I *have*." The West is experiencing the same phenomena Titus struggled with; we're being hijacked by a planeload of adolescent men.

Data from America, England, France, and Italy, as well as other westernized countries, is saturated with perpetual adolescence. In the page-turner *The Death of the Grownup*, the journalist/author catalogues a ten-year period of researching this issue. It isn't written from a Christian perspective but it is certainly applicable to the challenge facing not just the culture but the Church.

This ten-year research project discovered that in Great Britain, forty-six percent of adult couples regard their parents' houses as their *real* homes; in Italy, nearly one out of three thirty-year-olds never leave their parents' home to begin with. One case in Italy involved a young man who *successfully* sued to make his father responsible to give him financial assistance, not just because he was unemployed but because he couldn't find a job that he *want-ed*—he owned his own apartment, didn't live at home, and was in his *thirties*!

In America, the majority of eighteen to forty-nine-year-old males watch the Cartoon Network more than they watch CNN . . . which tells you how bad CNN must be. But you get my point.

The average video gamester in 1990 was eighteen; today he's going on thirty . . . or older.

In their first edition published in the twenty-first century, the National Academy of Sciences redefined adolescence (the period from the onset of puberty to adulthood) as continuing to the age of thirty-two. The MacArthur Foundation, after funding a major research project, argued that the transition to male adulthood does not *end* until age *thirty-four*.

Imagine, thirty-four-year-old men still thinking—and living—like middle-schoolers. This cultural shift comes with a mountain of implications. For one thing, it means that we now have a generation of young people who were parented by adolescents; little wonder the children cannot—or will not—make the transition out of adolescence into independent adulthood themselves until the age of thirty-five.

One secular journalist put it this way:

> Just look around—we are surrounded by grownups who haven't left childhood. With people in their forties and fifties, you can't find any clear demarcation of what's for parents and what's for the kids. Men in particular now dress like their sons—from message-emblazoned T-shirts to chunky athletic shoes—both equally at ease in the baggy rumple of perpetual summer camp.

We've seen this reflected in pulpit ministries over the past decade: even pastors evidently don't particularly want to stand in front of their congregations and look like a **dignified** adult. Why? Adult translates as *old*, and old must be resisted . . . so they preach in something that defies any evidence of age, as if they, too, are eternal summer campers.

The last thing men want today is to be addressed as "Mister" . . . or "Sir" . . . someone who has passed into the realm of an older age—imagine, into *adulthood*.

One author wrote that our civilization has a near religious devotion to perpetual adolescence.[11]

More radical now than ever, Paul says, "We need older men who are worthy of respect because they act like it . . . talk like it . . . even dress like it."

Paul knew the solution would involve a challenge to the older men to begin to pursue mature dignity and then turn around and mentor and disciple younger men who never had a father—or had an adolescent for a father who had never grown up himself.

The Church ought to be the place—it *must* be the place—where we have within our family circle older men who can literally provide for many younger men the *first* genuinely mature father figure they've ever encountered.

Again, this doesn't require older men to act like stuffed shirts; it *does* mean that older men successfully make the transition, shedding the silliness of adolescence and embracing the concept of being—and acting—**dignified**.

Sensible

Older men are to be temperate, dignified, **sensible** (Titus 2:2c).

Sensible is one of Paul's favorite descriptions for the family. It's the *only* term he applies to older men, young men, young women, and the entire church family (Titus 2:2, 5, 6, 12).

Sensible refers to a soundness of mind and thinking that shows up in a self-disciplined lifestyle.[12] In other words, you do the right thing, not because someone is telling you to or reminding you to, but because it is your own daily passion. You get up in the morning and pray, "Lord, I need to guard my steps today; I need to think clearly . . . grant me the wisdom to judge every issue soundly and sensibly."

The truth is old men have lived long enough to see just about everything. They're old enough to know that sin promises more than it produces. Older men have handled enough money to know that it doesn't bring happiness—in fact, it has wings like a bird and can just as easily fly away. Older men have owned enough stuff to know how quickly it breaks down or gets stored away in the shed. Older men have seen enough sickness and suffering to know that life is fragile and unpredictable.

They've grown in discernment and balanced thinking, which is evidenced in behavior marked by this word **sensible**. Frankly, older men are the perfect people to demonstrate with experience what it means to be **sensible** about life, family, work, and ministry . . . about what matters most.

IT'S ABOUT FIRM COMMITMENT

Paul isn't finished with older men yet. He continues further in teaching *how* these older men in the churches of Crete should behave . . . and believe.

Sound in Faith

> **Older men are to be temperate, dignified, sensible, sound in faith** (Titus 2:2*d*).

They are to be **sound in faith**—*healthy* and whole and uncontaminated in their faith. It describes a personal relationship with Jesus Christ . . . and an ongoing trust in Him.

Sound in Love

> **Older men are to be temperate, dignified, sensible, sound in faith, in love** (Titus 2:2*e*).

This requirement describes their personal relationships with others—their ongoing choice to demonstrate *agape* (the word Paul uses here): a selfless love and devotion toward others.

In contrast with the typical male, godly older men are to live for the needs of others. Their pure and wholesome love for other people would certainly gain a distinct hearing among so many hedonists on the island of Crete—and everywhere else.

Sound in Perseverance

> **Older men are to be temperate, dignified, sensible, sound in faith, in love, in perseverance** (Titus 2:2*f*).

This simply describes the older man as committed to pursuing these relationships, no matter what.[13] What Christian man wouldn't sign up for soundness in his walk with God and health in his relationships with others?

But how many would sign on for the **perseverance** demanded of him to pursue soundness and purity in faith and love . . . no matter what?

How many men today seem to be looking for a way out, their hand on the back door knob as soon as life's pressures and demands become overwhelming?

The greatest demonstration of **perseverance** in love was when Jesus Christ chose to endure the cross, not escape it. He satisfied the demands of holy wrath and even now perseveres in His agape love relationship with His Bride, the Church.

Though fully God, Jesus was fully man, and He has become for us the perfect model of an older man: a Man who matured and *grew in wisdom, stature and in favor with God and man* (Luke 2:52).

According to *Titus 2*, what each family and every church must have first and foremost are older men who treasure and model the persevering love of their Savior.

IT'S ABOUT ETERNAL CONSEQUENCES

A father wrote of learning the value of *treasures* from his young daughter:

> Molly gave me a paper bag to take to work with me. When I asked what was in the bag, she answered, "Just some stuff. Take it with you." I sat down for lunch at my desk and pulled out the paper bag. Its contents: two ribbons, three stones, a plastic dinosaur, a pencil stub, a tiny seashell, used lipstick, two chocolate Kisses, and thirteen pennies. I chuckled, finished my lunch, and swept everything off my desk into the wastebasket and went back to work. When I arrived at home that evening, Molly asked where the bag was. "I left it at the office . . . why?"
>
> "Well," she said, "those are my things in the sack, Daddy . . . things I really like. I thought you might like to play with them, but now I want them back." She saw me hesitate, and tears welled up in her eyes. "You didn't lose the bag, did you, Daddy?" I said I hadn't and that I would bring it home tomorrow. After she went to bed, I raced back to the office. Molly

had given me her treasures—everything that a seven-year-old held dear . . . and I missed [the meaning]. Not just missed it—I had thrown it away. I dumped all the wastebaskets out onto my desk. The janitor came in and asked, "Did you lose something?" "Yeah, my mind!" When I found the bag, I smoothed it out and filled it again with Molly's treasures. I took it home, sat down with Molly the next day, and had her tell me the story behind every treasure in the bag.

To my surprise, Molly gave me the bag once again several days later—same bag, same stuff inside. I felt forgiven. Over the months, the bag was given to me from time to time; it was never clear to me why I did or did not get it on a certain day. I began to think of it as the Daddy Prize. Soon, Molly turned her attention to other things . . . she was growing up. One morning she gave me the bag and never asked for it back. It sits in my office, left over from when a little child said, "Here; this is the best I've got; this is my treasure; and it's all yours." I missed it the first time, but it's *my* [treasure] now.[14]

Paul through Titus is calling a family meeting. And he begins by telling the Church that what they need first and foremost is older men who know what to throw away and what to keep; what to ignore and what to pursue; what to trash and what to trust; men who've grown old and, at the same time, been willing to grow up.

An older man who understands what lasting treasure is becomes a *living treasure* to all who know him.

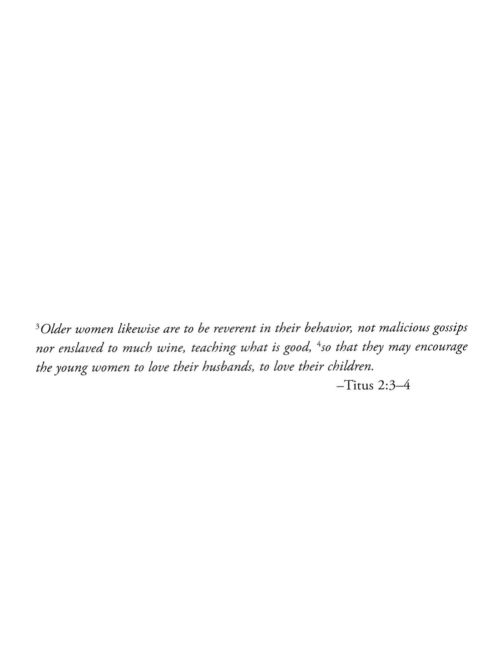

3 Older women likewise are to be reverent in their behavior, not malicious gossips nor enslaved to much wine, teaching what is good, 4so that they may encourage the young women to love their husbands, to love their children.

–Titus 2:3–4

CHAPTER TWELVE

RARE WORDS
FOR RARE WOMEN

Titus 2:3–4

A TOTALLY NEW WAY OF LIVING

George Gallup, founder of the American Institute of Public Opinion and The Gallup Poll, made this statement more than twenty-five years ago: "Never before has the Christian church made so many inroads into the society, while at the same time making so *little* difference."

I can't imagine what his comment would be today!

In this family talk, Paul is not telling Christians how to fit into their culture but how to radically create a new culture with new objectives . . . new desires . . . new lifestyles . . . new relationships . . . new distinctives.

Titus 2 is one of the most politically incorrect passages in the New Testament—it flies in the face of everything our culture says men and women of all ages should be living for . . . striving for . . . and acting like.

If you want to carve out the key verse from the chapter, here it is:

> [Jesus Christ, who] ***gave Himself for us*** [first] ***to redeem us from every lawless deed, and*** [second] ***to purify for Himself a people for His own possession, zealous for good deeds*** (Titus 2:14).

The Church tends to stop with the first reason: Christ came to redeem us. True! Just don't put a period there; we've not only been redeemed—we've been *assigned* to a totally different way of living.

Paul says for Titus to tell older women what they should do to fulfill their new assignment. Now, let's be honest, it's one thing to tell an older man what to do . . . it's another thing to tell an older *woman* what to do.

And to make matters even more challenging, both Titus and Timothy are *young* pastors; it would be an intimidating prospect to challenge older men . . . much less older women.

Pause long enough to feel the pressure Titus felt; he is commanded to enter established churches and determine a slate of elders and then, without any time to bandage his wounds from those encounters, he's to tell the older people in the church how to act!

I don't believe in luck, but I have to admit I find myself mentally saying at this point, *Good luck with that, Titus!*

Paul told Timothy earlier to treat younger men like brothers, young women like sisters in all purity, older men as fathers, and older women as mothers *(1 Timothy 5:2 paraphrase)*. There's great insight in that command: the church is a family and every person relates in similar fashion and respect to family members.

So, regardless of Titus's youth, he was to deliver this message with grace and tactfulness as if he were encouraging his own mother and father to grow into the likeness of Christ.

AGING TOWARD PERFECTION

***Older women** likewise . . .* (Titus 2:3).

Likewise does not mean that older women were to act like the older men; the word refers to Titus being told to teach the older women, *too.* In other words, they were not to be left out of this family talk.

Once again we need to answer the same critical question from our previous chapter: who qualifies as ***older women**?*

Perhaps they fit the following humorous profile:

> Four brothers had become successful in their careers of medicine, industry, and law. One evening, they reunited and talked over dinner about the birthday gifts they had given

their 95-year-old mother, who had just moved to Florida. The first said, "I had that big house built for Mother; I'm sure she's enjoying it immensely." The second said, "I completely outfitted a theater room inside her new home; she probably loves that room." The third said, "I had a brand-new Mercedes delivered to her garage." The fourth said, "You know how Mom loved reading the Bible more than anything, but reading is almost impossible for her nowadays, since she really can't see very well anymore. I met a preacher who told me about a beautiful parrot he had trained to recite the Bible. It took seven pastors more than ten years to teach that parrot to quote the entire Bible, references and all. It didn't come cheap, either—I had to contribute $100,000 to his church building program."

Eventually all four sons received thank you notes from their mother:

"Dear Milton, the house you built is so huge that I live in only one room, but I have to clean the whole house! Thank you anyway."

"Dear Michael, the theater with Dolby sound that can seat fifty people is nice, but none of my close friends live nearby, and since I've lost my eyesight I really don't watch much television. Thank you just the same."

"Dear Marvin, I am too old to travel and I have my groceries delivered, so I won't use that Mercedes, but the thought was kind. Thanks."

"Dear Melvin, you were the only son to have the good sense to put some thought into your gift to me! Let me tell you, that chicken was delicious. Thank you so much."

Yep, she qualifies.

In reality, the context of Paul's comments here focus on married women who are actually younger than you might imagine: old enough to have raised their children and become empty nesters, so to speak. They could be any-where from their early forties to their early sixties.

Frankly, the older the better, because Paul is referring to women who've lived long enough—like older men—to know what matters most.

They might very well be the widows Paul referred to who have *shown hospitality to strangers . . . washed the saints' feet . . . assisted those in distress . . . devoted* [themselves] *to every good work* (1 Timothy 5:3–10).

Older women in the early Church became known for their rescuing of babies left to die by their parents. In first-century Rome, these women went out at night and searched the city for abandoned newborns. They weren't the only ones on the lookout—others took the infants and raised the boys to be slaves or gladiators and the girls for prostitution.[1]

The Church in any generation has been blessed by the effort and energy, passion and service of older women. They've earned the right to teach the younger women who are in the middle of raising a family. These women know better than anyone the challenges and pitfalls of family life.

However, they earn the right to teach younger women only if four dis-tinctives are apparent in their lives . . . and the first one basically covers all the rest.

Sacred

Older women likewise are to be reverent in their behavior (Titus 2:3*a*).

Let me put it this way: there is *sacredness* about them. Several of the words used by Paul for these older women are actually rare Greek words. And this is one of those words.

The word for **reverent** never occurs anywhere else in the New Testament.[2]

The Greek and Roman world had their multitudinous temples and gods. Many of the temples were served by priestesses who were specially dressed, trained in their deportment, taught to serve their god within the temple and, even, how to advise visitors who had come to seek out this particular god. They acted as the god's representative.[3]

This is exactly the word picture Paul is describing for older women—their lives are sacred representatives of the Living God.

Notice, Paul writes that they *are to be* **reverent** *in their* **behavior**—another word so rare that the noun form isn't used anywhere else in the

New Testament. It refers to their *demeanor*: their **behavior** is appropriate for someone carrying out sacred duties.

One author asks the question, "What is Paul expecting mature women in the faith to project through their posture and personality, deportment and demeanor? Holiness!"[4]

Her life is lived in such a way that the King James Bible translates it *as becometh holiness*. They are old enough to know that the essence of life can't be bought or bottled. Life is more than fashion and features and status. Holiness is their primary objective and passion . . . an indication that they are uniquely qualified to teach younger women in the Church.

John Calvin said four hundred years ago that the problem with older women in his church was that they were trying to hold on to their youth and dress like young women. He wrote,

> They demean their own maturity and attempt to dress cultur-
> ally fashionable or even flirtatiously. Though there is nothing
> wrong with a woman adorning herself with pretty clothing, a
> line may be crossed.[5]

Some things never change . . . some temptations never go away.

The Church needs older women who've faced the tempter of Madison Avenue; older women who know, by now, that younger women are potential victims of shallow and short-lived promises.

One author put it this way:

> [Older women] know the dead-end despair of women who
> are all about high fashion on the outside but are settling for
> bargain basement on the inside.[6]

And the pressure's on—our culture has pressed young girls and young women into its mold. We have a generation of women chasing after an image that refuses to stand still. Like older men who need to say farewell with dignity to their younger years, we need older women who will say farewell with reverence to theirs.

Paul's challenge is as fresh today as it was to the churches in Crete. The Church must have older women who've finally figured out that their greatest contribution has never been their physical attributes but their spiritual ones—women who've grown up to learn that *charm is deceitful and beauty is vain, but a woman who fears the* LORD, *she shall be praised* (Proverbs 31:30).

And by the way, men, it would encourage our sisters tremendously if we honored them and respected them—not because of the beauty of their face but because of the beauty of their faith. We're on a runaway train; in this country alone, Botox has reached annual sales of one billion dollars. We would serve our sisters in Christ well if we attached more attention to their faithfulness than their figures or fashion.

Paul says through Titus that they are looking for some rare women with a passion for holiness.

One author described them this way:

> The tenor of their lives displays a consecrated holiness to God; they exceed the ethical and moral standards of surrounding society. The call upon [their] life comes not from their neighborhood or their nation, but from the nature of God.[7]

Sweet

Older women likewise are . . . not malicious gossips (Titus 2:3b).

Sweet is the opposite of what is described here as **malicious gossips**.

Simply put, she refuses to tear someone down and, instead, chooses to build others up.[8] She refuses to become a grape on the grapevine. And if she hears a story, she won't pass it along.

Paul doesn't pull any punches here. The word he uses can be literally translated *she-devil*.[9] In fact, the masculine singular form of this word is *always* used of the devil in the New Testament.[10]

He is effectively saying that older women shouldn't talk like the devil. And how does Satan talk? His primary verbal role is accusing the saints . . . running down the believers *(Revelation 12:10)*.

The devil is always interpreting someone's actions in the worst possible way—illustrated when he went before God and said, "I've been watching pious old Job, and I'm convinced that the only reason he worships You is because You treat him so well. In fact, if You took away Your blessings from his life, Job would curse You to Your face" *(Job 1–2 paraphrase)*.

Nothing is more destructive to harmony in a local church than gossip. Men are as guilty as women, but women tend to talk more to each other than men do; for that reason, perhaps gossip is particularly a besetting sin for women—especially the older ones who've seen it all.

When older women allow their words to divide and slander, they actually join in promoting the agenda, the work, and the enterprise of the devil—he doesn't even need to show up!

So Paul describes a godly woman as one who builds the body up instead of tearing it down.

Sober

Older women likewise are . . . [not] **enslaved to much wine** (Titus 2:3c).

These women Paul and Titus are seeking to instruct should be in control of not only what comes out of their mouths but what goes into it. The word Paul uses here for **enslaved** means exactly that—in fact, it's a word used to describe literal slavery.

It refers to someone being held and controlled against their will. In other words, this habit which they hoped would give them a place to withdraw from the pressures of life has become a prison.[11]

We could broaden addiction to include any controlling passion that masters someone's life—any habit that creates distance between a believer and holy living. It may not be something that is bad per se but something that is allowed to grow into excess. John Bunyan, the author of *The Pilgrim's Progress*, said that he stopped playing cricket because he found that he loved it *too* much.

A rare woman is not dependent on a substance or habit to face the day but is, instead, dependent upon the Holy Spirit.

And, by the way, this ought to be encouraging to us all: since Paul is issuing this challenge to older Christian women, he implies that some old habits die hard. Some of them may have to be battled over a lifetime.

With the Apostle Paul, godly women—and every believer—learn to say:

All things are lawful for me, but not all things are profitable. All things are lawful for me, but I will not be mastered by anything (1 Corinthians 6:12).

The island of Crete was known, according to historians, for its production of wine. Alcoholism and inebriation were rampant—like America today, where annual sales of alcoholic drinks bring in ninety billion dollars. The travesty has now swept up half a million alcoholics between the ages of nine and twelve. The moderation of many has led to the addiction of millions.

Even for Titus, there seemed to be difficulty finding older Christian women who weren't under its influence.

Serious

Older women likewise are . . . teaching *what is good* (Titus 2:3*d*).

This is the gracious ripple effect of a godly woman's life.

They were **teaching** both formally and informally—by word and by example.[12] Paul isn't talking about teaching here in terms of a post, such as a professor—this isn't a position but a pattern.

These older women have earned the right to speak . . . to mentor . . . to disciple . . . to model what it means to follow Christ in their particular world of influence.

In our culture, the pedestals are virtually empty and we are still struggling to find qualified older women to occupy this role of instructing and mentoring younger women.

EXPERIENCE IS THE BEST TEACHER

Older women likewise . . . *may* encourage *the young women to love their husbands, to love their children* (Titus 2:3*e*).

Paul expects a healthy church to have older women who have refused to put their lives on cruise control; older women who will train younger women for a brand-new way of thinking and living.

It's interesting to notice the implication of a ministry boundary for Titus. He is to teach and preach to *all* ages, but while he directly teaches older men and older women and younger men and bondservants, he is never commanded to directly mentor or train younger women. In fact, the word Paul uses in verse four for older women to **encourage** younger women is best translated *train*.

Train is a word related to the Greek word for *self-control*. In the original language, this verb to train *the young women* literally means to bring a person back to his senses.[13]

This is life-on-life . . . up-close-and-personal mentoring. Why? Because culture had so confused young women on the role of a self-sacrificing wife and mother that they would need nothing less than personal tutoring.

We're just as confused today. According to a recent study, song lyrics over the past thirty years have become increasingly self-centered. Researchers used a computer program to count the percentage of words in songs which refer to first-person plural pronouns (*we, us, our*) compared to first-person singular pronouns (*I, me, mine*). They found that *we* and *us* have declined dramatically and *I, me,* and *mine* have increased exponentially. One reviewer summed up the study by saying rather bluntly, "We might as well face it—we are addicted to self-love."

The first instruction by older women to the married younger women is that life isn't about self-love—it's about self-sacrificing love. In that kind of love, a person actually *finds* self-fulfillment and joy in marriage and family. It takes an older woman who has grown in Christ to be able to share that counterculture message, to teach it, and to model it.

The fact that Paul tells older women that they need to **encourage** [train] *the young women to love their husbands, to love their children* is because both things are impossibilities, at times. A younger woman has been married just long enough to learn how stubborn and difficult and insensitive and hardheaded her husband can be. And she's probably come to the wrong conclusion that she married the *only* man God made that way. It takes an older woman to come along and say, "That's how they come out of the box . . . God's got to work on your husband as He purifies him and makes him zealous for good deeds . . . and, by the way, He's got the same work to do on you."

Older women have the ability to pop the bubbles of misconceptions regarding marriage and family more effectively than any pastor can accomplish in a series of sermons. In fact, Titus has been effectively left out of the tutoring business.

Can any older woman accept the challenge? Who can qualify to be this kind of female tutor/mentor? Unlike what most churches unfortunately put forward, the flock doesn't need perfectly coiffed women with just the right taste in clothes, the right family pedigree, and impressive social connections. Isn't that counterproductive to the message of spiritual attributes trumping physical and material attributes? Aren't we going backwards when the female leaders in the Church sport the latest name brands and drop the biggest names?

The Church shouldn't seek to elevate perfect women but godly women who are demonstrating submission to Christ, exhibiting godly priorities as they pursue holy purity and good deeds.

For nearly twenty years, Elisa Morgan served as the president of MOPS (Mothers of Preschoolers) International—a mentoring program for young mothers that has encouraged many young women in a positive way. Elisa writes,

> I'm probably the least likely person to head a mothering organization that impacts thousands of mothers' lives for the Gospel. I grew up in a broken home. My parents were divorced when I was five. My older sister, younger brother, and I were raised by my alcoholic mother. While my mother meant well, most of my memories are of my mothering her rather than her mothering me. Alcohol altered her love. I remember her weaving down the hall of our ranch home in Houston, glass of scotch in hand. I would wake her at seven each morning to try to get her off to work. Sure, there were good times, like Christmas and birthdays, when she went all out and celebrated with us children. But even those days ended with the warped glow of alcohol. Ten years ago, when I was asked to consider leading MOPS International, I went straight to my knees . . . how could God use me—one who had never been mothered—to nurture other mothers? The answer came: *"My grace is sufficient for you, for power is perfected in weakness"* (2 Corinthians 12:9). God would take my

deficits and make them my offering to Him . . . and find His grace to be sufficient in my weakness.[14]

Titus would have signed her up. That's the kind of humility and grace God will use in this ripple effect of godly mentoring—a woman the Church needs to collectively encourage and promote. She has about her a demeanor of seriousness; of sobriety; of sweetness; of sacredness.

Her lips and her life are a testimony—not to herself, for she will see nothing in *herself* worthy of imitation. She will ultimately testify to the sufficient grace of God.

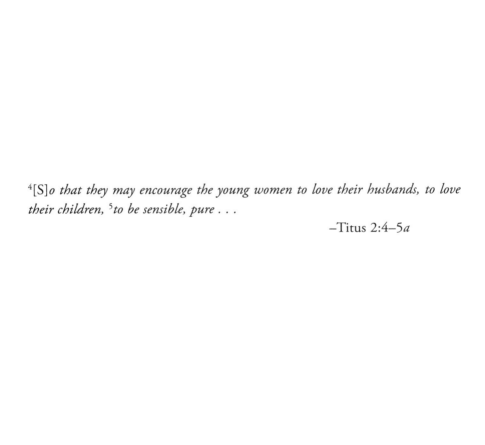

[4][S]*o that they may encourage the young women to love their husbands, to love their children,* [5]*to be sensible, pure . . .*

–Titus 2:4–5*a*

CHAPTER THIRTEEN

A MODEL
FOR MARRIED WOMEN

Titus 2:4–5a

A WISE RESOURCE

B y the time most adults reach age fifty, they've recognized that there has to be more to life than a career; a car that goes from zero to ninety in six seconds; a closet full of designer clothing; a credit card without a limit; a portfolio of high-yield investments.

Most people discover that relationships matter most; they find themselves watching young families with little children at restaurant tables, wondering if those parents even have a clue regarding the treasure they have within their family.

When we were children, we may have wanted to be able to fly through the air; later we couldn't wait until we could drive . . . graduate from high school . . . own a car . . . get a job . . . move into our own apartment.

Time just wouldn't move *fast* enough!

Now we don't want time to fly by—we realize that it *has*. We don't want to move into tomorrow—we want to replay yesterday. We want time to slow down . . . that's why we love looking at photos more and more—those moments that are frozen in time and can't completely slip away.

By the time we're fifty, we come to understand that our days are actually numbered. We begin to develop a greater level of wisdom regarding life— and time—when we finally realize how precious it is.

The Psalmist wrote:

> *So teach us to number our days, that we may present to You a heart of wisdom* (Psalm 90:12).

Knowing our days are numbered is fertile soil from which wisdom and discernment sprout, grow, and bear fruit. That kind of wisdom and perspective from the life of an older believer is actually desperately needed in the Church today. Older believers can become the most significant culture-shaping force within the body of Christ.

The older men are to model maturity, dignity, faith, and love. The older women are to model holy living and a sweet, sacred demeanor, serving as hands-on mentors of younger women.

Older women are not *less* valuable as they grew older but *more* valuable.[1] They are a powerful influence on younger women within the body of Christ as they perform a counterculture ministry.

A WORTHY RESOLUTION

[S]*o that they may encourage the young women to love their husbands, to love their children, to be sensible, pure, workers at home, kind, being subject to their own husbands, so that the word of God will not be dishonored* (Titus 2:4–5).

Keep in mind that Paul is simply dealing with the norm: men and women marry, and most married couples have children or choose to adopt them.

We know from *1 Corinthians 7* that Paul had a very high view of singleness. He didn't consider singles less than complete in Christ. In fact, being single doesn't somehow make us incomplete in our relationship with God the Father. If it did, then Jesus Christ was incomplete, since He never married.

Paul will stress in other passages the special opportunities for Christian service by remaining single.[2]

The point is make the most of whatever state in which we find ourselves—single or married—and go for it . . . maximizing it for the glory of God!

What Paul does in his letters, most often, is deal with the pattern God established for marriage and family, and his inspired instruction finds a hearing among the majority of the people in the Church. God's plan for marriage and motherhood will continually find less and less appreciation as culture moves away from God's design and chooses its own depraved, self-centered desires. Marriage as an institution in our culture is already entirely redefined.

Pastors and evangelists used to preach that the greatest danger to the institution of marriage was divorce. We now know that isn't true. The greater danger is that it ceases to *exist* with any real meaning.

According to a recently released Pew Research Analysis, barely half of all adults in the United States are now married. To put that into perspective, seventy-two percent of all adults were married in the 1960 census—today the number is fifty-one percent.

Why is this? One reason is the failure—or, perhaps, even the inability—of young men to grow out of their adolescent lifestyle and welcome the responsibilities of marriage. One secular journalist wrote that we are simply surrounded by grownups who haven't left childhood.[3]

But a greater reason for the lack of marital commitment is the moral digression in our culture. Why bother with a covenant and a commitment for life when you can have the physical and financial benefits of marriage—maybe even children—without shutting down your other options?

Another statistic from that research firm revealed nearly four out of ten Americans now say that marriage is becoming obsolete. This isn't news to anyone; we are simply observing the natural effects of a culture which has resisted and now, finally, has successfully banished the Bible from the public square. And when the Bible is exiled, any stigma with lifestyles and choices the Bible calls sinful disappears along with it.

Over the years, I've had couples in my office who, without any embarrassment, tell me that they see nothing wrong with living together without being covenanted together in marriage; it made sense financially, and there were benefits to getting to know one another before they married. Who was I to say they were living in fornication? In fact, before one meeting ended, one couple told me they felt closer to God than ever.

They'd better enjoy that close feeling while they can.

One secular author wrote that we are watching a tectonic shift in sensibilities within our culture today.[4] Right and wrong have been turned upside down. Marriage is no longer a covenant of self-sacrifice and responsibility between a couple as long as *life* shall last; it is simply a romantic union between two or more people as long as *love* shall last.

Welcome to the twenty-first century. And welcome to the island of Crete. This was their lifestyle, too:

- Homosexual marriage was practiced by emperors and statesman.
- Bisexuality was the norm and heterosexuality considered prudish.
- Older men were immature and self-centered, refusing to grow up and act their age.
- Older women were gossiping drunkards.
- Younger men were all about *I*, *me*, and *my*.
- Younger women were abandoning their husbands and children.

We are not living in a *post*-Christian world as much as we are living in a *pre*-Christian world, like the churches in Crete. The average person on the street doesn't know:

- which God is the living God;
- whether the Bible is any more sacred than the Quran, the Baghavad Gita, or the Book of Mormon;
- that there was a universal flood;
- whether Jesus is just another prophet in a long list of seers and wise men.

Do you know what this means? It means that we are living at the *perfect* time in a phenomenal age where we can display the Gospel of Jesus Christ and the kinds of pure relationships within a family and in the Church that mankind has abandoned.

The Light can *really* shine now.

Paul talked about the depravity of the Cretan culture and then provided his divinely inspired solution: older women encouraging the young women how to be wives and mothers. In other words, show them true wisdom; you could translate it *wise them up*.[5] In the upside down culture, here was the opportunity to turn everything right-side up.

Paul is providing the curriculum for mentoring young wives and mothers, and there are seven subjects to be taught. The first six are given in pairs, and the final one is a phrase which includes a mindset and a motivation. In this chapter, we'll deal with the first two pairs.

A WOMAN'S RELATIONSHIPS

[S]*o that they* [the older women] *may encourage* [train] *the young women to* love *their husbands, to* love *their children* (Titus 2:4).

The word for **love** here is *philos*: to show affection or, even, friendship. This verse brings up these questions: How can you command emotion? How can you summon affection?

What Paul is implying here is that **love** can be *learned*; that a person can live and act so that their emotions are ultimately conquered and corralled and governed by right thinking—and not the other way around.

God often commands emotional responses:

- rejoice evermore *(1 Thessalonians 5:16)*;

- respond with joyful resolve in the midst of trials *(James 1:2)*;

- give thanks about everything, for this is the will of God *(1 Thessalonians 5:18)*.

These are all commands that involve emotions which we might not have at the moment, but we obey and discover that our *biblical actions produce biblical emotions.*

We're living in a fallen culture with a fallen nature that tells us our actions should be the *result* of our emotions—that our emotions are the engine that pulls along our actions. God reverses all of that. He says, through Paul, to submit our minds to Him and act in faith according to His commands, and our feelings will eventually follow. The engine is action—the caboose is emotion.

That's exactly how we raise our children: when they *feel* like having candy for breakfast and *feel* like vegetables aren't worthy of attention, we have to push those feelings back with the command to eat the healthy things first.

There was a time when my mother told me to eat my vegetables. I didn't want to—I didn't feel like I needed them—I didn't like them, either. But she never gave me a vote; she knew what I truly needed, whether I felt like it or not. It would take most of my life before my feelings changed about peas and squash.

One evening when Marsha was at a church activity, I volunteered to fix dinner for our young children. How hard could it be? She made it easy for me by setting out a box of Tuna Helper: just boil water, pour in the box, stir, drain, add a can of tuna—dinner!

I boiled the water, opened the box, poured it in, and I saw all those little green peas . . . really hard, shriveled-up peas. They probably could have been shot from a BB gun. I thought, *Man, I wish Betty Crocker hadn't put those peas in there. I don't wanna eat 'em . . . but the kids will be watching.*

Seconds after I poured the contents of the box into the boiling water, all those peas floated right up to the surface . . . I was able to scoop them out easily. What a kind act of God's providence!

Fast forward two decades and now I *feel* differently about vegetables and salad and fiber and fruit. I still might not like the taste of green peas, but I know why they're good to eat, so regardless of emotion, I add a spoonful to my plate . . . right next to the mashed potatoes and gravy.

The command of Paul through Titus is for women to act in such a way that ultimately produces feeling a certain way. But acting in obedience always comes first. In everyday language:

> ***Younger wives and mothers, allow yourselves to be trained to* love *by acting toward your husband and children with the affections of* love** (Titus 2:4 paraphrase).

For the Jewish believers and most of the rest in their culture, we need to understand that their traditions of marriage and parenting would make this command all the more profound—if not difficult.

In America, we have the children's rhyme:

> *Johnny and Susie sitting in a tree,*
> *K–I–S–S–I–N–G.*
> *First comes love,*
> *Then comes marriage,*
> *Then comes baby in a baby carriage!*

For many people reading this letter in the first century, it was just the opposite: first comes marriage, then comes love. That's because marriages were most often arranged and the couple was betrothed long before they met. In fact, many times they didn't meet until just before the wedding.

One of our deacons and his wife, originally from India, met just before their engagement ceremony. I met a couple from Africa recently who was introduced to each other on the day before their wedding; the marriage was arranged by their Christian parents. In these instances, first came marriage, *then* came learning how to love each other.

Add children to the mix and it becomes even more challenging. Bearing children in Crete during the first century wasn't necessarily an expression of marital love but a duty. One author wrote that in Titus's day, bearing children was the result of "dutiful performance" . . . it was considered the duty of a wife to bear and raise the children *on her own*, with little help from her husband. She could easily resent her husband and naturally transfer that resentment to the children.[6]

With that in mind, consider Paul's profound instruction. These young wives and mothers who've come to saving faith in Christ are introduced to a new family called the Church—a fellowship of redeemed sinners. And they hear about new relationships and new priorities. The subject of a Christian home is something totally new to them, and they're going to need to be trained to a new way of thinking.

Paul wasn't telling them, "Listen, now that you're a Christian, here's how you can escape marriage and motherhood." No, Paul is saying, "Here's how you go back into all of that . . . and make a difference for the Gospel and the glory of God."

No wonder they would need to be trained to think entirely differently— just as men and women need to be trained in this generation.

ABC News aired the story of an all-female law firm that specializes in divorce. It created a billboard in the Chicago area, targeting the young and wealthy:

> LIFE'S SHORT. GET A DIVORCE. Next to that statement was a photograph featuring the six-pack abs of a headless male torso and a tanned scantily clad female's upper body. Within a week, the city took down the ad, citing technical problems.

The truth was that enough people complained. The law firm defended it, saying, "We find the advertisement refreshingly honest and insightful. It's true people are unhappy; there are plenty of options out there—get a divorce and get on with your life."[7]

If the primary purpose of marriage is self-fulfillment and sexual gratification, then the ad makes perfect sense and it can be praised as perceptive: if marriage or motherhood is ruining your life or your figure, get out as quickly as you can.

Paul slices through that cultural mindset with this new set of priorities—a new kind of discipline—a new list of commands . . . as well as a new set of privileges.[8]

And even though these young women are Christians, they would discover that Christianity wasn't some kind of miracle drug against marital and parental challenges. Marriage was still the union of two fallen sinners, and any children who were born to them or adopted by them would soon be found to be fallen sinners, too.

And to make matters even more challenging, the present tense of this verb **to love** means that this will be the *daily* decision and the *daily* challenge of these young wives and mothers.

Frankly, mothers have the toughest job on the planet. The phrase *working mother* is redundant. Mothers are underpaid, undervalued, overworked, and often simply taken for granted. When your children are hurt or not feeling well or need to throw up, they never call for Dad—they want Mom.

Mothers don't get much of a break, either. A fifteen-year-old came home from school and found his mom upstairs, lying on the bed. He was suddenly seized with genuine concern. He asked, "Mom, are you sick or something?" His mother responded somewhat weakly, "As a matter of fact, I'm not feeling very well." "Aw, I'm sorry about that, Mom." Then after a long pause he said, "Look, Mom, don't worry about going downstairs to cook dinner . . . I'm strong enough to carry you down there myself."

Here's the reality of Paul's challenge—it's a call for women to abandon their cultural training that led them into self-love, self-promotion, and self-centeredness. It's a call to embrace actions and decisions that are characterized by self-sacrificing love.

While Paul elaborates on how the husband is to love his wife *(Ephesians 5:25–30)*, here in Titus he expands on how the wife is to love her husband and children. And that's a startling thing that runs counterculture. One author summarized it: "Mature, godly love is not an emotion that wells up; it is a discipline that is worked up."[9]

And, I might add, *out.*

A WOMAN'S REPUTATION

[T]*o be* **sensible, pure,** *workers at home,* **kind,** *being subject to their own husbands, so that the word of God will not be dishonored* (Titus 2:5).

Just as the qualifications of an elder in *Titus 1* provide an excellent standard for how *every* man should live—whether he serves as an elder or not—these attributes here are for *all* women, not just those who are married or have children.

In fact, the word translated **sensible** is the same word Titus uses to challenge older men, younger men, and the entire church family. It has to do with balanced thinking—to think biblically—and then act.

Paul also adds that they should be **pure**. This word means *chaste* or *modest*. It originally referred to ritual cleanness, but over time it shifted to the moral realm.[10]

Purity in marriage doesn't automatically exempt women from either being attracted to other men or attracting other men to themselves. A wedding ring isn't a safety net.

Part of the curriculum for godly women being taught here is that they're not only part of a nuclear family but a larger family; it is to her glory to be chaste and discreet—to develop the reputation of being **pure**. Purity will be reflected in her commitment to modesty—a commitment to not purposefully attract attention to her body.

Paul knew that these young women wouldn't have a clue about this subject, having entered their spiritual family directly from the culture of Crete where sexual expression and freedom was flaunted, where prostitution—and everything else imaginable—was legal. Young women would come into the Church and need instruction from the older women in this very practical regard simply because they'd never benefited from modest mothers who modeled pure and chaste behavior.

This is why Paul openly challenged the women about their appearance in his letter to Timothy:

Likewise, I want women to adorn themselves with proper cloth-ing, modestly and discreetly (1 Timothy 2:9*a*).

Let me make the same appeal to our sisters in Christ, on behalf of their brothers in Christ. Men often lament, "If only women *knew* how difficult it is to try to focus on God, while at the same time battling our flesh when someone nearby comes into the assembly looking like they do . . . the entire worship service becomes a tug of war and we often leave the church more defeated than when we came in."

By the way, as fathers and husbands, we would do our brothers in Christ a great service if *we* counseled our wives and daughters with our honest opin-ion—which means we're going to have to take the blinders off and wake up to the way the women in our household are dressing. Think through the impact of their clothing—or lack of it—especially when we're heading out the door to a public worship service. Provide them insight and warn them, "Sweetie, you really look beautiful, but if you go to church wearing that outfit, the guys around you are going to have a really difficult time singing, *Holy, Holy, Holy.*"

Of *all* places, go the extra mile to be discreet and chaste and **pure** in the presence of your brothers in Christ.

This was a new message on Crete. For the women on that island and for women throughout every generation, getting attention is *exactly* the point . . . it's the name of the game.

Paul is basically instructing them, "Listen, if you want to make a mark for Christ—be known for the right thing—make sure it has to do with how you *live*, not so much with how you *look.*"

A WONDERFUL REVELATION

[T]*hat the word of God will not be dishonored* (Titus 2:5*b*).

The women came into the Church with a history that was anything but **pure**. They were fighting their own battles and many of them were probably wondering just how deeply the blood of Christ had cleansed them. After all, the island wasn't that big . . . and they had been wicked little Cretans.

Paul is effectively saying to these younger women, "You may not have had a reputation for being **pure**, but you can have one *now*. Purity may never have been associated with your past lifestyle, but that can change in the present. This is the Gospel of grace—no matter your past, the word **pure** can define you now."

This is the new challenge for chaste and holy living—older women will provide the pattern and the Holy Spirit will provide the power.

The pattern was set and would be reinforced as the older women taught the younger women about:

- growing and developing a deeper longing to live for the approval and pleasure of God instead of the approval and pleasure of men;

- letting purity affect everything, from the inside out;

- being sensible and governing their actions by their convictions instead of by their emotions;

- learning how to serve their husbands and children with self-sacrificing love instead of self-love.

Older women, you are to invite the younger wives and mothers into your lives so they may watch and learn that *your* life is life as God intended it.

Model for them a new way to love . . . a new way to live.

[W]*orkers at home, kind, being subject to their own husbands, so that the word of God will not be dishonored.*

–Titus 2:5

CHAPTER FOURTEEN

RETRACING OUR FOOTSTEPS HOME

Titus 2:5

THE BIG LIE

This verse is one of the most politically incorrect passages you'll find in all of the New Testament:

[T]*o be sensible, pure,* **workers at home,** *kind, being* **subject to their own husbands,** *so that the word of God will not be dishonored* (Titus 2:5).

It is, for the most part, avoided by the Church of our generation and by many pastors and leaders. In fact, several phrases that appear in the text are literally loaded with emotional fireworks. They will create an immediate inward response made up of preconceived notions and popular opinions.

The majority of the Christian world today has chosen to ignore the implications, explain them away, or assign them to a time long ago before society became so much more sophisticated and up-to-date.

Paul delivers these loaded phrases that refer to young married women who were to be **workers at home** and **subject to their own husbands**. That text not only raises eyebrows outside the Church but inside, as well.

The ideas of homemaking and submission for women are surely prehistoric, viewed by the majority of people as relics from the dinosaur age when men supposedly dragged their wives around by the hair, killed mammoths with clubs, and ate their meat raw . . . we're not talking sushi, either.

Surely Paul doesn't mean that this is for *today.*

Feminist thinking in the world outside the Church—and now securely inside the Church—actually *understands* what Paul means, which is one of the reasons the Bible is so troubling to our androgynous culture. No wonder there's so much heartburn and angst from those who would like to be perceived as biblical thinkers. No wonder so much interpretive gymnastics is employed to make Paul say something other than what he clearly says.

Feminist organizations such as NOW (National Organization for Women) have, since 1966, been calling for what constitutes the end of marriage and motherhood as we know it. They have demanded that corporations and the state take on more and more of the responsibility of raising children . . . and they've lobbied that marriage as an institution is an embarrassing leftover from our patriarchal past.

In fact, one feminist wrote, "We must fight the institutionalization of the oppression of women, especially the institution of marriage."[1] One feminist leader said, "Freedom for women cannot be won without the abolition of marriage."[2] And that's largely because they equate submission with slavery.

Granted, there are plenty of men who make that conclusion easy . . . I'll explain where it all started as we go further into our study.

For many years, there was a widespread slogan in the United States: MOTHERHOOD—JUST SAY NO![3] One of the greatest successes—and, to this day, the legacy—of the American feminist movement was the legal right granted to a woman to end the life of her preborn baby, regardless of the fact that now even medical science has conclusively proven that life begins for that baby long before birth.

By the way, feminist successes have not made men out of boys. Men have been all too willing to become acclimated to the new female culture of autonomy and sexual freedom. Why get married and have children when you can have the physical pleasures of marriage without a covenant of fidelity? When you can have the income of two breadwinners and continue the party lifestyle, why settle down and live off one income?

And if children should ever hit the radar screen, you can either abort or allow adoption, so your lifestyle is only minimally impacted. Children are viewed as a handicap that can easily be remedied.

Thus our culture digresses, believing it has found what it really wants in order to be progressive: freedom, individuality, autonomy, and gratuitous self-service—all in the name of sophistication and cultural advancement.

Who's fooling whom?

Hans Christian Andersen wrote a tale about an emperor so exceedingly fond of new clothes that he spent all his money on a designer wardrobe:

> In the great city where the emperor lived, many strangers came to town, and among them were two swindlers who let it be known they could weave the most magnificent fabrics imaginable. Not only were their colors and patterns uncommonly fine, but clothes made of this cloth had a wonderful way of becoming invisible to anyone who was unfit for his office or who was unusually stupid. *Those would be just the clothes for me,* thought the emperor—*I could tell the wise men from the fools.* Two looms were set up and the finest silk and gold thread was ordered (which promptly went into the swindlers' bags).
>
> The work progressed as the looms went back and forth, and the emperor anxiously awaited his new clothes. He sent several trusted advisers to observe the weaving of the cloth; each saw nothing but feared for his position, so they proclaimed they had never seen such beautiful material. When the emperor himself came with his retinue to examine the cloth, he saw nothing—although everyone else proclaimed the magnificence of the work. Wishing not to be made out a fool, he approved the fabric and ordered his clothes to be fashioned. A great procession was planned, and the day came for the emperor to be shown his new clothes. The "weavers" went to great lengths to point out each piece, commenting that they were as fine as a spider web, and it would feel as though he had nothing on. At last, robed in his new clothes, the emperor viewed his image in the mirror, saying that they were a remarkable fit.
>
> Off he went, striding under his canopy in the grand procession. The entire town knew about the cloth's peculiar power, and all were impatient to find out how stupid their neighbors

were. Everyone viewing from the streets and windows professed that these were the finest clothes the emperor had ever worn. But then a little child blurted out, "Look! The emperor has no clothes!" Surely the innocence of a child precluded all other opinions. One person whispered to another and another and another what the little boy had said. Finally, the whole town cried out in one voice, "The emperor has no clothes!"

And that was the end of the parade.

Who will dare to tell the truth about abortion and risk being cast outside the world of political and moral sophistication by saying, "They are taking the lives of human beings"?

Who will say, "To be rid of motherhood is to abandon the foundation of the family and lose the greatest potential role of influence known on planet Earth"?

Who will declare, "A woman who throws out the constraints and covenant of marriage is not going to be cherished by men—she will be exploited by men"?

Cohabitation . . . abortion . . . freedom from the rigors of motherhood and the constraints of purity—just look at our new clothes!

Our society has been buying these clothes in earnest for at least the past five decades. And everybody's saying, "But we feel so light . . . so unencumbered." There's a reason for that: they're naked.

The truth is that our politically correct culture is clothed in nothing more than its own imagination. All the opinions and messages and propaganda of our sophisticated world are *not* making people more content . . . fulfilled . . . at peace.

The clothing of the world is threadbare at best and nonexistent at the least. In fact, if the eyes of humanity were opened, they would discover—like Adam and Eve before them—their utter nakedness. In spite of their advertisements and endorsements and approval of the latest fashions, our world outside of God's design is no wiser than the deluded emperor, naked and strutting through town under his canopy . . . for all to see.

So where do we start to tell the world the truth about God's design for living?

We start with *ourselves*.

Paul told Titus to organize the churches on Crete. He knew that an active, committed-to-the-Gospel-of-Jesus-Christ Church would infiltrate her culture, and the believers would impact it as they went around turning on the Light with the innocence of their purity.

The illumination as it relates to marriage and motherhood shines on cultural ideas and expressions that many believe should be relegated to the first century. But they were not welcome *then*, either. These are timeless truths because:

1. We don't tinker with doctrine.
2. These truths are as fitting for the twenty-first century as they were in the first century.[4]

And they are no more welcome now than they were then.

Before we set off the fireworks display, remember that Paul told Titus to **speak the** things *which are fitting for sound doctrine* (Titus 2:1). What follows is a specific listing of those **things** pertaining to wives and mothers. And this is where it really gets interesting.

THE FIRST PRIORITY

Paul writes that the older women are to encourage the young women to be **workers at home** (Titus 2:5). This is a compound word: *house (oikos)*; *work* or *task (ergon)*—literally, houseworker.[5]

The wife and mother is to expend her energy primarily at home. She is to maintain a nest and a haven for both her husband and children. Obviously, in this context, she is a mother of young children.[6]

Some translations render **workers at home** as *keepers at home*. There are those who sarcastically opine that if she is required to be the keeper at home, then that means she must be *kept* at home. You conjure up a mental image of a mother chained to the kitchen sink with six crying children at her feet.[7]

That's not what Paul had in mind; he wasn't saying that the *only* place a wife and mother could work was in the home. In fact, a wife would have worked in the garden, the stable, the field—and while we're at it, she would have worked with other women to meet a variety of needs in the community, as well as in the church.

Study the *Proverbs 31* woman, who:

- hires her own staff,

- rises early and works late to produce her merchandise,
- barters in the marketplace with tradesmen,
- negotiates real estate deals with developers,
- expands her crop rotation system,
- assists the poor.

Her family isn't her only focus, but it is her *primary* focus.

Paul isn't so much defining the only place a wife and mother can work as he is defining the home as the number one workplace . . . the first priority for her energy and work.

This was the opposite of what the Cretan culture was all about—which is why Paul isn't just commanding but *commending* the roles of wife, mother, and homemaker.

The home is the place where the mother virtually impacts every member of society, as children begin to learn virtues, relational skills, compassion, honesty, respect for authority and, above all, the application of biblical truth to life.

No wonder there is so much pressure for young wives and mothers to adopt the ungodly precepts of radical feminism—the belief that wives and mothers at home are second-class . . . they've missed the bus . . . they're out of step . . . they're wasting their lives.

Add to that the pressure from their husbands who might want another stream of revenue—no matter what happens to the children or the home. Then factor in a fallen nature battling a never-ending wish list that grows with each television commercial or catalogue that arrives in the mail.

The pressure is on to *leave* the home and pursue a career—*regardless* of children and the home.

There are comparative statistics of the incredible rise of mothers of young children working full-time jobs outside the home: 1967 – 10%; 2012 – 71%.[8] Over twelve million infants and toddlers are in daycare centers nearly forty hours a week.[9]

Obviously we live in an imperfect world. There are definitely reasons mothers may have to work outside the home, whether for a season or for several years: single and divorced women; widows; wives of disabled men; wives of imprisoned men; women who have been deserted. These women may have few options for themselves and their families.

Wives without children or whose children are already grown obviously have fewer challenges in keeping the home. She and her husband may agree for her to work an outside job.[10] But let's not buy into the cultural full-court press for couples to raise their standard of living at the expense of their God-given responsibility. That responsibility of child rearing is really short-lived; it might feel like an eternity at times, but in the blink of an eye, it's over.

My wife was cleaning out a closet and found one of the little plastic toys our boys played with when they were toddlers—a tiny red and yellow guitar. All four kids eventually had their turn. They played with it, carried it around, strummed it and, of course, hit each other over the head with it. Marsha and I agreed that it was an absolute treasure worth keeping . . . and passing along to our growing brood of grandchildren.

I thought it was interesting that the National Institute of Child Health and Human Development—not necessarily the most biblical organization on the planet—conducted a hundred-million-dollar investigation of just over 1,000 children tracked from birth through preschool. The objective of the study was to trace behavioral problems that might surface in children primarily from being in full-time daycare. The result: "We have found that the total number of hours a child is without a parent (namely, their mother) from birth through preschool *matters*."[11]

Seriously? It matters? At the end of a hundred-million-dollar effort, they cough up the fact that Moms *matter*, and the more time mothers spend with their infants and preschoolers, the better?

We obviously know what our culture can barely bring itself to admit; of course, for our world to acknowledge much more than that would only invite the scorn of those who are convinced the emperor is wearing clothes.

No wonder Paul teaches that younger women's first and foremost priority is the home . . . and he didn't need to spend one hundred million to arrive at that conclusion.

The numbers are staggering, and they are rising: in 2009, 85.4 million U.S. women were mothers, yet in 2012, 74.8 million were in the civilian workforce.[12]

Psychology Today had an article on the pressure young girls are facing concerning their image:

Deprived of an internal compass, girls are competing to be everything, turning colleges into incubators for eating disorders and numerous unrealistic, self-imposed expectations. Those who aren't mentored by parents are not inoculated against peer pressure and wind up turning to their peers and the media for guidance. Girls' image obsession can be blamed on the culture of neglect—kids are raising [each other].[13]

There's never been a better time than now to shine the spotlight of truth on the subjects of motherhood and marriage.

We need to retrace our steps . . . back home.

THE RIGHT MENTALITY

[Encourage the young women to be] **. . . kind** (Titus 2:5).

Kind*ness* comes from a word that could be translated *goodness*. In our language, this word refers to being good-hearted or even having a heart that wants what is good. This would mean a woman's desire is to do whatever she can for the *good* of her husband and children.

Her thinking (or mentality) is reconditioned to ask herself whether something would be good for her husband, for her children. What would be good to do . . . or say . . . or provide?

Her mentality is refocused with **kind***ness* toward whatever is beneficial and good for her family.

THE PROPER HUMILITY

[Encourage the young women to be] **. . . subject to their own husbands,** *so that the word of God will not be dishonored* (Titus 2:5).

Paul uses the middle voice for this verb **(to be subject)** which means that he isn't telling men to command their wives to submit—he is actually telling the *wives* that this is a voluntary submission to the leadership of their husbands.

You could render this phrase *to continually place themselves under the authority of their own husbands.*[14]

Paul expands on this idea in *Ephesians 5*, where he refers to the wife as the Church, submitting to the leadership of her husband as unto Jesus

Christ. Then in the same chapter, to the husband loving his wife as Jesus Christ loves the Church.

Authority isn't a privilege to be exploited to build up a man's ego—it is a responsibility to be carried out for the benefit of those under his care.[15]

I know from personal experience that my wife would have a much easier time submitting to me if I acted more like Jesus. Still, the idea of wives submitting to their husbands, in our culture, is like drinking bitter water.

Think for a moment—*everyone* in a well-ordered society submits to *someone*. In fact, we're all told to *be subject to one another in the fear of Christ* (Ephesians 5:21):

- children submit to parents;
- students submit to teachers;
- athletes submit to coaches;
- employees submit to bosses;
- military service members submit to officers;
- citizens submit to town councils;
- drivers submit to policemen, etc.

Your submission doesn't relate to the *character* of the person to whom you submit—it has everything to do with the *kind* of authority he's been given. That police officer who pulls me over (speaking hypothetically here) may not attend church as regularly as I do or have as many verses memorized as I have. But he does have a role of authority that I haven't been given; an office that I am compelled to respect and obey. And every other driver is better off because I do.

Authority is part of God's arrangement for all of life. According to God's design:

- the wife is under the authority of her husband;
- the husband is under the authority of the elders of the church, as are singles, widows, young people, and everyone else;
- the elders are under the authority of Jesus Christ;
- Jesus Christ willingly submits to the authority of God the Father.

Paul clarifies to the Corinthians:

> But I want you to understand that Christ is the head of every man, and the man is the head of a woman, and God is the head of Christ (1 Corinthians 11:3).

For Titus (and for us), the difficulty with the concept of headship and submission runs against everything the women of Crete had been raised to believe—which is why Titus needed older women to teach the younger women who were new believers in Christ how this worked.

In our culture today, "equality" and "equal rights" have become the buzzwords of our generation. And the trouble with *equality* is that it can be deceptive, depending on who's using the word.

Erwin Lutzer points out that feminists have extended the definition of equality beyond equal treatment and equal value to equal *roles* for men and women—that is, the place of women should be interchangeable with that of men. Whatever men do, women should be free to do, and all gender-based roles should be abolished.[16]

Even now, the Church is growing more divided on whether women can preach or pastor—after all, surely they have equal rights to the highest level of authority in the Church. Aren't we all equal in Christ?

Yes, we are equal in our *essence*: both male and female are made in the image of God. We are both equal in our *salvation* and our individual *priesthood* before God: we can all go to God directly in prayer and worship. And we are equal in our *accountability* before God one day. Adam is no longer saying, "It was the woman." And the woman isn't even saying, "It was that snake." We will be *equally* individually accountable to God.

But equality in *essence* does not mean equality in *authority* or *function*. And what we've now inherited from fifty years of feminism and a few decades of evangelical feminism is not only the loss of God-ordained structure for the home, the family, and the Church, but the tragic failure to glory in the distinctions between men and women—to find satisfaction and contentment in God's created order of male and female.

The lines are all blurred; the picture is out of focus.

The problem isn't just recent history—it's ancient history! It really began in the Garden of Eden, and it's just been repackaged over the centuries in a variety of forms.

Both Adam and Eve were made in God's image. Adam's headship in marriage was established by God *before* sin occurred. In fact, it wasn't until after *Adam* ate the fruit that their eyes were opened to their shame. Distinctions in masculine and feminine roles were ordained by God as part of the created order—which means they echo in every human heart.[17]

But the digression of mankind into sin immediately introduced distortions in marriage, gender identity, and every other relationship. Part of the curse God pronounced on Adam and Eve had to do with their relationship and every marriage that would come after them. Before they were exiled from the Garden, God told Eve that part of her fallen nature would be *"your desire will be for your husband"* (Genesis 3:16*b*). That phrase is repeated in the next chapter, which provides clarity as God warns Cain that *"sin is crouching at the door; and its desire is for you, but you must master it"* (Genesis 4:7).

In other words, sin wants to master your life—it wants to manipulate and dominate your heart, but you must conquer it instead. God told Eve and her daughters after her—which includes every woman ever born—that women will struggle in their fallen nature with a desire that will no longer willingly respond to the leadership of men, but her desire will be to manipulate and master her world . . . especially her husband.

Then God says to Eve before she is exiled with her husband: *"[H]e will rule over you"* (Genesis 3:16*c*). In other words, Adam's default desire will no longer be to provide loving, nurturing leadership but, rather, exploitation and self-centered, self-promoting, self-pleasing rule over the woman. God created Eve to be at Adam's side, but now Adam will have the natural fallen desire to put her under his *feet*. And the woman is going to do her utmost not to just get back to Adam's side but to rule over his head.

Sin turned headship and submission into a battle over who will master whom! Some will quickly say, "But that is the Old Testament—what about *now*? There is a new body of believers . . . a new dispensation of grace. What about marriage now? What about men and women now? What about order and authority within the Christian community now?"

THE NEW PROPRIETY

Paul wants Titus to instruct the older women to teach the younger women that the Gospel returns them to the kind of relationship God intended *before* the fall of mankind. Man picks up the woman from the dust under his feet and places her at his side, lovingly leading her and caring for her and providing for her. She lovingly serves him and respects him and submits to his leadership.

Christianity is a restoration of relationships in the home—where the distinctive and God-ordained roles are not diminished or twisted or denied but honored and exalted and enhanced.

It's a return to the original home that God intended, where men are men and women are women—men are superior to women in being men, and women are superior to men in being women. All the differences and nuances and distinctives of gender and function are enhanced and enjoyed and reveled in as we honor our Creator.

When our daughter Candace was serving as a missionary in Santiago, Chile, she taught five-year-olds in a Christian academy. One week she posted on her blog the distinctives that she'd observed between the little boys and girls in her class—distinctives that are transcultural, because they are designed by our Creator:

- Boys want to color pictures of superheroes or a dog or a big scary animal.
- ➤ Girls want to color pictures of castles, princesses, flowers, and rainbows.
- Boys dodge my hugs but pick endless amounts of flowers for me.
- ➤ Girls hug me often but pick flowers to keep for themselves.
- Boys treat their schoolwork like competition.
- ➤ Girls offer help to whoever needs it.
- Boys flex their muscles in the bathroom mirror and see who can jump the farthest off the bench.
- ➤ Girls smile and giggle in the mirror and use their bench for twirling.
- Boys want to play ball with the older boys on the playground and believe they can keep up with them.
- ➤ Girls hover around the swing set, not giving a care to the ballgame going on a few feet away.
- Boys always want to be the first and the fastest.
- ➤ Girls hold hands and walk together.
- Boys play *in* the dirt and have to be asked to clean up.
- ➤ Girls play *with* the dirt and volunteer to wash up after recess.
- Boys go for the big cars and trucks and make motor noises at the play center; they make railroad tracks and battlegrounds out of anything they can find.
- ➤ Girls find the prince and princess and the big minivan and rearrange the furniture in the doll houses.

- Boys stick with the same thing for ten minutes, get bored, and are ready to switch to something different.
- Girls can spend the entire afternoon doing the same activity, perfecting or changing it.
- Boys tell me that I'm pretty.
- Girls ask me why I'm not married! (she is now, by the way)

Why the distinct differences? Because their Creator made them that way. Now I'm speaking in general terms; I know men who can make beautiful flower arrangements, and I know girls who can beat the socks off the guys in basketball. I grew up next door to a girl named Susan. On a rainy day, you'd find me in her garage, playing Barbies. I was fascinated by all the car doors that opened and the closets with little hangers—it was so creative. I just didn't want anyone to know about it and kept it a secret . . . until now.

Culture and fallen mankind will blur the lines and redefine the order that God has arranged for our benefit and well-being. And when we, the Church, follow God's arrangement, Paul tells Titus *that the word of God will not be dishonored* (Titus 2:5*b*). That includes God's name, His plan, His redemption, His glory, and His purposes for mankind.

The German philosopher Heinrich Heine challenged the Church in the nineteenth century: "Show me your redeemed life and I might be inclined to believe in your Redeemer."[18]

The world is watching—that's Paul's point. If we don't strive to live according to God's revelation, the world will dishonor God's Word. If Christians don't care about His Word, don't follow His Word, deny and disobey and rearrange the order of His creation, then why should they?

But we as Christians love the assembly—we love the unity of spirit and the joy of worship. We love the reminders of redeeming priorities and a redeemed mentality which produces an orderly, redeemed humility that insures that men and women alike live their lives with propriety *that the word of God will not be dishonored.*

Anything else is a lie . . . no matter how loud the applause as the emperor parades down the street. It's time to tell the truth—first to ourselves—and allow the Word of God to prompt us and prod us and pull us back to His created design . . . and by His strength, retrace our footsteps home.

⁶Likewise urge the young men to be sensible; ⁷in all things show yourself to be an example of good deeds, with purity in doctrine, dignified, ⁸sound in speech which is beyond reproach, so that the opponent will be put to shame, having nothing bad to say about us.

–Titus 2:6–8

CHAPTER FIFTEEN

A PATTERN
FOR YOUNG MEN

Titus 2:6–8

AN ENDANGERED SPECIES

S
o far, Paul hasn't pulled any punches in this family talk to each age group in the Church body, and he expects no less of Titus in all the churches on the island of Crete. His words have been both convicting and encouraging. He's raised our level of responsibility as well as our level of understanding. He has also elevated and distinguished and applauded the roles of older men, older women, and young wives and mothers.

Now, the Spirit of God will focus the lens of His microscope on the lives of young men—this group that is virtually hanging in the balance—and in our culture, young men between the ages of eighteen and thirty-four have been put on spiritual, emotional and, even, physical life support. Many of them may never be able to flourish on their own.

One of the most endangered species within the ministry of the Church is a vitally engaged, responsibly active, spiritually maturing young man. More than ever, the distractions of our deteriorating culture are claiming the attention of these core members of the Family.

One author writes:

> Today's Single Young Males (SYMs) hang out in a hormonal limbo between adolescence and adulthood. Once upon a

time, video games were for young boys and girls. But those boys have grown up to become child-man gamers, turning a small niche industry into a twelve billion dollar powerhouse. Men between the ages of eighteen and thirty-four are now the biggest gamers; according to Nielsen Media, half of the young men in that category are playing, on average, two hours and forty-three minutes a day. With no one to challenge young men to deeper connections, they swim across life's surfaces [without ever diving deeper]. Young men especially need a culture that can help them define worthy aspirations. Adults don't emerge. They're made.[1]

Long before the twenty-first century arrived with all its advancements, games, licenses, corruptions, and obsessions, the Apostle Paul actually agreed with that author's summary: adults don't just happen . . . they are fashioned. Spiritual maturity isn't guaranteed . . . it must be modeled.

THE PLAN FOR RESCUE

Paul begins his family talk to young men by giving Titus a loaded command: *Likewise,* **urge** *the young men . . .* (Titus 2:6).

Urge them. This is the same word Paul used when he wrote:

> *I* **urge** *you . . . to present your bodies a living and holy sacrifice, acceptable to God* (Romans 12:1).

This verb **urge** or *plead* is from *parakaleo* (*to call alongside; to call beside*). It's used in the New Testament for preaching, and it's also used for the ministry of the Holy Spirit *(John 14:16)* and the ministry of Jesus Christ *(1 John 2:1)*.

What Paul is commanding Titus to do is to come alongside young men in his preaching and in his personal pleading, urging young men to live the lifestyle he will describe—one that challenges everything they once followed on their beloved island.

Paul uses the present tense for this ministry of urging, indicating that this exhorting—this pleading—is ongoing. This is not a weekend seminar for young men.[2]

He understands that one of the greatest dangers for Christian young men—and every other Christian, for that matter—is not a sudden moral blowout that everybody notices but a slow leak that no one seems to observe.[3]

The Enemy isn't going to try to get young men to deny God at some moment in time . . . he wants them to *forget* about God over a period of time.

So Titus, this is your calling; give it everything you've got as you **urge the young men** to follow a godly pattern for living.

Here's the plan . . .

CHANGE THEIR BEHAVIOR

***Likewise urge the young men to be** sensible* (Titus 2:6).

You could translate this, "In every aspect of life, urge the young men to be **sensible**." Elders of the Church were to be **sensible** *(Titus 1:8)*. Older men were to be **sensible** *(Titus 2:2c)*. Young women were commanded to be **sensible** *(Titus 2:5a)*—eventually Paul will get around to commanding the entire church family to *live sensibly (Titus 2:12)*.

A synonym for **sensible** is *self-control*. Paul is effectively writing, "Urge the young men, in all things, to exercise self-control."

One author defined self-control (sensibility) rather perceptively: "Self-control is the ability to see a godly goal and choose that goal over and against competing desires."[4] This would be particularly challenging to young men who can be impulsive and passionate and ambitious.[5]

Self-control is choosing to pursue a godly goal . . . even when other desires get in the way. This is so important—especially for young men, when their company or their campus or their crowd offers temptation with a compelling voice.

This age group often has to study or work away from home—away from the influences of their heritage, and they haven't yet taken on the responsibilities of a home or a family.[6] They don't have the obligations that will help temper and anchor their emotions.

They have a cargo hold of confidence and only a crateful of experience. Is it any wonder that Satan and the world system spend so much time and energy snagging and enslaving and shipwrecking a young man? The world tells him that he's reached the legal age . . . he's on his own . . . he's arrived—that all depends on *where* he intends to arrive.

Paul implies that to arrive at a godly place in life where you establish patterns that make genuine contributions in life and for the Gospel, you must allow self-control to steer the ship of emotion and desire.

Self-control isn't exactly the most glamorous of virtues, but when a young man of passion and energy and vision and eagerness is matched and managed by self-control, something great will come from that life.[7]

I love the way Chuck Swindoll paraphrased these verses to young men:

> Titus, help younger men learn how to apply the brakes to life. Help them understand how to bridle their tongues and control their tempers. Help them know how to curb their ambition and to purge themselves of greed. Show them how to master their sexual impulses and how to follow their minds instead of their glands. Teach them to be responsible stewards of money rather than squanderers. Show them the rewards of unselfish leadership and the folly of self-centered pursuits.[8]

Self-control—this is the pattern for how they are to act.

Paul adds a personal challenge to Titus (a young man himself) and through Titus, he delivers more challenges to young men in general:

[I]*n all things* **show** *yourself to be an example of* **good deeds** (Titus 2:7*a*).

If you are going to be any help to young men—or to any younger believer in Christ—you have to **show** them . . . demonstrate these principles. There is no such thing as armchair Christianity. So *become* an example . . . live it out. A generation of younger believers is watching.

In fact, knowing the Bible without living it will produce a generation that really doesn't want to *know* the Bible, much less *live* the Bible.[9]

Paul wasn't telling Titus to call the plays from his La-Z-Boy.© He was commanding Titus to get into the game and show the pattern of godly service in living color—don't just urge them, **show** them. Don't just plead with them—provide examples of what life looks like when you stop playing games and start doing **good deeds**.

Good deeds, by the way, is a theme in Paul's letters to young pastors Timothy and Titus:

- Women are to adorn themselves by means of good works *(1 Timothy 2:10)*.

- Widows are to have a reputation for good works *(1 Timothy 5:10)*.

- Wealthy people are to be rich in good works *(1 Timothy 6:18)*.
- Christians who live lives of daily confession will be useful to the Master and prepared for every good work *(2 Timothy 2:21)*.
- The Bible equips the believer for every good work *(2 Timothy 3:17)*.
- Young men are to be an example of **good deeds** *(Titus 2:7)*.
- The Church at large is to be zealous for **good deeds** *(Titus 2:14)*.
- Christians are to be ready to perform **good deeds** *(Titus 3:1)*.
- Christians are to be careful to engage in **good deeds** *(Titus 3:8)*.
- Christians are to learn to engage in **good deeds** *(Titus 3:14)*.

Now don't misunderstand this emphasis. Paul is not defining how we *become* a Christian—he's describing how we *live* like one. In fact, later in this letter, Paul will make it crystal clear that:

> **He saved us, not on the basis of deeds which we have done in righteousness, but according to His mercy . . . so that being justified by His grace we would be made heirs according to the hope of eternal life** (Titus 3:5a, 7).

Our salvation is not earned by good works. None of us could do enough **good deeds** to compensate for our own sins, anyway, and if we could, the crucifixion of Jesus Christ on behalf of the guilt of our sin would be unnecessary agony.

Paul isn't telling Titus to urge unbelieving young men to live this way so they can *be* redeemed; he's telling those who've been redeemed to show the world they *have* been. And it isn't about themselves—it's about doing good things, **good deeds**, for other people.

CHANGE THEIR THOUGHTS

[I]n all things show yourself to be an example of good deeds, with purity in doctrine, dignified (Titus 2:7b).

Pure **doctrine** literally means uncorrupted **doctrine**.

Young men are more likely to be carried away by doctrinal novelty than older men who've arrived at their conclusions after years of careful study. Paul is urging young men to get a head start on acquiring a comprehensive understanding of sound **doctrine**.[10]

This doesn't mean answering questions on a test—it's a reference to developing a Christian mindset. Paul knew that it was impossible to live like a Christian unless you think like a Christian. Christian thinking is determined by and governed by sound doctrinal truths revealed in the Bible.

Our generation—of all generations in modern history—is in the process of abandoning doctrinal instruction and doctrinal preaching and teaching. Everything today has to be relevant and creative and funny and fast.

Today's generation is suffering from spiritual anorexia: a loss of appetite for doctrinal substance.[11] This is nothing less than the loss of appetite for the truth of God's Word.

Read the thinking process of the Psalmist:

> *Oh, how I love your law!*
> *Your commands make me wiser than my enemies,*
> *For they are ever with me.*
> *I have more insight than all my teachers,*
> *For I meditate on your statutes.*
> *I have more understanding than my elders,*
> *For I obey your precepts* (Psalm 119:97–100 NIV).

> *My soul weeps because of grief;*
> *Strengthen me according to Your word.*
> *Remove the false way from me,*
> *And graciously grant me Your law.*
> *I cling to Your testimonies;*
> *O Lord, do not put me to shame!*
> *I shall run the way of your commandments,*
> *For You will enlarge my heart.*
> *Teach me, O Lord, the way of Your statutes,*
> *And I shall observe it to the end.*
> *Give me understanding, that may observe Your law*
> *And keep it with all my heart.*
> *Make me walk in the path of Your commandments,*
> *For I delight in it* (Psalm 119:28–29, 31–35).

> *I shall delight in Your statutes;*
> *I shall not forget Your word* (Psalm 119:16).

Simply put, you cannot act like this unless you think like this, and you will never think like this unless your mind is saturated with biblical truth. Titus was to urge the young men to become devoted to sound **doctrine** and tell them that they cannot have the wisdom of God without being in the Word of God.

Why? Because you cannot be profoundly influenced by that which you do *not* know.[12] And let me add, men: read not only the Bible but books that illustrate and dramatize and illuminate the Bible—good devotional books and volumes that inspire Christian leadership and Christian thinking and living.

Three out of four books purchased from Christian bookstores today are purchased by women.[13] Our generation of men has stopped reading. The average man buys a book and never gets past the third chapter.

Think about it: you decided to read through the Bible, which is why all of us have read the Book of Genesis more than any other book in the Bible. Eventually you get to Leviticus and then into the Book of Numbers. It might be more profitable advice to encourage young men to take one book of the Bible and study it for a year instead of reading through the Bible in a year.

We will never become knowledgeable in sound **doctrine** unless we study it and read it and become acquainted with it.

I would recommend reading:

- *My Utmost for His Highest* by Oswald Chambers is a devotional with doctrinal teeth in it—then read the biography of Oswald Chambers.

- Hudson Taylor's *Spiritual Secret* has influenced a tremendous number of Christians; if you want more, read the two-volume biography written by his grandson Howard Taylor.

- *The Knowledge of the Holy* and *The Pursuit of God* were both written by A. W. Tozer.

- Read a chapter a week of Charles C. Ryrie's *Basic Theology: A Popular Systematic Guide to Understanding Biblical Truth.*

- Biographies of Christians from the past are beneficial; *50 People Every Christian Should Know: Learning from Spiritual Giants of the Faith,* by Warren Wiersbe, summarizes the lives of people of faith from the past.

- John MacArthur's *Right Thinking in a World Gone Wrong: A Biblical Response to Today's Most Controversial Issues* is powerful.

Biographies, doctrinal reading, biblical study with meditation and memorization, practical Christian reading, devotionals, church history—all of these have a way of creating a biblical filter through which we can rinse our thoughts and cleanse our perspectives and develop wise decisions.

And you have to stay at it—one author's words: "The mind is like a garden. If a garden is not carefully looked after and cultivated, it quickly becomes a wilderness. So it is with the Christian mind. Leave it alone and it will swiftly become worldly in its thinking."[14]

The mind apart from the guidelines of true doctrine can justify *anything* . . . even within the Church:

- How can something that has brought me such enjoyment be wrong?

- God's will is for me to be happy, and I've never been happier doing what I'm doing.

- We need to accept everyone in the Church, no matter their actions and misbehaving.

- The purpose of the Church is to meet my needs.

- My marriage was never God's will in the first place.

- The problem with Christians is that they're so judgmental—I'm not sinning any more than any other person.

Those are just a few perspectives and thoughts that can sink into someone's heart if unprotected by the filter of doctrinal truth.

The problem with the Church is not that we're teaching too much—we are teaching too little. If we want young men to think correctly and to grow in Christ, they must learn of Christ, become acquainted with the doctrines of Christ, and understand the commands of Christ.

Paul adds at the end of our verse that young men are to be **dignified**. We've already encountered this word in our discussion on older men. The word refers to a bearing of gravity, sanctity, dignity.[15] It speaks of a willingness to be viewed as someone who is growing older and growing up. It describes someone who is worthy of respect.

Again, this doesn't mean a Christian young man is a wet blanket wherever he goes. It doesn't mean he can't have fun and laugh . . . but it does determine what he considers fun, and it certainly guards what he laughs at.

The dignity that Titus is to model for the young men on Crete is the balance of wisdom and decorum that ultimately earns the right to be heard; to this day, our culture isn't going to take our Christianity seriously if we don't.

CHANGE THEIR SPEECH

Likewise urge the young men to be . . . sound in speech *which is beyond reproach, so that the opponent will be put to shame, having nothing bad to say about us* (Titus 2:6, 8).

Sound in speech: from the words *hygiene* (*clean, healthy*) and *logos* (*word*). In other words, young men should be known for their clean speech. For Greeks, the term *logos* could have a number of connotations. Jesus Christ is called the Logos—the Word from God *(John 1:1)*.

In *Ephesians 4:29* Paul uses *logos* to refer to daily conversation. Likewise, here in **Titus 2**, the context is one of normal conversation. This is day-to-day speaking with others.[16] Paul is simply referring to a young man's *vocabulary*. The pattern for a godly young man goes far beyond how he acts and how he thinks—it gets down to the nitty-gritty of how he *talks*.

Older men are to set the example and raise the bar. Men of all ages should pray with the Psalmist, *Set a guard, O LORD, over my mouth; keep watch over the door of my lips* (Psalm 141:3).

Our world brags: *"Our lips are our own; who is lord over us?"* (Psalm 12:4). In other words, "Who's gonna tell me how to talk? I can say whatever I wanna say. Besides, haven't you ever heard of the First Amendment—freedom of speech?"

The maturing Christian understands that our freedom of speech is not a license to say things that discredit the Gospel and hurt the reputation of Christ and His Church. Notice the direct incentive for a man's clean vocabulary: *so that the opponent will be put to shame, having nothing bad to say about us* (Titus 2:8*b*). There is this surprising pronoun at the end of the verse. You'd think Paul would have written *so that the opponent will be put to shame, having nothing bad to say about* you. But that's not what he says . . .

Whenever you pursue and develop a godly reputation, guess what? The Church ends up with a godly reputation. It works the other way around, too. Whatever you're like, the unbelieving world around you will think that's what *all* Christians are like. Our reputation as a body of believers is tied directly to each one of us; the integrity of the Church as a whole depends on each of us individually.

If you are not thinking like a Christian, acting like a Christian, and talking like a Christian, please don't tell *anybody* where you go to church.

THE CHALLENGE TO CHANGE

God's method has always been to take a holy person and drop him into an unholy culture. There he can demonstrate through his clean conversation and clear thinking process and careful dignity what it means to be a disciple of Jesus Christ.

Here's the exciting challenge: a maturing young man will live with a growing awareness that it isn't just about him—*it's about all of us!*—and ultimately, and primarily, it's about the character and reputation and glory of our Redeemer.

I love the way the Apostle Peter phrased it in his first letter:

> *Keep your behavior excellent among the Gentiles* [the unbelievers] *so that in the thing in which they slander you as evildoers, they may because of your good deeds, as they observe them, glorify God* (1 Peter 2:12).

We ultimately show our world by our thinking and acting and speaking that there's something more to live for . . . something far better—and the world can't help but tip its hat to the amazing God who brought about such a holy improvement in us.

I recently met a former professional football player for the Chicago Bears. After our initial conversation, I invited him to church. He laughed and told me he was unavailable. I asked why, and he shared with me his commitment to Christ involves preaching the Gospel every weekend throughout the state of North Carolina on a circuit that includes prisons and juvenile detention centers. I asked Carl to share his testimony with me, and this is what he said:

> I made it to the top of my professional career. I was living the dream. I was signed early in the NFL draft and played

several years of winning seasons. The pinnacle of my career was against the Dallas Cowboys. During that game I rushed Troy Aikman, the Cowboys quarterback, and caused him to fumble the ball. I picked up the fumble and ran for a touchdown. I remember spiking that football in the end zone—right on the Dallas Cowboys star; it had been my dream since I was a young boy to do that very thing. But in my hotel room that night, after the euphoria of running that fumble back for a touchdown and being responsible for my team's victory—when I was finally alone—I was overwhelmed with the emptiness that I felt. I realized then and there that there had to be something bigger and more important in life than running touchdowns. It wasn't long afterward that I picked up a Bible and began to read it . . . eventually giving my life to Jesus Christ. And let me tell you, that moment in the Dallas stadium cannot compare with seeing young men and women give their lives to Jesus Christ . . . there's nothing greater than that.

Paul is reminding the young men of Crete, as they live their lives and chase their dreams:

- Nothing is more important than the credibility of your testimony.
- Nothing is more vital than the delivery of the Gospel.
- Nothing is more critical than the reputation of the Church.
- Nothing is more glorious than bringing honor and attention and praise to our God and Savior, Jesus Christ.

[9] Urge bondslaves to be subject to their own masters in everything, to be well-pleasing, not argumentative, [10] not pilfering, but showing all good faith so that they will adorn the doctrine of God our Savior in every respect.
                                                                    –Titus 2:9–10

CHAPTER SIXTEEN

THE SACRED CALLING
OF WORK

Titus 2:9–10

A MATTER OF PERSPECTIVE

There is a Latin word which came into our language and, over time, lost its true meaning in the English world: *vocation* (a *calling*). As early as the 1500s, it was used to refer to every kind of labor—every vocation—as a *sacred calling* from God.

Martin Luther, the sixteenth-century Reformer, used the word to refer to any and all occupations. He wrote:

> God could populate the earth by creating each new generation of babies from the dust; instead, He ordained the offices of husband and wife and parent as sacred vocations. All our work in the field, in the garden, in the city, in the home, in government—these are the masks of God, behind which He is hidden and does all things.[1]

Luther explained, "God Himself is milking the cows through the vocation of the milkmaid."[2] Every vocation was a sacred calling through which God fulfilled His divine purposes.

Behind the term *vocatio* was the idea that every legitimate kind of work or social function was a distinct calling from God, utilizing God-given skills and talents and gifts. God *Himself* was and is active in everyday human labor, responsibilities, and interactions.

Reformation leader and theologian John Calvin wrote in the 1500s that the workplace was to be considered a place of worship.[3]

The Reformers were actually wrestling the concept of a sacred calling away from the Roman Catholic clergy and giving it equally to the tradesman, the mother, and the milkmaid, where it belonged. Their sermons and writings pointed out that every Christian, whether a student, a teacher, an artist, a housewife, or a farmer has a sacred calling from God.

So it doesn't matter if you're the Chief of Surgery or the Chief of Police or the chief custodian—you are fulfilling your *calling* from God . . . a sacred duty.

For the Christian, this was a revolutionary application. Nothing was wasted. Even the mundane act of milking a cow was touched with magnificent and sacred meaning. It's all in your perspective:

> Three men in the Middle Ages were working on the grounds of the building site where, for decades, a cathedral had been under construction. All three men were chipping away at rock, squaring stones to be used. One afternoon each was asked, "What are you doing?" One replied, "I'm cutting stones." Another said, "I'm making a living as a stone mason." The third man enthused, "I am building a magnificent cathedral."

The Reformers were simply fleshing out what the Apostle Paul had already written 1500 years before them, as he encouraged Christians:

> *Whatever you do, do your work heartily, as for the Lord rather than for men . . . it is the Lord Christ whom you serve* (Colossians 3:23–24).

Unfortunately, in today's workplace, *vocatio* has been lost. We talk about our careers, vocations, and skills independently of anything sacred. Today the motive for work has been reduced to a paycheck, and the incentive for work has become the weekend. The ultimate goal for work is retirement, and the average American dream is to be done with work, never having to serve anyone ever again.

The Apostle Paul is about to clarify the meaning of work for the Church as he addresses one particular member of the average household on the island of Crete: the ordinary household servant.

It will be to the *slaves* that Paul will explain that common, everyday work is worship—a platform upon which the glory of Christ can be seen and honored and exalted. Even a servant was endowed with *vocatio!*

A CHANGE OF HEART

Urge bondslaves to be subject to their own masters in everything, to be well-pleasing, not argumentative, not pilfering, but showing all good faith so that they will adorn the doctrine of God our Savior in every respect (Titus 2:9–10).

When Paul wrote this letter to Titus, there were as many as fifty million slaves in the Roman Empire. In fact, estimates indicate that as much as one-third of the population of the Roman world was occupying the place of servant or slave.[4]

In Paul's day, people became slaves in numerous ways: prisoners of war, punishment for certain crimes, debtors, kidnapped and sold into slavery, voluntarily becoming indentured servants, farm laborers, clerks, craftsmen, teachers, soldiers, even doctors.[5]

They were human beings without personal rights—they could be treated with or without mercy. Aristotle called the slave a living tool . . . a possession with a soul.[6]

It will be the Gospel that will topple the tyranny of slavery. It is, to this day, the Gospel that has men treating others with equal dignity and justice.

While Paul does not call for an end to slavery (nor the open rebellion of slaves—for which liberals have made much in discrediting Paul), what they miss is the patience of God's wisdom. Paul actually lays the groundwork for the elimination of slavery. He plants the truth which will eventually bear the fruit of freedom in any country and in every generation from that day forward.

He writes radical things, such as believing that slaves and their Christian masters are actually brothers *(1 Timothy 6:2)*; that in the sight of God, slaves and freemen are one in Christ *(Galatians 3:28)*.

When Paul meets and leads to faith a runaway slave named Onesimus, he writes to Philemon, the master of Onesimus (a believer in the church in Colossae), and he tells Philemon to welcome Onesimus back, not as his servant but as his beloved *brother (Philemon 1:16)*.

When the Roman Empire disintegrated and eventually collapsed, the system of slavery collapsed with it, due in great measure to the influence of Christianity. In fact, before its demise, so many slaves were being set free that the Roman Emperor introduced legal restrictions to curb the trend.[7]

The Gospel made the difference.

It is critical to understand that the New Testament wasn't written to give instructions on how to rebel against or reform human institutions—it introduced all that was necessary to change the human heart.[8]

Social reform is a matter of the heart. And reformed, spiritually redeemed human hearts have challenged, impacted, and reformed human institutions throughout history. A civilized Europe did not produce Christianity; Christianity *civilized* Europe.

What I find especially fascinating in this text from Paul to Titus is that Paul is challenging the *servant* to have a change of heart, not the master. Paul will tell the servant that his station in life is a divinely ordained *vocatio*—a sacred vocation—through which he will influence his world for the glory of God.

And for those of us who live in a free world, there are six distinguishing characteristics that will revolutionize our own personal vocation. They are for every modern-day employee and they will dramatically alter our perspective regarding *work*.

Humble

Urge bondslaves *to be* subject *to their masters in everything* (Titus 2:9*a*).

The word translated **subject** was used by the military to designate a soldier's relationship to his superior officers.[9]

It's the concept of lining up in rank, in file. In other words, **urge bond-slaves** to make sure they are in order, which sounds rather redundant. Why would Paul tell a bondslave to line up behind his master when he obviously is already?

Paul is using the passive voice, indicating that servants then—and employees today—are to *voluntarily* come under the authority of their employer. It isn't a matter of being bullied into submission but of being willing. No matter how difficult . . . no matter how unfair . . . no matter how oppressive.

In other words, the faithful believer perseveres with humility and self-sacrifice as long as he is employed in his task. While others at the worksite roast the management, talk about the boss, and run down the company, the Christian stays in his *place* . . . willingly and graciously doing the hard task—even if he is never thanked by his supervisor or paid what he believes he's worth.

In fact, the word Paul uses for master (employer) is the Greek word *despotes,* from which our word *despot* is derived. A despot is a tyrannical, arbitrary ruler with absolute authority, who often is unkind, unreasonable, and overbearing.

Paul paints the worst picture possible. He isn't suggesting submission to a job or to our supervisor because he has our best interests at heart; because they love us at the company; because they care about us or show their appreciation for our labor. He has in mind the exact opposite scenario: to willingly submit, even when we work for an overbearing, uncaring despot.

Why would anybody *willingly* and, even further, *graciously* work for someone like that? Because—and here's Paul's ultimate point—this is how the Christian reveals himself, shining like a candle in a dark room.

Believers understand that our supervisor isn't our final authority—we are enabled to carry on and stay in our place because we embrace our job as a *sacred calling* from the living God who works through us to fulfill His purposes and reflect His glory. Only this empowers us to serve with humble and gracious perseverance.

Reliable

***Urge bondslaves . . . to be* well-pleasing** (Titus 2:9*b*).

The word **well-pleasing** was almost always used in the New Testament to mean well-pleasing to God.[10] Again, Paul is hinting at a grander perspective for any employee. That's why he wrote:

> *Therefore we also have as our ambition, whether at home or absent, to be pleasing to Him* [Christ] (2 Corinthians 5:9).

Christ is our ultimate supervisor. Being an employee has to do with our status, whereas being **well-pleasing** has to do with our spirit.

A Christian employee has no excuse for half-hearted work . . . cutting corners . . . laziness . . . lack of initiative . . . carelessness. That person will never please his boss. What Paul wants us to know is that we're not pleasing the Lord, either.[11]

Martin Luther was approached by a cobbler who wanted to know how he could best please his Savior now that he was a Christian. He asked Luther, "How can I serve God?" Luther asked him, "What is your work?" The man said, "I am a shoemaker." Much to the cobbler's surprise, Luther replied, "Then make good shoes and sell them at a fair price."[12]

What Paul was doing in Crete is what the Reformation attempted to reignite: instill in believers a higher motive for work—a standard of excellence because of the Person who is ultimately represented.

Kent Hughes put it this way:

> It is then possible for the housewife to cook a meal as if Jesus Christ were going to eat it, or to clean the house as if Jesus Christ were to be the honored guest. It is possible for teachers to educate children, for doctors to treat patients, for nurses to care for them, for salesmen to help clients, for shop assistants to serve customers, for accountants to audit books, and for secretaries to type letters as if they, in each case, were serving Jesus Christ.[13]

That's why the Christian does the hard task—volunteers to go the extra mile—works extra hours to help someone out. Christianity makes that cubicle, that desk, that home, that shop, that classroom nothing less than a holy of holies where God's Spirit touches earth.

Paul effectively demands that if Titus wants to revolutionize the island of Crete (or we, our corner of the world today), it won't result so much from a series of sermons as from the testimony of reliable employees.

Non-Combative

Urge bondslaves to be . . . **not argumentative** (Titus 2:9c).

This might be the hardest characteristic yet. Paul switches to the negative here: *not* contrary, *not* quarrelsome, *not* contentious, *not* belligerent. He keeps raising the bar, doesn't he?

Frankly, the slave in Paul's day had no choice but to be submissive—that's just the way it was. But now he's told not to grumble about it, either. In today's culture, this one characteristic would effectively shut down most of the interoffice conversation. What in the world is there to talk about at the water cooler if we can't gripe about our supervisor—or the company—or the low wages—or the unfair treatment?

Paul actually uses a verb that means *to speak against*—or, in our vocabulary, to talk back. It means mouthing off.[14]

So the issue isn't that we simply agree to fulfill a task or that we plan to do it with excellence—it's that we don't complain about it in the process.

Paul is getting under our skin . . . he's challenging our spirit.

When our children were young, they had daily and weekly chores. My wife eventually decided that she would deal with our children's hearts and not just their hands. So she informed them that from that time forward, they not only had to do their chores in order to get their allowance, they had to do them with a good attitude. Now that was tough.

All of sudden taking out the trash had an entirely new challenge to it. It was six months before I got *my* allowance!

In case you're wondering, being non-combative doesn't mean you can't express a grievance through legitimate means. It doesn't mean that unethical or immoral dictates of management are to be complied with if you have to sin to obey them, even if your boss demands it. You might need to find another job in order to keep your conscience clean.

Paul is referring here to an employee being asked to perform a legitimate task which he doesn't want to do, and he snaps, "Okay, I'll do it, but I'm going to let you know I don't like it one bit." That Christian employee has forgotten he is actually on a sacred mission, designated by Christ as His representative on earth and through whom the living God fulfills His purposes.

Thus far, Paul has challenged our will, our heart, and our attitude; now he speaks about our hands.

Honest

Urge bondslaves to be . . . **not pilfering** (Titus 2:9–10*a*).

Another negative is interjected—a word used in the Grecian world for *embezzlement*—literally *laying on one's side.*[15] It means that we're putting something aside that doesn't belong to us. The Greek word also refers to someone being light-fingered.[16] He's stealing from his employer.

According to the U.S. Department of Commerce, employee dishonesty costs American businesses over fifty billion dollars a year, and the U.S. Chamber of Commerce reports that one in every three business failures is the direct result of employee theft. And it isn't necessarily big stuff—it's a lot of little stuff: resources, personal use of equipment, false expense reports—it all adds up to theft.

What could happen in our world if everyone began living honest lives?

A revival swept through the tiny country of Wales during the early 1900s. Over 100,000 people responded to the Gospel and came to faith. They began making restitution by returning things they'd stolen—which unexpectedly created severe problems for the shipyards along the coast. Over the years, workers had pilfered all kinds of things, from wheelbarrows to hammers. However, as people sought to make things right, they began returning what they'd stolen and the result was staggering! Soon the shipyards were overwhelmed with returned property. There were eventually such huge stockpiles of tools and machinery that several of the yards actually put up signs asking the men to *stop*. One sign read, "If you have been led by God to return what you have stolen, please know that the management forgives you and wishes you to keep what you took."

Paul told Titus how to impact the island of Crete: start by having all the employees who have stolen things return them and steal no more.

The world really wouldn't know how to handle that kind of honesty.

Loyal

Urge bondslaves to be . . . **showing all good faith** (Titus 2:9–10*b*).

You could translate this *showing yourself completely faithful in goodness.* This is another show-and-tell word; *showing* means *to show for the purpose of demonstrating or proving something.* In other words, you prove to your employer that you have the best of intentions for the place where you work.

One commentator wrote that the Christian employee is not to leave his loyalty in doubt but is to give ample evidence of it. Tragically, good-faith loyalty to one's employer and to one's fellow employees is a common casualty of the modern work ethic, even among Christians.

By the way, this mark of loyalty is the very characteristic that raised Daniel from middle management to a senior role in the kingdom of Babylon. The king appointed him over all the political leaders so that he would not suffer loss *(Daniel 6:2).* That's a nice way of saying so the king wouldn't be robbed blind.

King Darius needed an honest man who would be loyal to the crown and the kingdom. Why would Daniel even care about the king or this foreign kingdom? He had been abducted as a teenager, taken as a prisoner of war, and against his will made a eunuch, which would keep him single the rest of his life. He was put through the royal academy for political and business training because of how he distinguished himself early on.

Eventually Darius, Daniel's new Persian king, promoted him. For some reason, this exiled Jewish man did his best at whatever job he had, even if it meant the advancement and betterment of a kingdom to which he didn't really belong.

Keep in mind that Daniel never went back home. His faithful record didn't replace all the things he'd lost. But because of Daniel's loyalty to the king and the king's assignment for him, God was glorified. In fact, Daniel's legacy of integrity would so set him apart that he would eventually become the leader over all the other Magi who served with him in office.

Daniel would use his position to teach the Gospel through Old Testament prophecies so effectively that six hundred years later, his spiritual legacy was seen in the entourage of Magi who traveled from Persia with their gifts of gold, frankincense, and myrrh, arriving in Jerusalem to worship the newborn King of the Jews *(Matthew 2:2)*.

Before we tell our world what the Gospel means *to* us, they need to see the difference the Gospel makes *in* us.

Lustrous

Urge bondslaves to . . . adorn the doctrine of God our Savior in every respect (Titus 2:9–10c).

The word **adorn** is *cosmeo*, which gives us our word *cosmetics*.[17] The believer's life serves as a beautiful cosmetic for the truth of **God our Savior**. This word was used by the ancient world to describe setting jewels in such a way so as to highlight the beauty of the wearer.

One commentator writes, "So live a life that adds luster to the Gospel of God our Savior."[18]

Why should we? Because our boss needs a Savior, and we know that our fellow employees and friends are going to live somewhere forever. We also know there are only two eternal destinations: heaven or hell—and no one gets into heaven without **the doctrine of God our Savior.**

Justin Martyr wrote in the second century that those who live around believers should be ready to hear about Christ by either watching the Christians lives or by doing business with them.[19]

I wonder how many people would be receptive to our Gospel after having done business with us.

A REASON TO CHANGE

Jonathan Edwards, a faithful pastor and the Father of the First Great Awakening, prayed that God would stamp eternity on his eyes so that all that he viewed would be seen in the context of its eternal consequences.[20]

That doesn't mean we have to go out and do something big . . . or amazing . . . or great—just do our job:

- Show up!
- Work hard!
- Smile often!
- Stay out of trouble!

- Stay away from troublemakers!
- Don't talk back!
- Tell the truth!
- Live for something greater than the weekend!
- Point people to the Savior whenever possible!

There are a lot of Christians willing to do great things for God . . . not as many are willing to do *little* things for God. According to Paul's letters, even little things are events where God touches earth and moves His hand to perform His will.

A pediatrician named David Cerqueira wrote about his encounter with a little girl named Sarah:

> It all started with my wife's Sunday school class; she had prepared a lesson on being useful to the Lord and taught the children that usefulness was actually serving God. The kids quietly listened to my wife's words, and as the lesson ended, a little girl named Sarah spoke up. "Teacher, what can I do? I don't know how to do many useful things." Not anticipating that kind of ready response, my wife quickly looked around and spotted an empty flower vase on the windowsill. "Sarah, you can bring in a flower and put it in that vase. That would be a useful thing, and God would be pleased with the difference that would make in this room for everyone who sees it." Sarah frowned, "But that's not important." My wife replied, "Well, it is if it helps someone—even in a small way."
>
> The next Sunday Sarah brought a dandelion she had picked and placed it in the vase. She continued to do it each week, without reminders or help, and she made sure the vase had a bright flower. When my wife told our pastor about Sarah's faithfulness to this small task, he took the vase upstairs in the main sanctuary, placed it next to the pulpit, and used it as an illustration for serving others.
>
> That next week, I had a call from Sarah's mother. She worried that Sarah seemed to have less energy than usual and didn't

have an appetite. I saw Sarah the following day. After putting her through a battery of tests, I sat numbly in my office with the paperwork on my lap. The results were in: Sarah had leukemia. On my way home, I stopped to personally give Sarah's parents the news. Sarah's genetics and the leukemia that was attacking her small body were a horrible mix. Sitting at their kitchen table, I explained that nothing could be done to save her life.

Time passed and Sarah became confined to bed. Then it came—another phone call from Sarah's mother, asking me to come. After a short examination, I knew that Sarah did not have long to live. That was Friday afternoon. On Sunday morning, near the end of his sermon, the pastor suddenly stopped speaking and stared at the back of the sanctuary. Everyone turned to see what held his attention. It was Sarah. She was being carried into the sanctuary, bundled in her blanket. In her hand she held a bright flower. Her parents had brought her to church one last time. They walked to the front of the church where the vase still sat on the pulpit. She put her flower in the vase and then placed a piece of paper beside it.

The following Thursday Sarah passed away. The pastor asked me to stay behind after the funeral service. We stood together at the cemetery as everyone walked to their cars. He said, "Dave, I've got something you ought to see." He pulled from his pocket the piece of paper that Sarah had left by the vase. Holding it out to me he said, "I want you to keep it." I opened the folded paper where Sarah had written in pink crayon: "Dear God, this vase has been the biggest honor of my life. Sarah."

She understood . . . a simple task was the greatest honor of her life.

I am convinced that there will be some surprised first-century household servants standing before God, receiving honor and reward for the simplest of tasks—and there will be some surprised twenty-first-century Christians, as well. I'll be among them, discovering there were a thousand duties and tasks—and a thousand more—we never imagined would be considered an honorable thing to perform.

We have far too many Christians waiting to do something great for God; we need more Christians willing to do something small for God . . . something simple . . . something unremarkable . . . something ordinary, like putting a bright flower in a vase on a windowsill in a classroom.

This is the way we are to live and work—and in so doing, we display the beauty of the Gospel . . . the treasure found in **God our Savior**.

So do something useful where the glory of God can—through you, a willing servant—turn some mundane place into sacred space . . . a place where the Spirit of God touches earth.

Even if it's milking a cow.

[11]*For the grace of God has appeared, bringing salvation to all men,* [12]*instructing us to deny ungodliness and worldly desires and to live sensibly, righteously and godly in the present age,* [13]*looking for the blessed hope and the appearing of the glory of our great God and Savior, Christ Jesus,* [14]*who gave Himself for us to redeem us from every lawless deed, and to purify for Himself a people for His own possession, zealous for good deeds.*

–Titus 2:11–14

CHAPTER SEVENTEEN

LEARNING TO SAY
THE RIGHT WORDS

Titus 2:11–14

EXIT STRATEGY

Tales of death and despair in the frozen north are not new in Alaskan folklore, but seldom have men recorded their own fatal adventure as graphically as Carl McCunn. He was a likeable Texan with a love for the outdoors. A strapping six-foot-two 240-pounder, he'd spent four years in the navy before making his home in Anchorage in 1970. In 1976, he went alone into the Alaskan wilderness on a wildlife photography expedition. Now he was returning and had taken a year planning his trip. He solicited advice and purchased supplies. The thing he'd overlooked was the one detail that would eventually cost him his life:

> In March 1981, as winter was ending, Carl was flown to a wilderness camp in an isolated valley near a nameless lake 225 miles northeast of Fairbanks. He took two rifles, a shotgun, 1,400 pounds of provisions, and 500 rolls of film. There he would spend the next five months hiking, hunting, fishing, and photographing the splendor of his surroundings.

> By early August, with his supplies dwindling, his concern grew. "I think I should have used more foresight about

arranging my departure," he wrote in his diary, "I'll soon find out." Every day he searched for food and scanned the skies for rescue. Meanwhile, concerned friends asked for help to check on McCunn. Trooper David Hamilton flew over the camp and testified that he had seen Carl waving a red bag. He said he circled, and McCunn "waved in a casual manner and watched us fly by." Later, Carl recorded in his diary, "I recall raising my right hand, shoulder high and shaking my fist on the plane's second pass. It was a little cheer—like when your team scored a touchdown or something. Turns out that's the signal for ALL O.K. DO NOT WAIT! Man, I can't believe it!"

Snow came and the lake froze over. Hiking out to Fort Yukon was now impossible. By October, Carl was competing with wolves and foxes for the rabbits he snared. In November, he ran out of food. He was found by authorities nearly a year after he had set up his camp and begun his expedition. The details of his final days are known because of a 100-page diary found near his body, where he recorded those last months of starvation and freezing cold. Perhaps the greatest understatement of his life was made when he wrote, "I think I should have used more foresight about arranging my departure."[1]

He never made plans for his exit. He'd planned everything for his expedition . . . he'd planned nothing for his departure.

That is the story of most human hearts today: they think only of living and not about leaving. Nearly two people die every second on planet Earth—more than 6,000 an hour—155,000 every day—around 57 million a year. All the while the grace of God has made every provision for not only *living* in this wild world of ours but for *leaving* it.

The truth is that the grace of God is critically necessary for us to live in this world, headed in the right *direction*, and to leave this world, headed for the right *destination*.

GRACE, GRACE, GOD'S GRACE

We are saved by **grace** . . . we live by **grace** . . . we are taught by **grace** . . . we go to heaven on the promise of God's **grace** for those who've believed His

Gospel *(Ephesians 2:8–9;* ***Titus 2:11).*** In other words, the **grace** of God is our way out of here; it is our eternal exit strategy!

Whether you're older or younger, a man or a woman, a household servant, or a slave, ***the grace of God has appeared, bringing salvation to all men*** (Titus 2:11). The question remains: What has the world done with the gracious offer of salvation from God?

Paul is *not* saying that all men are saved—don't misunderstand him. He's not preaching universalism here. The connective conjunction that begins this very long sentence that stretches from verse eleven all the way through verse fourteen is a word that ties into the context of the previous verses where Paul has addressed different categories of people.

We can understand Paul to be saying here that ***the grace of God has appeared, bringing salvation to all*** [kinds of people]—whether man or woman; young or old; bond or free; rich or poor; Jew or Gentile; married, single, or widowed; parent or childless; citizen or foreigner.

Anybody can become a member of the family of God, and if we are already a member, we received our membership card solely by believing in the Gospel of the **grace** of God.

And when we get saved, **grace** isn't finished. We're going to grow in **grace** *(2 Peter 3:18)*—that is, in the gracious character of our living Lord. Paul is effectively saying, "What I want to do for a few sentences is to explain to every member of the family of God how **grace** impacts every aspect of your life."

He then gives three different expressions in which **grace** teaches us how to add to the vocabulary of our life. In fact, if we want to measure how we are growing in **grace**, just ask ourselves: *How often am I saying one of these three things?*

Leaving Our Past Life

The first word to learn how to say, by the **grace** of God in our life, is a two-letter word: *no*—N-O. In other words, **grace** is impacting our lifestyle to the point that we are actually learning how to reject the wrong things on a daily basis:

> ***For the* [G]*race of God has appeared, bringing salvation to all men,*** [now watch what **Grace** does first] ***instructing us to deny ungodliness and worldly desires*** (Titus 2:12*a*).

Paul personifies **Grace** in this text and watches as **Grace** shows up and begins teaching us how to say *no*. We might think **Grace** is all about saying *yes*—it will include that, but the *first* thing **Grace** teaches us to add to our vocabulary is the critical word *no*.

The word translated ***instructing*** has wonderful implications from God's Spirit through Paul. He could have chosen the word *didasko*, which refers to a more formal classroom setting for instruction; however, *didasko* typically works when you show up at a certain time for the lecture. Paul doesn't use that word here; instead, he uses the verb *paideuo*, which gives us our word *pedagogy*. This often refers to teaching a toddler—a young child—typically by a parent.[2]

This kind of teaching is informal, most often, and throughout the day, whenever teaching opportunities arise. In other words, God's Grace is a teacher that finds us where we are, daily instructing us whenever teaching moments arise.

This means that **Grace** condescends to teach us at our own personal speed. **Grace** is the kind of teacher who reinforces truth according to our own personal needs and style of learning. **Grace** is the perfect tutor.

Paul writes that **Grace** is ***instructing*** us—the tense of the verb is the present tense, which indicates that this is a continuous education.[3] If you missed a lesson or two yesterday, **Grace** will show up and teach you today. And if you didn't quite get that lesson (which none of us ever masters, since the subject of our lesson is the character and nature of our gracious God), **Grace** will show up again and again and again to lead us through the lessons. In fact, for the rest of our lives we will have the companionship of this teacher named **Grace**.

Her curriculum will tutor us in how to say—and live—the little word *no*, as in ***to deny ungodliness and worldly desires***. The words ***to deny*** mean to refuse; to renounce; to disown.[4] Paul is effectively saying, "This is the kind of life you're leaving behind." We reject it—we daily renounce it—we leave it behind.

A young couple in our church told me that they decided to literally renounce everything in their lives that might stand in the way of their commitment and growth: they poured their brandy down the sink; threw away their music collection, books, and magazines; began spending their money differently; made an immediate shift in their view of life. They said, "We're finished living on the fence." They were saying *no*—renouncing their past life.

Paul expands this same concept to the Ephesian believers:

> *Walk no longer as the Gentiles* [unbelievers] *also walk, in the futility of their mind, being darkened in their understanding, excluded from the life of God because of . . . the hardness of their heart; and they . . . have given themselves over to sensuality for the practice of every kind of impurity with greediness. But you did not learn Christ in this way* [**Grace** didn't tutor you to live this kind of life as a Christian] *. . . in reference to your former manner of life, you lay aside the old self, which is being corrupted in accordance with the lusts of deceit, and that you be renewed in the spirit of your mind, and put on the new self, which in the likeness of God has been created in righteousness and holiness* (Ephesians 4:17–20, 22–24).

Learning to walk in Christ, tutored by **Grace**, means that we will, first of all, be taught how to say *no* and what to say *no* to. The person who says, "I'm under **grace** and that means I can say yes to everything" isn't really being tutored by **Grace**, because **Grace** teaches us in this text how to say *no*.

[Growing up in Christ], one author wrote, is impossible without the discipline of refusal.[5] If you have children, you know you spend more time telling them, "No, no," as you're raising them and training them and protecting them. And when they're older, you say, "N-O!" *No* may be the first word your child learns to spell.

Early on, your little angel toddles over to a vase on the living room table and reaches out his pudgy little hand to grab it . . . and you say, "No, no." He looks over at you and without blinking an eye—staring you directly in the face—grabs it. He has just decided that you aren't as tough as you look. *I'll show you what I think of your "No, no."*

No wonder Mark Twain said, "When a child reaches the age of two, put him in a barrel and feed him through a knothole . . . when he turns thirteen, plug up the hole." I'm not recommending that, but Mark Twain did have four children, so he knew a little something about self-will.

Part of the challenge of growing up is responding to the word *no*. Without that word, it would be difficult for kids to survive—I mean, what's wrong with playing in the street, walking on the roof, eating candy for supper, or playing in the rain when it's lightning? Every one of those things is a blast when you're a kid. But somebody said *no* . . . and ruined the party.

The truth is we need **Grace** to teach us what to say *no* to, because our parents won't be around forever. They may not have taught us in the first place, and our peers certainly won't teach us. The world system is designed to erase every *no* and replace it with *yes . . . now!*

Francis Schaeffer, Christian philosopher and author, wrote forty years ago:

> We are surrounded by a world that says "no" to nothing. We have a society that holds itself back from nothing. Any concept of the word "no" is avoided as much as possible . . . absolutes and ethical principles must give in to selfish [pursuits]. Of course, this environment fits exactly into our natural disposition because, since the fall of man, we do not want to deny ourselves either.[6]

No wonder we need the daily tutoring of **Grace**, for **Grace *will teach us to say no*** [which we have difficulty saying] ***to ungodliness and worldly desires*** (Titus 2:12*a* paraphase).

What exactly are ***worldly desires***? Simply put, they are anything that we as a growing disciple of Christ might do or say or desire or pursue or participate in where we would be embarrassed if Jesus came along for the ride.

Saying *no* is how we are to leave our old life.

Living Our Present Life

[I]*nstructing us to deny* ungodliness *and* worldly desires *and* to live sensibly, righteously *and* godly *in the present age* (Titus 2:12).

Don't just stop with *no* . . . **Grace** will teach us when to say *yes*. In fact, the tense of this verb **to live** indicates that it takes place at the same time we are denying our old life.[7] We're saying *no* to **ungodliness** and **worldly desires**, while at the same time saying *yes* to living **sensibly**, **righteously**, and **godly**.

Part of the misconception of Christian maturity which can become discouraging is the opinion that believers arrive at some point where they never have to say *no* again . . . where everything good and right will be an easy *yes*.

We think, *Surely a mature, wise, committed Christian gets to the point where she never has to bother saying "no"; those temptations will give way at some point and she'll only need to say "yes"—and then she'll be on easy street.*

Not according to Paul. And not according to the rest of the Bible. Even Paul, as a mature believer, transparently admitted that he struggled with doing things he didn't want to do and *not* doing the things he knew he should be doing: *O wretched man that I am!* (Romans 7:24).

We are never beyond temptation; we will never outgrow the need to say *no* to something—and, at the same time, we are never beyond the need to affirm something. While we cannot live the Christian life without saying *no*, we certainly can't live it without saying *yes*.

Christianity isn't just about denial—we don't only shun ungodliness . . . we embrace godliness in its place.[8]

We don't just *put off* the old man . . . we *put on* the new man *(Ephesians 4:22–24)*.

Paul tells us that **Grace** will tutor us to say *yes* to three different attributes; the first one in *Titus 2:12* is living **sensibly**—the attribute of *sensibility.*

This word has shown up several times already in this letter to Titus:

- elders *(Titus 1:8)*;

- older men *(Titus 2:2)*;

- young wives and mothers *(Titus 2:5)*;

- young men *(Titus 2:6)*.

But now Paul broadens the application of this word to the entire church family. No one is exempt from saying *yes* to this characteristic. It literally means to live with discretion . . . to think and act with self-control.

It's a word that refers to someone who has a sound mind. That is, the believer doesn't allow his mind to be controlled or distracted by either circumstances or culture.[9] In other words, a believer is daily making up his mind to follow the truth.

Paul then adds another course in the curriculum of **Grace**: a believer is to live **righteously**. This word is used only two other times by Paul in his letters: to defend his own actions as upright *(1 Thessalonians 2:10)*, and to describe the believer's moral obligation to stop sinning and live righteously *(1 Corinthians 15:34).*[10]

Living **righteously** simply means that we live by the divine standard of what is *right*.

People are quick to talk about their values: family values . . . personal values . . . cultural values . . . those who share their values, etc.

The word *values* means absolutely nothing, because it can be defined any way a person wants to define it. We may *value* human life, but another person with equal passion may *value* the right of people to die whenever they want to. We may *value* traditional marriage, but others with equal intensity may *value* same-sex marriage.

Values are subjective—they are determined by whatever a person believes, feels, and wants to do, which is why values are as varied as opinions.

What has been lost to the English language in our generation is the word which *values* replaced . . . and we didn't notice it until it was gone: *virtues*. There's a world of difference between the two. Webster said it best when he defined *virtue* as *conformity to a standard of right*.

No wonder that word had to go.

Objective standards of rightness—or righteousness—are replaced by a relativistic culture that doesn't want to conform to any ethical, moral or, even, spiritual absolutes.[11]

Values, by definition, do not conform to any external standard of right or wrong—they are merely created by the person claiming them in order to be perceived as a person of virtue. A man says, "I hold firmly to these values," and people think, *He has such fine character*. Not necessarily . . . he's just a person of values, and a person of values is not necessarily a virtuous person. Someone who holds to values is simply holding to a standard he feels good about . . . at the moment!

Values can change—virtues do not.

William Sangster, a well-known pastor in England during the time the *RMS Titanic* sank, gave this illustration of how values can change quickly:

> As the *Titanic* began to sink, a wealthy woman had already taken her place in one of the lifeboats that was to be lowered into the North Atlantic. She suddenly remembered some-

thing she'd left behind and was so desperate about it that she was allowed to get out and run back to her stateroom. There were only minutes before the boat would be lowered without her. When she reached her cabin, she rushed to the shelf above her bed. There her jewelry box sat, filled with diamonds and precious gems. She shoved it aside, and it crashed to the floor. Behind the box were three small oranges; she grabbed them and ran back to the lifeboat and climbed onboard. The danger of death had boarded the *Titanic*; one blast of its awful breath had transformed all values . . . priceless things had become worthless and worthless things had become priceless.[12]

There is coming a day when the world will stand before God and discover that according to *His* standard of rightness, many of their values were not all that valuable. And they certainly were not virtues.

Paul warns, through Titus, "Now that you're a believer, let the grace of God teach you, through the Word of God and by the Spirit of God, what is valuable, virtuous, and right."

Paul adds a third word: **godly**—the opposite of ungodly, which the believer is to deny. This is an appropriate attitude toward God and the things of God. It is *God-likeness* in perspective and spirit. Paul adds that we're to live this way in **the present age**.

Christians live in this present age. We don't live for it; we shouldn't live like it . . . but we do live in it.[13]

And this is how we're taught to live.

Looking For Our Future Life

[L]*ooking for the blessed hope and the* appearing *of the glory of our great God and Savior, Christ Jesus* (Titus 2:13).

Among other truths, this verse is one of the strongest statements on the deity of Jesus Christ in all the New Testament. Some might argue that Paul is referring to both God the Father *and* God the Son: **our great God and** [our] **Savior, Christ Jesus**.

That argument fails when you observe only one single definite article in this title. In other words, ***our great God*** is also the ***Savior***, who happens to be ***Christ Jesus***.[14]

We could just as correctly reverse the reading of the title to capture the idea: Jesus Christ is the Savior and our great God. Further bolstering this translation is the fact that the nouns referring to Jesus Christ are singular. Throughout the Old Testament, God is often referred to as ***great***. In the New Testament, the reference to God's greatness is always attached to God the Son.

Additionally—and just as importantly—whenever the New Testament speaks of God **appearing**, it is never used of God the Father or God the Spirit but always in reference to God the Son.[15]

This makes sense, given the fact that we're told that Jesus Christ is the embodiment of deity: He is the physical manifestation of the invisible God *(Colossians 1:15).*

And Paul tells us that Jesus Christ, our great God and Savior, is going to **appear!** We're looking for Him even now. This is a reference, in this context, to the Church in any age, looking for the rapture of the believer by the sudden appearance of Christ:

- The Thessalonian believers were commended for waiting for God's Son who was coming from heaven to take them up to meet Him in the clouds—not receive Him when He descends to set up His kingdom *(1 Thessalonians 1:10).*

- Paul further told them that believers would be delivered from the wrath to come *(1 Thessalonians 1:10).*

- Paul wrote that he expected to be *alive* when Christ came to catch away [Latin: *rapturo – to rapture*] the Church that was still living *(1 Thessalonians 4:17).*

- John adds the insightful vision that Christ returns to earth to set up His kingdom reign for a thousand years, and He is pictured descending from heaven *with* the redeemed *(Revelation 19).*

Paul is telling us here to look for that time when Christ will come *for* His Church. Christ will fulfill His promise to protect His Bride from the wrath of God which will engulf mankind for seven years—a time of trouble called the Tribulation Period. And afterward, the redeemed, with Christ, will descend from heaven and establish Christ's kingdom on earth where we will rule with Him for a thousand years.

NO . . . YES . . . *MAYBE TODAY!*

Paul says us that **Grace** will instruct us on how to say *no, yes,* and *maybe today.*

Grace is teaching us to look up—to look forward to the coming of Christ. There's our exit strategy—He's it! He's our escape from death unto life. Most people will say with empty confidence, "I'm set for my expedition through the wilderness and savagery of life; I have all the provisions I need." That's not going to be enough. Have you planned a way out?

That way is embodied in ***our great God and Savior, Christ Jesus***. He is *the way, and the truth, and the life; no one comes to the Father but through* [Him] (John 14:6). And Paul says, "While we're on the subject of our ***great God and Savior***, let me tell you what He's done for those who've placed their faith in Him alone":

> [He] ***gave Himself for us to redeem us from every lawless deed*** (Titus 2:14*a*).

He did it to ***redeem us***; every slave in the world of Titus would understand this terminology—it came directly from the slave market. In that day, a buyer would approach the auction block upon which a slave stood and where buyers bartered. Having won the bid and paid the price, the owner would remove the slave's chains, and that slave would belong to him.

Jesus Christ bought us out of slavery to sin and purchased us as His own slaves . . . which is why Paul began this letter by telling Titus that he considered himself nothing more than a slave belonging to God ***(Titus 1:1)***.

He ***redeemed us***—did you notice—***from every lawless deed***. The tense of the verb ***redeemed*** refers to the act of Christ on the cross—a previous act with ongoing power and implication.

From every lawless deed means that we cannot commit an act of sin tomorrow—or next year, for that matter—where Christ will say, "I didn't know about that sin . . . I didn't know you were going to commit that one." No, ***every***—without exception—***lawless deed*** thought and act and desire has *already* been paid for in the past, on the cross by our Savior's own death—with ongoing power and implication. Christ paid the price **to purify for Himself a people for His own possession** (Titus 2:14*b*).

He redeemed us in the past.

He's purifying us and cleansing us in the present.

He's making us **zealous for good deeds** all around us as we move into the future.

The Puritans would call Christians "empowered with new affections."[16] When we understand the sacrifice and love of Christ, the lavish gift of His **grace**, can we be anything but zealous people for God?

Woodrow Kroll wrote of a convicting moment inside a taxi as he headed toward an airport near Chicago:

> My cabby was a Muslim and I engaged him in conversation. We passed a large building that had been converted into a mosque, and I asked him how many men attended there for prayer. He said, "The 4:00 p.m. service has about 1,500 worshippers. The 4:00 a.m. service is not as well attended— only around 900 men come to pray." Can you imagine 900 Christians praying at 4:00 a.m. in the city of Chicago—or anywhere else, for that matter?[17]

Although most Americans claim to believe in God, they evidently don't believe in attending church. At least not like Muslims attend their prayer services. In fact, if you took all the unchurched in America—those not attending church anywhere—and made them into their own separate nation, it would be the eleventh most populated nation on earth today.[18]

What kind of message are *we* communicating to our world today? Are they hearing us say *no* to ungodly and worldly desires? Are they watching and listening to us say *yes* to righteous and godly things? Do they hear us talk about the return of Jesus Christ, and do they see us living with the sense of anticipation of *maybe today*?

A physicist wrote in the commentary section of *The Wall Street Journal* about people clinging to hope . . . false hope, I might add:

> The latest data from space satellites is unmistakable: the universe will eventually die. Galaxies are being pushed apart.

Someday, when looking heavenward, we'll be quite lonely, with other galaxies too far away to be observed. Worse, it will be deathly cold. As the universe accelerates, temperatures will plunge throughout the universe. Billions of years from now, the stars will have exhausted their nuclear fuel, the oceans will freeze, the sky will become dark, and the universe will consist of dead neutron stars, black holes, and nuclear debris. Is all intelligent life on earth doomed to die? It seems as if the iron laws of physics have issued a death warrant. But there's still one possible exit strategy: leave the universe itself. Do the laws of physics allow for the creation of wormholes connecting our universe to a younger, more hospitable universe? In 2021, a new space probe, LISA (Laser Interferometer Space Antenna) will be launched which may be able to prove or disprove these conjectures. Can a gateway be built to connect our universe with another? For intelligent life, there is no choice. Either we leave for [another] universe, or we die in the old one.[19]

Can a gateway be built to travel from our universe to another? The answer is a resounding *yes*! Paul writes,

Looking for the blessed hope and the appearing *of the glory of our great God and Savior, Christ Jesus* (Titus 2:13).

Some day . . . one day . . . maybe this day . . . He will come for His Church. Human history is even now speeding toward the return of Christ and the soon-coming kingdom of God.

In the meantime, let's practice saying and living these three different expressions—**Grace** will teach us how:

No . . . Yes . . . Maybe today!

These things speak and exhort and reprove with all authority. Let no one disregard you.

–Titus 2:15

CHAPTER EIGHTEEN

IN THE COUNTRY
OF THE BLIND

Titus 2:15

THE BLIND LEADING THE BLIND

English author H. G. Wells, famous for his culturally provocative novels such as *The Time Machine* and *The War of the Worlds*, once wrote a lesser known short story entitled "The Country of the Blind." In a luxurious, inaccessible valley in Ecuador, everyone was born blind. There was no sight, no color, and no news of an outside world. The people who lived there had everything they wanted in their hidden, fertile valley—everything except sight. But then, a visitor from the outside world suddenly arrived:

> A young man was exploring the region and accidently fell off a cliff, sliding down, down into the deep foliage of the forest. He survived and stumbled into this forgotten country. Before long, he encountered the people and realized every person he met was blind. He gathered as many as would listen and began to describe things around them—the color and beauty of creation. He told them of another world beyond the valley. They sat with him and listened . . . but in the end, they chose not to believe him. They came to the conclusion that his sight had caused him to lose his sanity. He was simply out

of his right mind. In spite of this, the young man decided to stay and work among them. He fell in love with a girl from a prominent family, wanted to marry her and settle down in this Country of the Blind. Her father went to a respected elder—and doctor—to talk about the proposal. They concluded it would never work unless something radical occurred: in order to cure the young man of his insanity, his eyes must be removed. The father asked, "Then he will be sane?" "Oh, yes, he will be perfectly sane and quite an admirable citizen." Upon hearing that he could marry the daughter if he submitted to an operation that would blind him for life, the young man left to think it over. He fully intended to go to a lovely place where the meadows were filled with flowers and remain there until the hour of his sacrifice, but as he looked around at the beauty of creation and saw the sun rising like an angel in golden armor as its light flooded the meadow, he realized then and there that the valley was nothing more than a trap of ignorance and futility. He escaped with his life and sight intact from this Country of the Blind.[1]

In a very real way, Crete was a country of the blind. It was enslaved to sin and enveloped in spiritual darkness, given over to drunkenness and immorality—it was a spiritually blind culture.

The remedy would involve a living, dynamic, unified, Gospel-saturated, Christ-exalting body of believers who were willing to sacrifice everything—except their spiritual sight—to fulfill their mission.

THE LIGHT DAWNS

Paul's solution to false teaching and false teachers was to put the Church family on special assignment. The change wouldn't be sudden . . . it would take a lifetime and require the daily influence of salt and light.

The difference between the believer and the young man in Wells's novel is that we do not escape with our lives—we *give* our lives. We throw our lives into the darkness around us, where we shine as light in our culture. We are living in the Country of the Blind, describing for them another world and another life. We are speaking of spiritual sight to those who are *perishing, in whose case the god of this world has blinded the minds of the unbelieving so that they might not see the light of the gospel of the glory of Christ, who is the image of God* (2 Corinthians 4:4).

It won't be easy . . . our world thinks we've lost our mind. Further, they are determined to silence any revelation of another world beyond their limited understanding; determined to remove any semblance of spiritual sight and light.

Powerful forces are at work to remove any vestige of Christianity from public view. One U.S. District Court judge proposed a solution to the case brought before him by the American Civil Liberties Union. It was bringing suit against a high school that had displayed the Ten Commandments for the past decade on the wall of one of the buildings on school property. The judge ruled that the display could remain only if the four commandments that explicitly referred to God were removed. He ordered the school into mediation to work out a compromise with the ACLU.[2]

The inhabitants of our world don't want anybody to *see* any reference to our Creator. And all who help remove any sight of God become good citizens in this Country of the Blind. If ever there was a time for the Church to recognize the blindness of her world—if ever there was a time for the Church to display the glorious light of the Gospel—it is now.

Where do we begin? Paul provides the answer as he writes, **[S]***peak the things which are fitting for sound doctrine* (Titus 2:1), and ends the chapter with a similar command:

> ***These things* speak *and* exhort *and* reprove *with all authority*** (Titus 2:15).

In other words, tell people the truth. And while you're at it, notice how Paul wants Titus to start with the Church. In this verse, Paul uses three imperatives: **Speak! Exhort! Reprove!** And do all three with ***authority***! These are not suggestions or options—these initiatives form the job description of every obedient shepherd . . . and for the flock at large.

Conversation

***These things* speak** (Titus 2:15a).

Paul uses the word *laleo* for *speak*, which can be translated *to announce, reveal, disclose something*; it can be used for careful teaching.[3]

Paul isn't referring to sermon manuscripts, apologetic discourses, and theological dissertations. He means the ordinary conversation that takes place in the lunchroom; over the backyard fence; in the hallways at work; with friends on the deck; with children, as we sit on the edge of their bed before we tuck them in at night.

This might sound simplistic and not all that strategic, but this is the plan: *talk* about Jesus Christ. Bring *Him* into our conversations . . . let Him be the subject of our discussion on the golf course or at the restaurant or on an airplane.

By the way, it also happens to become a wonderful way to meet other Christians, enjoying surprising moments of fellowship between strangers.

My wife and I met believing skycaps who helped us with our baggage while coming and going when we traveled to South America. We were prepared to drop the seed of the Gospel, but they both responded with, "I already know what you're talking about," and we enjoyed the fellowship of two brothers we didn't know were part of the family of God.

Paul more specifically writes, ***These* things *speak*.** What **things** is Paul referring to? He's saying, "Speak about the **things** I brought up in the previous verses; **things** that fit hand in glove with sound doctrine.

Talk about what it means:

- to be a dignified older man;
- to be an older woman committed to sobriety;
- to be a wife and mother who honors God;
- to be a responsible, godly young man;
- to be an honest employee;
- to be a man or woman of your word.

Talk about that stuff—and not just in church; take the conversation out there . . . shed some light for the sake of a world that is wandering around in the dark. Talk about these things with the citizens of the Country of the Blind. The subjects that make up Christianity are not to be reserved for Sunday. Make them part of our daily conversation.

Motivation

***These things speak and* exhort** (Titus 2:15*b*).

This verb is more intense. It's a favorite of the Apostle Paul, and it forms the compound verb *parakaleo*, which means *to call to one's side.*

He uses the word nine times with Timothy and Titus and sixty-four more times in his other letters.[4] Depending on the context, it can be translated with the nuance of encouraging or counseling or commending or, even, admonishing.

This verb involves more than simply stating and explaining truth; it embodies the added nuance of entreating or pleading.[5] It encompasses the passion of someone trying to persuade or convince or invite someone to come along. This is not just conversation—it's an invitation. It's the difference between casually informing someone there's a forest fire in California and telling them their backyard is on fire. It is emotionally passionate because it is absolutely personal.

We are in the Country of the Blind, and we should be passionate that the citizens understand there are things they *must* know and understand . . . there *is* another world out there. The grace of God has appeared, bringing the offer of salvation to all men *(Titus 2:11)*. Our exhortation is for spiritually blind people to join us, to receive the gift of sight . . . and then to wait with us as we look for the appearing of the glory of our great God and Savior, Christ Jesus *(Titus 2:13)*.

Paul's command to exhort those around us can only take place when our conversation includes an element of motivation. To simply have a conversation with someone might mean that we never become personally involved.

To plead (exhortation) is impossible without personal involvement. We simply cannot passionately exhort—plead with or commend or counsel or encourage someone—without personally becoming involved in their lives. And there's a difference between being available for good deeds and being zealous for good deeds.[6]

Abraham Lincoln received a letter in 1850 from his stepbrother John D. Johnston, who wrote asking yet again for money so he could settle his debts. On numerous occasions in the past, Lincoln simply gave him the money so he wouldn't have to get too involved, and that was the end of it . . . until the request arrived again. This time, lawyer Lincoln decided to get involved more personally in an effort to plead with his brother to change his lifestyle and stay out of debt.

He wrote this letter:

Dear Johnston,

Your request for eighty dollars I do not think it best to comply with now. At the various times when I have helped you a little you have said to me, "We can get along very well now"; but in a very short time I find you in the same difficulty again. Now, this can only happen by some defect in your conduct. What that defect is, I think I know. You are not *lazy*, and still you are an *idler*. I doubt whether, since I saw you, you have done a good whole day's work in any one day. You do not very much dislike work, and still you do not work much merely because it does not seem to you that you could get much for it. This habit of uselessly wasting time is the whole difficulty; it is vastly important to you, and still more so to your children, that you should break the habit. It is more important to them, because they have longer to live, and can keep out of an idle habit before they are in it, easier than they can get out after they are in. You are now in need of some money; and what I propose is, that you shall go to work, "tooth and nail," for somebody who will give you money for it. . . . I now promise you that for every dollar you will, between this and the first of May, get for your own labor, either in money or as your own indebtedness, I will then give you one other dollar. . . . Now, if you will do this, you will be soon out of debt, and, what is better, you will have a habit that will keep you from getting into debt again.

Affectionately your brother,

Abe Lincoln[7]

That is an excellent example of *involved* exhortation.

Alteration

These things speak and exhort and reprove (Titus 2:15c).

The word Paul uses here for **reprove** means to correct or, even, to convict.[8] Again, these verbs become progressively more intense and strong.[9]

The truth of *these things* eventually cuts a path to the heart and demands nothing less than observable change. It might help to think of the Church as a tailor's shop: you go in with your coat or pants because you need something altered . . . it doesn't fit . . . something's not right. And it needs to be changed.

You wouldn't go back to a tailor if the alterations didn't make the garment fit better . . . that's *why* you went in the first place. But can you imagine the tailor saying, "I didn't want to offend you by suggesting that anything you owned needed changing, so all I did was iron it . . . it looks so much better now." You'd find another tailor.

What about the assembly? We don't go to church to look better . . . we go to be altered. That's what genuine worship performs in our lives. Genuine, biblical edification doesn't mean we *feel* better—it means we *live* better.

One Puritan defined good worship as that which enlivens our conscience by the holiness of God; feeds our minds with the truth of God; purges our imaginations by the beauty of God; opens our hearts to the love of God, and causes us to devote our will to the purpose of God.[10]

Does anybody ever go to church to have their imagination purged? Their conscience enlivened? Do we really want to have an encounter with the Word? Do song and prayer and Scripture on the love and beauty and holiness of God cause us to devote ourselves more fully to the purpose of God? He should be our tailor, working in us to make alterations. The trouble is we most often want Him to simply iron out a problem or two.

Titus 2:15 is actually the job description of a true shepherd. He, like his Lord, doesn't just iron out problems, either. He is all about making necessary alterations. The Church follows suit, giving priority to offering our world life-altering, heart-changing truth in the Country of the Blind.

And the truth isn't always polite conversation or even passionate exhortation. Sometimes the truth creates a collision: our life and our message become a direct confrontation to our generation, demanding nothing less than demolition and reconstruction.

Martin Luther the Reformer commented on this command in Titus when he wrote this in the sixteenth century:

I find it impossible to avoid offending guilty men, for there is
no way of avoiding it but by our silence or their patience; and
silent we cannot be because of God's command, and patient
they cannot be because of their guilt.[11]

Times haven't really changed all that much.

Authorization

These things speak and exhort and reprove with all authority (Titus 2:15*d*).

Paul has now overreached. He's actually gone so far as to expect people
to submit to someone else's authority. Surely he understands the impos-
sibility of this implication. We can talk to people about Christianity, we
can even exhort them to change—but don't tell them we have any kind of
authority over them.

Authority is a dirty word in our culture today. **Authority** stands in our
way; it stops us from doing what we want to do; it interrupts our personal
freedom.[12]

Pastors today refuse to deliver the authoritative truth of sin or judgment
for fear of losing influence and popularity. Parents today are guilt-tripped
into thinking that if they act with any **authority**, they will lose the love of
their children.

Authority is simply a bad word today. To suggest that one thing is right,
another is wrong; something is godly, another is sinful might prove to be
embarrassingly awkward. Those living in the Country of the Blind are much
more comfortable with opinions than with ultimatums.

The Enemy wants to silence the **authority** of God's message through
us: "This is the only way to heaven and every other way leads to hell." Yet,
as Paul understood it, doing so is to deliver the authoritative words of God.

And when we speak *these things*, Paul assures us that we have the back-
ing of God's **authority**. So, *speak and exhort and reprove* with all authority.

Consider the worldview that must be reproved and challenged:

* The universe began by random events.
* Life begins by chance.

- Human beings are animals.
- A fetus isn't a baby.
- Sex outside of marriage is safe.
- Whatever is legal is right.
- Pornography is for the mature adult.
- Divorce doesn't harm children.
- Religions are all the same.
- There is no such place as hell.
- There are many ways to God.

SPEADING THE LIGHT

William Barclay, a Scottish theological leader of the last century, wrote:

> The eyes of the sinner must be opened to his sin; the mind of the misguided must be led to realize its mistake; the heart of the heedless must be stabbed awake. The Christian message is not opium to send men to sleep; it is [a] blinding light which shows them as they are and God as He is.[13]

In this land of the spiritually blind we must tell its inhabitants of the glorious Gospel, which will give them everlasting sight.

Paul linked Jesus to one of the strongest statements of hope in regards to our future; it is a statement that is under attack all over again:

[L]*ooking for the blessed hope and the appearing of the glory of our great God and Savior, Christ Jesus* (Titus 2:13).

In the Country of the Blind, everyone believes that Jesus is simply one among many ways to heaven. He's one of any number of saviors—so long as a person is sincere in following one of them. And there are plenty of pseudo-pastors and pseudo-spiritual leaders preaching that message of universalism today. You can watch them on television or pick up a bestselling book by them in the Christian bookstore.

A Christian journal that pointed out—with some courage, I might add—the disguise of universalism in the writings of "influential church leaders" commented on a book entitled *A New Christianity*. In it, the author rejected the claim that the Bible provided certainty. He presses that one of the troubling things about Christianity is its dogmatism . . . its certainty.[14]

Another author agrees and writes that what we need to do is keep the big questions alive because that's really more important than answering them. Really? Is the question of eternal destiny more valuable than the answer? And is it unsophisticated to speak with biblical certainty? The Apostle John answered that question 2,000 years ago:

> *These things I have written to you who believe in the name of the Son of God, so that you may **know** that you have eternal life* (1 John 5:13).

That you may **know** . . . sounds rather certain, doesn't he? Dogmatic, even.

Another former evangelical pastor wrote a bestseller (fortunately) that repackaged the heresy of universalism (unfortunately) with a clever twist: every sincere person is going to heaven by way of Jesus, even though he/she doesn't actually believe in Him. As long as their heart is fine or their actions measure up, they'll be okay.[15] That's like telling a cancer patient, "As long as you wear nice clothes and shine your shoes, you're going to be just fine."

To Titus, Paul isn't writing about uncertainties or options; he is delivering the truth to a country where no one can see—truths that challenge someone's conversation, motivation, alteration, and authorization. Just don't expect any bouquets of thanks in response.

Having aired our sermons for a number of years, I have received all sorts of responses:

- demands that I make apologies on the air for what I've taught;
- persuasions to change our doctrine;
- accusations that I am maligning their doctrine, their church, and their beliefs;
- gifts of books to read to change my mind;

- suggestions that I should take a hike—only in more colorful language.

Perhaps that's why Paul concludes this chapter by telling Titus and everyone else who teaches the truth of God's Word, **Let no one** disregard **you** (Titus 2:15e). Don't let anybody write you off; keep telling the truth, regardless.

The word for **disregard** only appears here in all of the New Testament. It's a compound word that literally translated means *to think around something*.[16] Paul is telling Titus, "Don't let anyone run circles around you; don't let anyone off the hook on some philosophical loophole—make sure your teaching is clear and biblically defensible."

In fact, Paul uses the second person singular pronoun *you*, which lays emphasis on the shoulders of Titus. *You*, Titus, make sure that *you* don't let anyone get around *you* and deceive the flock or turn your own mind away from the truth. The role of the shepherd is to passionately and persistently preach and teach the blinded who have been deceived.

So here's the plan—the way to daily impact the lives of people on Crete and in Cary or Chicago or Cheyenne or wherever we live and work and play:

- Make Jesus Christ part of our daily conversation.
- Make Christianity our motivating challenge to others.
- Make the truth of Scripture the basis for our alteration.
- Make the Scripture our authorization as we deliver the ultimatums of the Gospel.

And don't ever forget . . . we happen to live in the Country of the Blind. Be encouraged that we are inviting them to join us as we look for the Country of Everlasting Light, where there's beauty and joy and worship forever.

And be aware that Paul writes these initiatives in the present tense. In other words, "Don't stop . . . keep on delivering the truth . . . every single day."[17]

Shepherds, especially—stay the course!

Remind them to be subject to rulers, to authorities, to be obedient, to be ready for every good deed, ²to malign no one, to be peaceable, gentle, showing every consideration for all men.

–Titus 3:1–2

CHAPTER NINETEEN

LIVING IN THE CITY OF MAN

Titus 3:1–2

IN IT . . . NOT OF IT

Planet Earth is home to two very real worlds.[1] And the Christian is in contact with both of them. Augustine referred to them in his monumental work *The City of God*, which largely shaped how the Western world thought of itself for well over a thousand years. It was written after the fall of Rome in the fifth century. Roman pagans argued that the city fell because it had abandoned its old gods when it adopted Christianity. Augustine responded that the problem wasn't that Rome was *too* Christian—it wasn't Christian *enough*. He argued that there were two "cities" in this world: the City of Man, dominated by self-love and built around the lowest common denominator in society—self-indulgence—and the City of God, built around love of God and, therefore, love of neighbor.[2]

The City of Man is the physical world around us—a world we engage through sight, sound, smell, taste, and touch. But at the same time, the Christian is very aware of another world—invisible, though just as real . . . in fact, eternal. The Designer and Creator of *both* worlds is the same Person: our Creator God.

Augustine explained that we connect to the City of God by means of the Spirit instead of our senses. Most in our world would agree with everything written so far . . . except the part about a Creator. They like to think of *something* out there in the vast universe—just don't talk about a Designer or a Sovereign Creator.

William Irwin Thompson likened our unbelieving world to flies crawling across the ceiling of the Sistine Chapel, blissfully unaware of the magnificent shapes and colors and designs that surround them.[3]

Certainly Evolution's brush has attempted to eliminate the concept of a Master Painter responsible for all the creative shapes and colors and designs that surround us. Some even study the complex patterns of the paintings but deny there ever was a Painter—Someone outside their world of cells and insects who actually designed and painted the beautiful landscapes of Earth.

Educators are busily washing any reference to Him off the walls of history and science. The politically incorrect crime of our time is to state with any sense of certainty that a Painter exists, much less One who is responsible for the painting. And if we really want to shake things up, suggest that it's not only His painting but *His* ceiling in *His* chapel with *His* ground underneath; that it's *His* earth and *His* universe, too, while we're at it.

That would be inconceivable to our world. Over the past several decades, we've watched our world remove the signature of the Painter from the mural of His universe.

In May 2012, the U.S. Court of Appeals ruled against a town (the case of Town of Greece, NY v. Galloway) for opening its council meetings with prayer. And we automatically think, *We knew that was coming.* But what makes this decision so bizarre is that the town had already tried to be politically correct by inviting a variety of religious leaders to pray. They even brought in an atheist and a Wiccan priestess to pray. The court found in its majority opinion: "The town's prayer practice had the effect of affiliating the town with Christianity." Even the *concept* of prayer was too Christian and it had to be abandoned.[4]

If I were God, I would not remain so quiet about all of this. I would at least start writing messages in the clouds, make them purple and the rain pink . . . send Skittles cascading from the sky so everyone has to admit that, at least, there's *Someone* up there!

God evidently isn't intimidated by unbelief. He doesn't seem to be anxious about being ignored or disrespected. We are. In fact, we can become infuriated and bitter.

One author wrote:

> In reaction to the rapid and pervasive escalation of immoral-
> ity and ungodliness [in our culture], believers have become
> both saddened and angered. Hostility among some of them
> has been intensified still further when they learn that their
> taxes are being used to fund ideas and practices that only a
> few generations ago were condemned even by most secular-
> ists. They fear for their children and even more for their
> grandchildren because of the kind of world into which they
> will be born, educated, and have to live.[5]

There is a growing spirit of antagonism toward government; a growing pessimism toward institutions; a growing attitude of isolation among
believers, abandoning the culture entirely and basically heading for the hills,
saying, "This City of Man is going to hell, so I'll just give my attention and
time and money and energy to the City of God."

Has it ever occurred to you that the reason Jesus Christ did *not* take
us immediately to heaven after our salvation is because He wants us to live
in the City of *Man*, demonstrating the reality of the City of *God*? And the
clearer the distinctions are between these two cities, the more remarkable
our Gospel becomes.

Keep in mind that the world is not our enemy—it is our mission field.
And it's doing nothing more than what we should expect. So what do we
do about it? How do we live in the City of Man while we wait for the City
of God?

The believers on Crete must have wondered the same thing: "What's
next, Paul? You told us how to act in church and how to relate to one
another. Is that it?—is that the end of our responsibilities and obligations
while living temporarily in the City of Man?"

With somewhat startling implications, Paul begins to inform believers
that Christianity does not remove the Christian from society—it makes the
Christian a productive member *of* society.

Christianity doesn't make us isolated citizens—it makes us better citizens; Christianity doesn't relieve us of civic duties—it enforces them.[6]

Paul can't be serious! He is *very* serious . . . get ready to discover that Christianity should make every one of us remarkable standouts in the City of Man as we ultimately represent the City of God.

RESPONDING TO RULERS

Remind *them to be subject to rulers, to authorities,* to be obedient (Titus 3:1*a*).

The opening verb **remind** is in the present tense; Paul is telling Titus, "*Keep on reminding* the believers of these responses." And first among them is the response to civil authority: **to be obedient**.

Respecting the Law

If we traveled back to the island of Crete, we'd discover a citizenry who had earned an empire-wide reputation as a dissatisfied, disgruntled people; they were always involved in some sort of plotting and conflict—and they hated Roman rulers. Plutarch, the first-century historian, wrote that Cretans were always on the verge of revolt.[7] The large Jewish population wouldn't have hesitated to lend a hand, either.

Crete had also become a haven for pirates.[8] Imagine an island that reveled in a swashbuckling, self-serving, independent lifestyle that answered to *no* authority.

We've already learned that "Cretan" had become a nickname (given by their own prophet) for *"liars, evil beasts, lazy gluttons"* (Titus 1:12)—not exactly the kind of people who respond well to authority.

Paul tells Titus to remind these believers—and then keep on reminding them—that they're not to act like their forefathers. They may have pirate blood in their veins, but as new creatures in Christ they must demonstrate a remarkably different attitude toward authority.

In the original language, Paul uses two infinitives and two nouns in such a condensed fashion so as to read, *to be subject, to be obedient to rulers, to authorities*.

Here's a radical idea: Christians are not above the law.[9] Believers can't say, "We, as citizens, belong to the City of God—so forget all you people in the City of Man."

If we went over to Paul's fuller explanation in *Romans 13*, we would discover mind-altering principles related to the issue of secular government. The first is that obedience to governmental rulers and authorities is not an option but a command. We don't need to pray over whether we'll pay our taxes, meet city codes for buildings, operate our businesses according to state regulations, pay our employees minimum wage, get our cars inspected, or pay the registration fee after standing in line for a month at the local DMV.

Christians don't get a free pass—they pay the same full price as everyone else.

Respecting the Authorities

Paul introduces the concept that the institution of government is the creation of God:

> *Every person is to be in subjection to the governing authorities. For there is no authority except from God, and those which exist are established by God* (Romans 13:1).

Every civil and political power has actually been appointed by God. The Apostle Peter wrote:

> *Submit yourselves for the Lord's sake to every human institution, whether to a king as the one in authority, or to governors as sent by him . . . For such is the will of God that by doing right you may silence the ignorance of foolish men* (1 Peter 2:13–15).

While we engage in due process as citizens of this country, voting and speaking our conscience, we can rest with complete confidence that God's purposes are never thwarted—He has every office under His control. Every judge is a minister of His providential direction, and the heart of every king (president/prime minister/dictator) is in the palm of His hand.

There is never a reason for the Christian to panic. In fact, resentment toward the culture around us may be an indicator that we don't think God is keeping up . . . that He's letting things slip out of His control.

But the truth that every candidate who wins an office is actually God's choice keeps the believer from giving up. Instead, the believer may run for office; write a gracious, informative letter to the Editor; serve on an advisory board; plant trees in the local park; volunteer in some capacity in the community. Like Daniel and Joseph, the believer benefits his pagan culture by merging his integrity with the valid needs of his own community.

Christians benefit their culture as living ambassadors *on assignment* from the City of God.

Respecting God's Command

Should a Christian obey civil authorities, regardless of their attitude toward the Gospel? The answer lies in the timeline of Paul's own letters. While Nero was on the throne and society was as depraved as ever, the apostle was urging respectful obedience, so long is it didn't involve directly violating God's commands. By the time of Nero's reign, culture had completely abandoned any semblance of sexual norms: heterosexuality was considered prudish; the emperor was bisexual; pedophilia, adultery, idolatry, abortion, prostitution, and drug addiction were not only empire-wide—they were *legal* and absolutely *acceptable.*

This was the century in which Jesus Christ planted the living Church . . . and it exploded into existence. Why? Among other reasons, Christians were so remarkably different from everyone else. They had a respect for authority, even when that authority hated the very ground the Christian walked upon.

Rome would eventually demand that Christians express their allegiance to the City of Man by annually offering a pinch of incense and declaring, "Caesar is Lord." Many Christians died as martyrs rather than attempt to overthrow the emperor . . . they simply refused to deny that Christ *alone* was Lord.[10]

Is Paul implying that it would never be right to disobey the law of the land? No; whenever the will of the law demands that a believer violate the Word of God, the Christian stands with the apostles when they were told they must stop preaching the Gospel of Christ: *"We must obey God rather than men"* (Acts 5:29).

At the same time, the apostles didn't mount an insurrection to try to impeach the high priest. Nor is Paul suggesting that the believers band together to overthrow Nero. Instead, Paul is informing the Church in Crete, Rome, and elsewhere that they are to respect the authority of the land—pay their taxes, keep the laws and codes of the land . . . even to the point of dying for their faith, should they be required to violate Scripture.

Christians could sing on the way to their execution, with the clear conscience that they had served the City of Man as best they could for the glory of God . . . and now they were about to enter the City of God. The world only shakes its head in wonder at those remarkable Christians.

So, what's our attitude toward those in authority:

- Parents?
- Teachers?
- Supervisors?
- Elders and church leaders?
- Town councils?
- the IRS?
- the Wildlife Resources Commission when we've met our hunting or fishing quota?
- the State when we write the check for property taxes?
- the police officer who pulls us over?

The problem with responding to authority isn't new . . . and it starts young:

> Kids were brought into a room, one at a time, where they found a table and chair, toys, and a plate of homemade cookies. They were told they couldn't eat the cookies until they had permission. When the adult left, the camera began to roll . . . the agony was terrible. Some kids walked over to the plate of cookies and just stared . . . and stared. One child began to repeat, "Don't eat the cookies . . . don't eat the cookies." One kid went over to the corner and stood there bumping his head against the wall. Another child simply ate a cookie.

The camera is rolling and people around us are watching. What does our spirit communicate to others about our view of authority? If they observe respectful obedience, that's terrific, but be prepared—the Apostle Paul is just getting started.

RELATING TO OTHERS
Going the Extra Mile

Remind them . . . to be ready for every good deed (Titus 3:1*b*).

In other words, Christianity is more than simply obeying; it's certainly more than begrudging the letter of the law. Paul says **be ready**, be *eager* to go out of our way to serve our community leaders and the people that surround us in this City of Man.

Paul's attitude is remarkably different from the status quo. The Jewish community on the island of Crete—in fact, throughout the Roman Empire—urged separation from local culture. They huddled together and ignored those around them.

In the first century, Jews living outside Israel formed tight-knit communities which included no one from the outside Gentile world. They were slow and reluctant to submit to local laws and authorities; they felt they were above it. One author wrote that they treated the people around them with thinly veiled disdain.[11]

Rather than live among the people and demonstrate the glory and character of God, they kept to themselves and did nothing at all in what they would have defined as "secular society." They simply didn't mix with the locals.

Maybe you're thinking that here in this text Paul is merely telling church members to be eager to do good deeds *to one another*. Certainly that's a biblical principle, and Paul required as much when he wrote the Galatian believers:

> [L]*et us do good to all people, especially to those who are of the household of the faith* (Galatians 6:10).

However, Paul is going to end the sentence in **Titus 3:2** with the clarification that the believer was to perform good deeds **for all men**—not just for believers.

At any moment on the island of Crete, a citizen could feel the touch of the flat side of a Roman spear on his shoulder and know right away that, according to the law, he was compelled to carry that soldier's gear for one mile.[12] Everyone despised the practice, especially the Jewish population; no doubt, believers wouldn't want to interrupt their schedule or go out of their way to help an idolater, either.

A Roman mile was considered a thousand steps. The person would undoubtedly pick up the gear and begin counting out loud as he walked along: 1, 2, 3 . . . 999, 1000. *Plop*—there's your gear . . . I'm outta here.

But Jesus Christ preached in His Sermon on the Mount:

"Whoever forces you to go one mile, go with him two" (Matthew 5:41).

Can you imagine the surprise of the soldier when he heard, "Hey, listen, I know I've already walked my thousand steps, but I'm willing—because of my obedience to Christ my Savior—to carry your gear another mile." That soldier and everyone who witnessed it would scratch their heads in amazement. It was this spirit of eager service that gave us the expression we still use to this day: "going the extra mile."

Are we ready to demonstrate remarkable Christianity? Then go the extra mile!

Avoiding the Grapevine

Remind them . . . to malign no one (Titus 3:1–2*a*).

This verb is from the Greek word *blasphemeo*, which gives us our word *blasphemy*. Only in this context, it refers to slandering another person.[13] And note that Paul doesn't add a loophole: **malign no one** *if it isn't true. If it's true, don't hold back!* No—simply put: **malign** [absolutely] **no one.**

Paul's directive for the believer couldn't be clearer. We can't abuse or insult with our lips. We can't run down politicians, fellow believers, colleagues at work, or family members and ever hope to elevate the reputation of the Gospel.[14] That activity is rampant in the City of Man. It's a dog-eat-dog world out there . . . they are skilled at swinging the sword and carving a path to the top of the heap.

One historian said of Crete and first-century culture, "Verbal slander was practiced as a fine art.[15]

This verb (*to malign*) is subordinate to the opening command, which unfortunately implies that the believers in Crete were already involved in maligning others. Paul effectively says, "Titus, remind them and remind them and keep reminding them not to drag other people through the mud."

Delete words from your vocabulary like "stupid"—"jerk"—"fool"; you're never going to impress upon anyone that you're a Christian when you use names like that for another driver, your boss, or a colleague . . . not to mention another Christian.

We live in a crass, vulgar, rude society where we can demonstrate our Christianity with remarkable distinction by refraining from verbal abuse.

No Swinging Back

Remind them . . . to be peaceable (Titus 3:1–2*b*).

It could be rendered *not contentious.* The word literally translated means a *no-brawler.* Yes, Paul was a fighter, but he wasn't a brawler.[16] He didn't put on his gloves whenever offended. Remarkable Christianity doesn't swing back. Even when we have what many would call a good reason to take a swing, we don't do it.

Consider the apostle writing this letter to Titus. Roman governors, through pride and incompetence, had kept him in prison for years; Roman authorities had illegally bound him, beaten him with rods, delayed hearing charges against him and, when the charges were presented, left him under house arrest for several more years.[17]

If anybody had good reason to write a letter, it wouldn't have been to Titus—it would have been to the Roman senate. Paul could have growled in his cell at every changing of the guard. He could have demanded better treatment as a freeborn Roman citizen. On another occasion he would sit in a jail nicknamed The Rat's Nest and write, [I]*n everything give thanks* (1 Thessalonians 5:18*a*).

Paul will practice what he penned. He will witness to these soldiers, and they no doubt said to each other, "That man is absolutely remarkable . . . there's got to be something to this Christianity."

I recommend to my seminary students the biography of Robert Chapman, a pastor in nineteenth-century England:

> He was single his entire life, pastored a small church his whole ministry, yet made a deep impact on his community. Charles Spurgeon called him the saintliest man in England. But not everyone liked Robert Chapman. A grocer in the community hated him; he became so infuriated by Chapman's open-air preaching that on more than one occasion, he spit on him as he walked past.
>
> For a number of years, the grocer verbally abused Chapman whenever he came around. Chapman never retaliated—never struck back. One day when Robert's wealthy relatives came to visit him, they insisted on buying groceries and cooking

meals while there. Being single and with little money, he agreed. When asked where he would recommend they purchase the groceries, Chapman insisted they go to the grocery of the man who had insulted him for so many years. His relatives knew nothing about that drama, and Robert was insistent that they travel to the other side of town to do their shopping. More food was purchased than could be carried, and they asked that it all be delivered to the home of the Reverend R. C. Chapman. The stunned grocer asked them to repeat the address, then said it had to be a mistake—they must have come to the wrong shop. Chapman's relatives assured him that Robert insisted they come there. When the grocer arrived with the delivery and Chapman answered the door, he broke down in tears. That very afternoon Chapman led the grocer to faith in his Lord.[18]

What wonderful fruit from the life of a believer who refused to swing back.

Staying the Course.

Remind them to be . . . gentle (Titus 3:1–2c).

That word **gentle** doesn't quite translate the depth of character bound up in its construction. It's an adjective found only five times in the entire New Testament, and it refers to someone who is patiently steadfast—someone who is able to submit to injustice, disgrace, and maltreatment without hatred or malice . . . trusting God, in spite of it all.[19]

That's why Paul effectively says that remarkable Christianity stays the course—and you could add—*sweetly.* Easy for Paul to say? Hardly. He will use this same word again while under house arrest: *Let your* **gentle** *spirit be known to all men* (Philippians 4:5a).

The Apostle Peter used the same word when he wrote:

> *Always be prepared to give an answer to everyone who asks you to give the reason for the hope that you have. But do this with* **gentle***ness* (1 Peter 3:15b, c NIV).

This is how we respond when we're questioned for our faith; when our testimony is ridiculed or challenged; when our lifestyle is mocked and insulted.

Frankly, our entire culture could use Paul's counsel. One author pointed out the problem that is now culture-wide:

> Reasoned discourse is now imperiled. It is giving way to in-your-face sound bites; playing hardball is the dominant metaphor for American [dialogue]. Our interchanges are confrontational, divisive, and dismissive. Balance and fairness are casualties on evening shows as two, three, and sometimes four voices contend simultaneously for dominance. Volume and stubbornness are the new civic virtues.[20]

This is good news only in that remarkable Christianity can be all the more distinctive when practiced.

No Playing Favorites

Remind them to be . . . showing every consideration for all men (Titus 3:1–2d).

A literal understanding of that word translated **all** means just that—**all**. In fact, it can be expanded to mean *every kind of; all kinds*.

All; regardless of race, religion, political leanings—even if they're to the left and we're tempted to push them over the edge; regardless of social status or salary or education or age or ethnicity.[21] Be humbly considerate—***showing consideration***—toward them **all**!

If they have a need, it doesn't matter who they are . . . be eager and ready to meet it.

George Whitefield, a spiritual leader in the 1800s, learned of a widow with a large family whose landlord had recently taken all her furniture because she couldn't pay the rent:

> Whitefield immediately rode the great distance to her village with a friend. When they arrived at her home, he gave her five pounds; it was enough money to pay her rent and get her furniture back. Riding home, Whitfield's friend chided

him for giving away such a large mount, to which Whitefield responded, "When God brings a need before us, it is that we may relieve it."

Suddenly the two men were startled by a highway robber, who confronted them and demanded their money. Having given all his money away, Whitefield had none, but his friend still had money in his purse. After the thief rode away, Whitefield turned the tables on his friend and reminded him how much better it was for the poor widow to have his money than the thief. Continuing their journey, the robber returned and demanded Whitefield's coat. Whitefield graciously agreed but only if he could have the bandit's tattered coat in exchange, since the day was cold. After trading coats, the thief rode away again. After some time, Whitefield and his friend spotted the robber galloping towards them as fast as he could. Fearing for their lives, they gave their horses the spur and arrived at some cottages before the robber reached them. The thief had to turn away or be apprehended. As Whitefield sat by the fire, he removed the tattered coat and found his five pounds in one of the pockets, plus nearly five hundred pounds more![22]

In today's economy, Whitefield gave the widow five hundred dollars and received fifty thousand in return.

Now that's my kind of Christianity . . . sign me up!

Remarkable Christianity means that we sign up to go the extra mile; to avoid the grapevine; to refuse to swing back; to stay the course . . . and to refuse to play favorites, treating *everyone* with gracious consideration along the way.

[3]For we also once were foolish ourselves, disobedient, deceived, enslaved to various lusts and pleasures, spending our life in malice and envy, hateful, hating one another. [4]But when the kindness of God our Savior and His love for mankind appeared, [5]He saved us . . . according to His mercy.

–Titus 3:3–5*a, c*

CHAPTER TWENTY

REMEMBER!

Titus 3:3–5a, c

THOSE REMARKABLE CHRISTIANS!

About seventy-five years after Paul wrote his inspired letter to Titus, a church leader living in Athens wrote his friend:

> The difference between Christians and the rest of mankind is not a matter of nationality or language or customs. Christians do not live in separate cities of their own, speak any special dialect, or practice any eccentric way of life. They conform to ordinary local usage in their clothing, diet, and other habits. Nevertheless, they do exhibit some features that are remarkable and, even, surprising. For instance, even though they obey the prescribed laws, in their own private lives they transcend the laws. They show love to all men— and all men persecute them. They are misunderstood and condemned; they repay curses with blessings, and abuse with courtesy.[1]

Sounds familiar, doesn't it? It seems the inspired reminder of the Apostle Paul made it from the island of Crete to the city of Athens. I wonder if it made it from Crete to the town of Cary . . . or Atlanta . . . or Denver . . . or Los Angeles. This letter has every one of our addresses on the label. And we might not have caught it, but right in the middle of this letter, Paul remarks that Christians were now living with some rather obvious distinctions. They stood out.

Much of Paul's letter to Titus included what believers were to be doing, but he also reminded them of what they *used* to do.

DREDGING UP THE PAST

For *we also once were foolish ourselves, disobedient, deceived, enslaved to various lusts and pleasures, spending our life in malice and envy, hateful, hating one another* (Titus 3:3).

The verse begins with the connective conjunction **for**, which implies that the believer might be wondering why in the world he should ever treat unbelievers with kindness and love and courtesy and humility and deference. Paul anticipates that response by effectively saying, "You need to act like this toward the unbelieving world because of what you used to be like when God in *His* kindness and grace intercepted your lives."

In other words, remember the pit you were dug from . . . remember the slime you used to wallow in . . . remember the sinful acts that dragged you through the mud, while you loved every minute of it.

Remind them—that's how this chapter opened. Remind these believers how they are to act and what makes them so remarkable, then remind them what once made them so despicable.

There aren't many counselors who could keep a practice going if they reminded people what they *used* to be like as an incentive for what they *ought* to be like. Imagine challenging your client how to live for Christ by reminding him how he once lived as a slave to sin. What kind of counseling session is that?!

But that is exactly what Paul is doing. *Why* he does it will become clear only after he takes us back through the swamp that emptied us out at the cross.

Biased

For we *also once were* **foolish** *ourselves* (Titus 3:3*a*).

As Paul begins, it's insightful—and encouraging—to recognize how he shifts from talking about *them* to talking about *us* . . . he goes from *you* to *all of us*: **For** we *also once were* . . .

Paul never forgot his past. The people who never completely get over their past are people who never get over their conversion. Unfortunately, too many Christians have.

Paul begins to list how *we also once were*, and the first characteristic is **foolish**. The word that translates as **foolish** doesn't refer to silliness or irrational thinking.[2] Paul doesn't mean someone who lacks intelligence but someone who is intellectually biased against any talk of God—certainly any idea or suggestion of accountability before God.

Paul had this kind of person in mind when he wrote:

> [B]*eing darkened in their understanding, excluded from the life of God because of the ignorance that is in them* [note this], *because of the hardness of their heart* (Ephesians 4:18).

This person scorns the wisdom of God, Solomon wrote in *Proverbs 28:26*. The foolish person is literally in a deliberate state of folly, by his own choosing to trust in himself.[3] He is effectively the opposite of *Proverbs 3:5–6*, for the biased rebel is determined to trust in himself, to lean on his own understanding, and to acknowledge his own will in everything.

Paul is saying, "We need to remember that this is who we once were. In fact, now that we're Christians, we still need the daily reminder to trust in Him, not to lean on our own understanding, but in all our ways acknowledge Him . . . put Him first."

An unbeliever doesn't want to put God first because he *himself* is first.

Belligerent

For we also once were . . . **disobedient** (Titus 3:3*b*).

This word describes a person who deliberately chooses to rebel—not only against the concept of God but the idea of a moral standard created by God. And this attitude isn't just belligerence against God but against all authority.

One author wrote that this kind of person chafes under any kind of authority.[4] This word is the perfect caption for our culture: BELLIGERENT. Those in authority in our land are trying to control a runaway, disobedient, belligerent culture by passing more laws and handing down more court rulings . . . and the culture is simply not responding.

We've watched legislative bodies weigh in across the country, passing bans on all sorts of things that parents once decided . . . before they evidently abandoned ship. Now there are laws against body piercing for minors; the sale or rental of violent video games to minors; the purchase of junk food from machines in school lunchrooms.

The lower house in the Texas legislature even devised a ban on overtly sexually suggestive cheerleading [for high schools].[5] How ironic is that, given the provocative image of the average NFL cheerleader? What's even more ironic is that every state in the union would never think of banning or even discouraging sexual activity *after* the game—just keep the cheerleaders from suggesting it *during* the game.

One author wrote that we now have more and more children who are arriving in the classroom without any moral compass.[6] And that would probably be because their parents didn't have one to pass along. Little wonder that lawmakers don't even know where to begin.

You can't watch an argument take place on the floor of congress or on primetime television relating to whether God should be mentioned in the public square, and then expect the next generation to care about Him—much less obey His moral and ethical laws.

Here's the digression:

- develop a personal bias against God;
- develop a cultural bias against God;
- develop a personal belligerence against the boundaries of God;
- develop a cultural belligerence against the boundaries of God.

This eventually leads to a culture-wide **disobedient** spirit—literally a chafing under any kind of moral or ethical authority . . . and it only grows more and more obvious.

One revealing incident involved one hundred twenty-five university students from a prestigious ivy league school who were caught collaborating in groups and on email to come up with answers to exam questions. They clearly violated a no-collaboration policy that was printed on the exam itself. But—get this—many of the students were shocked by the charge of cheating, claiming they didn't know it was cheating, even though it was described *on* the exam. Other students threatened to sue the school. One reporter responded tongue-in-cheek when he wrote, "Are we meant to assume that students who are smart enough to get into this university don't know what cheating is? Will the school [need to] offer a course on why it's a bad idea to pour gasoline on a flaming toaster oven?"[7]

Perhaps.

Recently, Brazil became embroiled in an ethical dilemma when a notary approved the country's first three-way civil union: one man and two women. The notary claimed she hadn't broken any law. In fact, she argued that Brazil had already approved gay marriage, and since there were no laws on the books against polygamy, the definition of marriage was obviously flexible—so why not.[8]

Indeed.

Reports such as these simply highlight the fact that apart from the Moral Lawgiver, there are no moral guidelines. Dismiss God and *anything* is permissible.

Blind

For we also once were . . . deceived (Titus 3:3c).

The word Paul uses here to describe our fallen condition is a word that can be translated *misled*—literally, *duped*.[9]

The world thinks it's found the answers, but Paul reveals it has actually been *duped*. Not a very flattering description, but the truth nonetheless. Dismiss God, follow your own path, and the Bible promises that you will stumble from bad to worse *(Romans 1)*.

The trouble is God isn't the only spiritual voice out there. There's another voice, even more interesting to the unbeliever. While God speaks only the truth, there's a fallen angel who is the father of lies *(John 8:44)*; he's called the angel of light *(2 Corinthians 11:14)* who deceives the whole world *(Revelation 12:9)*—he is a *master* deceiver.

Paul warned Timothy that *evil men and imposters will proceed from bad to worse, deceiving and being* **deceived** (2 Timothy 3:13).

They look good . . . they sound religious . . . they might even wear a collar or stand behind a pulpit. Paul wrote earlier for Titus to be alert to those who have turned away from the truth and are misleading people *(Titus 1:10–11)*. They are teaching things that uplift the spirit and perhaps encourage the heart and certainly please the ear. Jesus characterized them, saying:

> *"And if a blind man guides a blind man, both will fall into a pit"* (Matthew 15:14).

The world is rejecting Creator God and is duped . . . misled . . . blind . . . following the wrong spiritual guide—heading toward a precipice.

Bound

***For we also once were* . . . enslaved to various lusts and pleasures** (Titus 3:3*d*).

The word **lusts** is *epithumia*: strong desires.[10]

Keep in mind that this activity exists only in the mind and heart. You could call it forbidden fantasies. We can be enslaved to fantasy, according to this letter from Paul, whether we physically do anything about it or not.

Paul would counter the argument that violent and/or sexually provocative video games or internet pornography really isn't sinful because the gamer or viewer isn't physically involved . . . it's just in the *mind*. He would respond, "No, it all must be called what it is: **various lusts and pleasures**. In fact, Paul writes here that the partaker is **enslaved**, whether it stays in his mind or ends up being acted upon.

Paul issues a severe warning because we eventually act out our fantasies. In fact, the next word Paul uses is **pleasures**. This moves beyond mental fantasy into physical actions. The word for **pleasures** is *hedone*, which gives us the word *hedonism*.

Hedonism is simply the pursuit of self-satisfaction, whatever it might be.[11] It is the number one religion on the planet. And Paul adds the adjective **various** to both **lusts** and **pleasures** to inform us that all of it comes in a variety of forms, fashions, disguises, and allurements. The word **various** literally means multicolored.

Just how many colors are there? Wait until your wife wants to paint a room in the house and you make a run to the home improvement store. Walk up to the guy at the paint counter and say, "My wife sent me over here to pick up some blue paint . . . where do you keep it?" He'll double over in laughter—and that's when you know you're in trouble.

"Let's see," he'll say with a smirk, "is that royal, teal, powder, aqua, steel, navy, cobalt, baby, periwinkle, Carolina, cerulean, or Mediterranean blue?" You had no idea there were so many shades of blue paint!

That's the idea here: multicolored. We have no idea there are so many ways to sin . . . so many *kinds* of sin.

And notice that the word for **pleasures** here isn't just immoral or sexual sin. Paul actually uses it in his letter to Timothy for covetousness.[12] Label that one *materialism*, and add it to the color palette with all its hues and possibilities.

The truth is the world is **enslaved**, always wanting more. It thinks about it and dreams about it and lusts for it and lives for it; I want that shade, and that one, and two of those, and that color . . . no, that one. Oh, all right . . . I want them *all*.

The world is free as a bird to think anything, do anything, want anything, pursue anything—it's free! But Paul effectively announces that the world is actually **enslaved** to what it has; **enslaved** to what it doesn't have; **enslaved** to what it shouldn't have, and **enslaved** to what it can't have. It's a downward spiral that chokes the unbeliever with terminal discontent.

Paul is writing to us all—this activity represents our *old* life, not our *new* life. It belongs back in the pit, even though it wants to keep crawling back out. So put an iron cover over the opening of the pit to keep those forbidden **lusts**, **pleasures**, and greed where they all belong.

Bitter

For we also once were . . . spending our life in malice and envy (Titus 3:3*e*).

It makes sense: if our life is spent nursing lust in our heart and longing for whatever it is we want, **malice** and **envy** will be the driving factors in every relationship . . . in every setting.

Just look at what they have . . . look where they live . . . look what they wear . . . look where they work . . . look at their kids . . . they have the life I want.

The word **envy** represents more than that, however; it harbors the feelings of displeasure when someone else has it . . . when someone else is honored or promoted.[13]

Parents in Tennessee complained that posting the Honor Roll "embarrassed" the kids who were excluded, so on the advice of the school counselor, the Honor Roll in that school was entirely eliminated.[14] The issue was not embarrassment over not being on the list—the issue was the envy of parents whose kids weren't on it. I read recently that one high school graduating class acknowledged more than one hundred valedictorians!

Don't overlook the rather chilling word Paul used first: **malice**. This word means that someone will be willing to make another person suffer in order to get what they want. It doesn't stop with arguing over the Honor Roll. One father was so angry that his daughter was suspended from the school softball team that he attacked the coach with an aluminum bat, sending him to the hospital.[15]

Just think of the last episode of road rage that you witnessed. Where does that come from? **Envy and malice**. He got in *my* way . . . that's *my* spot . . . he'll pay for that!

One of my sons was behind a slow-moving car, and when the dotted line allowed, he passed the car. And that's when the guy came alive, sped up, and passed my son. Just as soon as he was in front, he slammed on his brakes. Fortunately there were no cars coming, and my son was able to swerve into the other lane. The other guy sped up and passed him again, trying to do the same thing. My son slowed down and backed way off; eventually the guy sped away.

Infuriated at being passed on the road, a person becomes willing—at his own peril—to cause a crash and spill blood. Can **envy** cut that deep? Can a person become *that* malicious?

Absolutely. It was **envy** that led the Sanhedrin to deliver Jesus over to Pilate *(Matthew 27:18)*. **Envy** plus **malice** led them to mock Him and spit on Him as He made His way up the brow of Calvary's hill. He had taken *their* place of favor with the people . . . He had taken *their* place in the temple traffic . . . He dared to get in *their* way.

He would *pay* the ultimate price.

Bad-Tempered

***For we also once were* hateful, hating one another** (Titus 3:3*f*).

People are at each other's throats—and not just in Crete. Think for a moment of the shallowness of human relationships where you work or go to school. Think how quickly the behind-the-back comments break out whenever someone is not around.[16]

You could outline this textual progression downward in three steps:

1. our attitude toward God: *foolish* (biased) and *disobedient* (belligerent);

2. our attitude toward ourselves: *deceived* (blind) and *enslaved* (bound);

3. our attitude toward others: filled with *malice and envy* (bitter), and *hatred* (bad-tempered).[17]

We have to admit that Paul has most fully and realistically described the awfulness of our sin and the depths of our own depravity; he, indeed, has every right to say that this list includes us all. We are entirely and utterly hopeless—deserving nothing but the wrath of God.

That's exactly the place Paul wants us to be as he begins to describe our deliverance.

LOOKING TOWARD THE FUTURE

But *when the kindness of God our Savior and His love for mankind appeared,* He saved us . . . *according to His mercy* (Titus 3:4, 5*a*, *c*).

Right about the time we became sick at the description of who we were—and what we still battle—Paul delivers one of my favorite words in the English Bible. It's the little conjunction **but**.

But: contrary to expectation. In other words, having been shown to be guilty of everything on that list of evil attitudes and actions, Paul writes, **But . . .** Contrary to what we might think God will do to us, **He saved us . . .** *according to His mercy. The kindness of God our Savior and His love for mankind appeared*—God came looking for us.[18]

Biased, belligerent, blind, bound, bitter, and bad-tempered—**but** in His kindness and love, **He saved us**. What an incentive to love Jesus Christ back . . . and to live for Him, too. To make Him our Master and Lord—to make our lives one giant exclamation mark of gratitude!

The following illustrates the response of gratitude:

> Every Friday evening, almost without fail, when the sun resembled a giant orange and was starting to dip into the blue ocean of Florida, old Ed came strolling along the beach to his favorite pier. Clutched in his bony hand was a bucket of shrimp. He was alone on the end of the pier with his thoughts and his bucket. Before long, however, white dots came screeching and squawking, winging their way toward that lanky frame, enveloping him, their wings fluttering and flapping wildly. Ed tossed shrimp to the hungry birds, smiling and saying, "Thank you, thank you." In a few short minutes the bucket was empty, but Ed stood there, lost in thought, transported to another time and place. When he finally turned and began to walk back toward the beach, a few of the birds hopped along the pier with him until he came to the steps, and then they, too, flew away. Old Eddie Rickenbacker quietly made his way down to the end of the beach and went home.
>
> He was famous in World War I—a Medal of Honor winner and ace fighter pilot with the most victories (26) in the war. During WW II, the Secretary of War asked the retired pilot, now a 52-year-old airline executive, to travel to the Pacific theater as a nonmilitary observer. On the flight across the Pacific, he and the seven-member crew went down. Miraculously, all the men survived, crawled out of their plane, and climbed into three rafts. They floated for days on the rough waters of the Pacific. They fought the sun. They fought the sharks. Most of all, they fought hunger. By the eighth day, their rations were gone. No food. No water, and hundreds of miles from land. No one knew where they were. They needed a miracle. That afternoon they had a simple devotional service and prayed for one. They tried to nap. Eddie leaned back and pulled his military cap over his nose. Time dragged. All he could hear was the slap of the waves against the raft.

Suddenly, Eddie felt something land on his cap. It was a seagull! He sat perfectly still, planning his next move. With a flash of his hand and a squawk from the gull, he managed to grab it and wring its neck. Then he tore the feathers off, and he and his starving crew made a lifesaving meal of it. Using the intestines for bait, they caught fish, which gave them food and more bait . . . and the cycle continued. With that simple survival technique, they were able to endure the rigors of being shipwrecked until they were rescued . . . after twenty-four days at sea.

Eddie Rickenbacker lived many years beyond that ordeal, but he never forgot the unintentional sacrifice of that life-saving seagull. And he never stopped saying thank you. That's why every Friday night he walked to the end of the pier with a bucket full of shrimp and a heart full of gratitude.[19]

If the world got close enough to us, would they hear our gratitude to the God who saved us from the record of our vile sin and the wreckage of a meaningless life and a horrible future?

What an incentive to leave our old life and pursue a new one! Go out there and say with Paul and those remarkable Christians on the island of Crete, "Lord, we remember:

- We remember who we used to be—thank You!
- We remember where we were headed—thank You!
- We remember why we needed a Savior—thank You!

⁴But when the kindness of God our Savior and His love for mankind appeared, ⁵He saved us, not on the basis of deeds which we have done in righteousness, but according to His mercy, by the washing of regeneration and renewing by the Holy Spirit, ⁶whom He poured out upon us richly through Jesus Christ our Savior, ⁷so that being justified by His grace we would be made heirs according to the hope of eternal life.

–Titus 3:4–7

CHAPTER TWENTY-ONE

AMBUSHED BY GOODNESS

Titus 3:4–7

DEBTORS, ALL

An unforgettable event occurred in the lives of three graduating seniors at Azusa Pacific University, in Southern California:

A special gathering of alumni, new faculty, and board members had been convened. John Wallace, the president of the university, invited three graduates, as well. Upon graduation, those particular students were planning to spend two years serving in India among the Untouchables. The students assumed that they were being invited to the meeting of the university leadership in order to be commissioned and encouraged. They would be. Something else had been planned of which they were unaware. Dr. Wallace called the three students forward and then said, "I have some exciting news for you. Someone you don't know has appreciated what you're planning to do over the next two years as you sacrifice your time and talents to help less fortunate people. These friends of the university have chosen to give gifts to the school in your names and on your behalf." The university president then turned to the first student and said, "On behalf of the donor, you are forgiven your $105,000 debt to this institution—it is now completely paid." The president turned to the second student and said, "And you also are forgiven your debt of $70,000"; and to the third student he said, "You are forgiven your debt of $130,000 to this university, as well." Everyone applauded . . . many wept; especially the three students, stunned by the news of these gifts. They were ambushed by grace—blown away that someone they didn't even know would pay off all their debt.[1]

In many ways, this is what it means to be ambushed by the grace and goodness of God. The only difference is that we didn't sign up for two years in India to become the benefactors of His goodness. In fact, we don't deserve it at all. We are forever in His debt.

But the truth remains: the more we learn about our redemption in Christ, the more we are dumbfounded by the goodness of God.

ONE WORD CHANGES EVERYTHING

We—pirates and rebels at heart—are nothing more than the benefactors of a remarkable gift. We've been ambushed by the grace and goodness of a remarkable Savior.

> But *when the kindness of God our Savior and His love for mankind appeared, He saved us, not on the basis of deeds which we have done in righteousness,* but *according to His mercy, by the washing of regeneration and renewing by the Holy Spirit, whom He poured out upon us richly through Jesus Christ our Savior, so that being justified by His grace we would be made heirs according to the hope of eternal life* (Titus 3:4–7).

That's one long, uninterrupted sentence, and I remind you that it begins with the little contrastive conjunction **but**.

That conjunction changes everything.

We've already learned that whenever we hear **but**, we begin to really tune in to what follows it:

- We really like your resumé and your work experience, **but** . . .

- The buyer agreed your house was worth the price and he really wants it, **but** . . .

- I like you and I think you're a really nice guy, **but** . . .

Forget what came in front of that conjunction—it's what follows that matters.

Charles Hughes served as Secretary of State in 1921 under President Harding and later as a justice on the Supreme Court. As Secretary of State, he attended a Pan-American conference where he would have to depend on a translator for the Spanish and Portuguese speakers. He wisely instructed his translator, "While a running translation is important to me, what I really want you to do is give me every word after the speaker says **but**—because that may change everything."[2]

Paul is saying that we have nothing to offer God beyond our sinful lives, **but** . . . there's something that changes everything.

A REMARKABLE REDEEMER

*But when the **kindness** of God our Savior and His **love** for mankind appeared, He saved us* (Titus 3:4–5a).

Paul takes special note of God's **kindness** and **love. Kindness** uniquely appears in the letters of the Apostle Paul. It refers to the goodness of God. It can actually be thought of in terms of generosity.[3]

And it's not a surprise that the next noun used as a subject in the clause is **love.** Both are remarkable gifts from a remarkable Redeemer. Paul uses a compound word here for **love,** combining *philia* (love) and *anthropos* (man)—*to love mankind. Philanthropia* is where we get our transliterated word philanthropy.[4]

Mankind has always been highly impressed by philanthropy—acts of **kindness** toward mankind. In fact, to give away something we could keep for ourselves is something even the ancient Greeks highly valued; it was considered one of the highest virtues ever demonstrated toward another.[5]

Salvation is actually the philanthropy of God's goodness and grace.

Perhaps you've read of the pact made by several billionaires to give away half of their fortunes to different causes while they are still alive. One man promised to give away half of his personal fortune—some thirty billion dollars. Of course, he retained the remaining thirty billion and change—to muddle through. Truthfully, I admire that decision; whether he knows it or not, he is reflecting the law of God written on his heart.

God is the *ultimate* philanthropist. He doesn't just give away *some* of His fortune—gold is nothing more than asphalt to Him . . . future roads and sidewalks—He gave the *life* of His only Son. The ultimate act of philanthropy would be to sacrifice our life for another.

In his commentary on Ephesians, John Phillips included an incident that happened when he visited a friend:

> My friend's daughter was an alcoholic and while I was visiting in the home one day, the daughter was delivered to the door. She had consumed nearly an entire bottle of whiskey. Her temper was flaming and abusive. Her face was flushed, her manner belligerent, her actions violent. I looked at the picture of the young, unspoiled girl that still hung on the wall of her parents' home. I pitied her with all my heart for the terrible shipwreck she had made of her life and for her slavery to such a cruel and relentless tyrant. Yet I watched as her father took her gently by the arm, ignoring her abusive [language]. He steered her unsteady footsteps outside to his car. He carefully settled her in, his face drawn and his eyes filled with pain. He patiently strapped her into the seatbelt, then drove her home and put her to bed. I pitied her . . . but he *loved* her.[6]

Multiply that young woman's slavery and wretchedness and abusiveness by ten thousand and the love of that father by infinity and you have the love of our Redeemer. He did not simply pity us from galaxies away—He *loved* us.

Paul adds that God's love **appeared**—this is a reference to His incarnation when He came to die and settle forever the matter of atonement for sins past, present, and future.

Christ came to our sewer; He moved into our slave quarters; He inhabited our slums. We weren't looking for Him—He came looking for us . . . and He ambushed us by His grace and goodness.

A REMARKABLE REDEMPTION

He saved us, *not on the basis of deeds which we have done in righteousness, but* **according to His mercy** (Titus 3:5a–c).

In the Greek New Testament, the words **not on the basis of deeds** appears first in the sentence to show the emphasis of Paul's statement: literally, **Not from works, He saved us.** Which means true, biblical salvation is not only freely given, but it has a built-in component of humility:

> For by grace you have been saved through faith; and that not of yourselves, it is the gift of God; not as a result of works, **so that no one may boast** (Ephesians 2:8–9).

If we could sew one stitch of righteousness into our garments of eternal splendor, we would spend all eternity admiring that one stitch: "Beautiful robe, huh? Did you see this stitch? *I* did that one."

Think about what we do with our young children. The day is coming to an end and we tell them, "Okay kids, it's time to clean up the playroom . . . get all your toys and put them into the toy box . . . pick up those Cheerios you dropped on the floor, and get all those Legos off the stairs and your tricycle out of the hallway. C'mon . . . hop to it!" We know they'll not be able to get it all done perfectly, but we want them to make the effort. And then after we tuck them in, we go back through the house and take care of everything they didn't do.

A lot of people think that's how God saves us—we do everything we can do and God will appreciate all the help we give Him, and when we're finished, He'll take care of everything else we couldn't do.[7]

But Paul says *apart* from works, He saved us. Nobody's going to run around heaven bragging that they did their fair share and God took care of the rest. Our remarkable redemption was paid in full by Christ Himself—with no help from us. Salvation is a gift we receive, as undeserving sinners, **according to His mercy.** Paul adds this to make sure we get it right. He writes along this same progression to the Ephesians:

> Among them we too all formerly lived in the lusts of our flesh, indulging the desires of the flesh and of the mind, and were by nature children of wrath, even as the rest. **But God** [there it

is again], *being rich in* **mercy**, *because of His great love with which He loved us, even when we were dead in our transgressions, made us alive together with Christ (by grace you have been* **saved***)* (Ephesians 2:3–5).

It can't be any clearer than that! Christianity doesn't give us room to gloat, but it leaves us plenty of room to be grateful.

A REMARKABLE RECONSTRUCTION

By the washing *of regeneration and renewing* **by the Holy Spirit** *whom He poured out upon us richly through Jesus Christ our Savior, so that being justified by His grace we would be made heirs* (Titus 3:5d–7a).

Paul's use of the phrase **By the** washing *of regeneration* has led many to believe that the ordinance of baptism is in view. A lot of ink has been spilled over the viewpoint that a person can't be saved until they've been baptized. And they roll out this text as one of their favorite supports of that position. Unfortunately for them, all one needs to do is keep reading. The church—or pastor—isn't doing the baptizing. Paul writes, **By the** washing *of regeneration and renewing* by the Holy Spirit.

Paul is referring to the internal, spiritual cleansing of the heart at the moment of regeneration. Certainly water baptism depicts outwardly what has already happened inwardly. In truth—and I'll take up the argument of those who believe in baptismal regeneration, for just a moment—in the mind of the apostles and the early Church, there was no such thing as a non-baptized believer. One was so closely linked to the other that they couldn't imagine one without the other.

Why would anybody follow Jesus Christ and not want to publically identify through the ordinance He instituted whereby the disciple displays his belief in Christ's death, burial, and resurrection?

Some say, "But I get nervous in front of a crowd. I don't like speaking in public. I really don't want to be seen with my hair plastered to my head. What if water gets up my nose?"

The physical demonstration of **washing**, which illustrates the internal spiritual act of cleansing, is a wonderful testimony, indeed. And every excuse should be set aside in obedience to Christ's clear command.

However, let's not make it part of the definition of regeneration. If we do, we've added something *we do* for God in order to be saved—which according to the Bible is something *Christ does* for us.

And keep in mind that if someone must be baptized in order to ratify their salvation, we are asking them to depend on someone else. What if the pastor forgets to baptize you? What if the water pipes are frozen? What if the drain is opened and the baptismal tank empties? What if the person doesn't make it to the church? Will their eternal hell be the consequence of these unfortunate circumstances?

In all seriousness, the text explains itself beyond question. In fact, the word Paul uses here for **washing** is not *baptizo* but *loutron*. It's a reference to taking a bath—the kind we take on Saturday night, whether we need it or not. It's a complete bath.

Salvation is an admission of how dirty we are . . . we don't need a quick shower, a little **washing**—we need a full bath in Christ's regenerative power.

When our twins were around four years old, we lived in a house with a wood-burning fireplace. Out behind the house next to our deck, there was a little iron door about two feet from the ground that could be opened, and the ashes from the chimney could be shoveled out. Our boys found that little door, and what do you think they did? Kept it closed and tidy? They considered it an open door from God.

It was summertime, but I hadn't cleaned it out from the previous winter, allowing my boys to discover its treasure. They threw the ashes into the air . . . they shoveled ashes all over each other . . . they played in it. I mean, how much fun can two little guys have? When my wife asked me to call the kids in for supper, I stepped out onto the deck and saw two aliens from outer space—large eyes peered up at me from layers of ash. They were covered from head to toe.

I called to Marsha to come out on the deck—I wanted her to see the boys doing something I hadn't put them up to. When she saw them, she said, "What are we going to do?" My first thought was adoption. Then she said, "They can't come in the house like that." I replied, "Let me take care of it." I grabbed the garden hose and sprayed them, then had them take off their clothes—all the way down to their Superman underwear—and I hosed them down from head to toe and back again. The twins thought it was a blast . . . and they were finally clean.

That's the idea behind **washing** (*loutron*). In fact, the only other time this word **washing** appears in the New Testament is when Paul uses it to refer to taking a bath in the water of the Word *(Ephesians 5:26)*.[8]

Paul isn't referring to the public ordinance of baptism, he's referring to the deep cleansing, regenerating work of the Holy Spirit who effectively uses the truth of the Word of God to hose us completely down.

This verse contains three key doctrinal words.

Regeneration

By the washing of regeneration (Titus 3:5d).

Regeneration literally means to have *another* birth. This is what Jesus Christ referred to in *John 3* as being *born again*. It is a compound of *palin* (*again*) and *genesis* (*beginnings*).[9] The Book of Genesis simply means the Book of Beginnings.

Paul is referring here to a brand-new beginning . . . a new birth. The believer has had one birth already—it was physical; now, Paul says, by means of the Holy Spirit, we have experienced a second birth—which is spiritual. Salvation is the moment of our new birth. To get into heaven, we have to be born, as it were, twice.

No wonder Satan has counterfeited this concept, going all the way back in Old Testament days. He copied the idea of animal sacrifice and atonement and good works and spiritual death and resurrection long before Paul ever delivered the genuine Gospel of a new birth.

The heart of man, energized and educated by the deceiver of mankind—Satan—has created a variety of beliefs and exercises that tie into some truth found in the Gospel. In this way, Satan counterfeits and confuses the genuine item of **regeneration**.

For instance, one mystery religion required its followers to go through a ceremony where they dug a pit (a symbolic grave), and over the pit they placed wooden beams in a lattice formation. They then killed a bull and dripped the blood of the bull through the lattice, onto the person below who was ceremonially dying. The blood gave him new life—a new birth—and he was brought up out of the grave. Further, following this event, they gave the initiate a drink of milk to signify that he was a newborn babe.

The Stoics adopted this word **regeneration** and used it to refer to Earth, which they believed was thoroughly burned by God every 3,000 years, then given a new birth.[10]

All of these mystery religions and cults illustrate the Apostle Paul's characterization of *always learning and never able to come to the knowledge of the truth* (2 Timothy 3:7).

God alone created the heavens and the earth, and God alone is the One who creates spiritual life:

> *For by Him all things were created, both in the heavens and on earth, visible and invisible, whether thrones or dominions or rulers or authorities—all things have been created through Him and for Him* (Colossians 1:16).

> *Therefore, if any man be in Christ, he is a new creature* (2 Corinthians 5:17a).

According to the Apostle Paul, **regeneration** is not the turning over of a new leaf or a mystical rite for initiates; it is the birth of a new life by means of the Holy Spirit, and it happens to all who've come by faith to Christ alone.

Renewal

By the . . . renewing by the Holy Spirit (Titus 3:5e).

There is a difference between regeneration and renewal:

- Regeneration takes place in a moment in time—**renewing** is a lifetime process.

- Regeneration is a once-in-a-lifetime spiritual bath—**renewing** is a daily shower.

Paul writes to the Corinthians that the inward man is renewed day by day *(2 Corinthians 4:16)*. He uses the same word when writing to the Romans:

> *And do not be conformed to this world, but be transformed by the **renewing** of your mind* (Romans 12:2a).

This is the ongoing activity of surrender to the Holy Spirit, who uses the Word to daily cleanse our minds, hearts, and lives.

Justification

But when the kindness of God our Savior and His love for mankind appeared, He saved us, not on the basis of deeds which we have done in righteousness, but according to His mercy, By the washing of regeneration and renewing by the Holy Spirit whom He poured out upon us richly through Jesus Christ our Savior . . . being justified by His grace (Titus 3:4–7*a*).

In this one sentence from the Apostle Paul, we clearly see the distinctive presence of the Trinity. If anyone asks for a text revealing the Trinity, here's a great one. We have **God our Savior**, then **the Holy Spirit**, and then **Jesus Christ**.

This is also a wonderful verse on the equality of Jesus Christ with God the Father. Notice how Paul refers to **God** as **our Savior**—a reference to God the Father—and moments later refers to **Jesus Christ** as **our Savior**.

Which is it? Is God the Father our Savior or is Jesus Christ our Savior? And while we're at it, we're told that the agent involved in the act of regeneration is the **Holy Spirit**—so is He our Savior, too?

The answer is *yes*, *yes*, and *yes*. Salvation is the perfect work of cooperation between God the Father, God the Son, and God the Holy Spirit.

Now . . . back to this idea of being **justified**. Paul describes it here as that part of the transaction of our new birth where God the Judge declares us to be righteous. The righteousness of Christ is imputed (credited) to our account, and the atonement of Christ is fully sufficient to pay for the record of sins we've committed against Him. To be **justified** is when God the Father, acting as the Judge sitting on the bench with all the evidence brought before Him, is unable to locate any record of sin against us. He strikes the desk with his gavel and says to us, "**Justified!**"

This means the believer is more than acquitted. It means that the believer has every single sinful thought and deed completely purged from his biography. His record is as spotless as the righteousness of Christ.

Several years ago, I was driving through a small town, going six miles an hour faster than I should have been. It was a borrowed vehicle, and the wheels were larger than the original factory wheels, which caused the calibration of the speedometer to be off (that's my story, and I'm sticking to it).

Instead of going 70, I was doing 76—which was really bad because I had entered a township where the speed limit had just dropped to 55 miles per hour.

Obviously I was in trouble, traveling 21 miles over the speed limit. The police officer kindly made an appointment for me with a local judge. As I stood in line that afternoon with all the other race car drivers, the courtroom resembled a classroom—a small room where the judge sat at a folding table with a stack of papers on top.

My name was called, he asked me how fast I had been driving, and I told him. He scribbled something on his notepad and then looked up at me and said, "Sir, I am doing you quite a favor." Now I hadn't even said anything. I didn't know what he was doing at the time. He handed me a piece of paper, and again said, "I'm doing you a *big* favor." I said, "Thank you, sir" and walked toward the door. As I opened the door, he hollered after me: "*I am doing you a big favor!*"

I would later learn that he gave me a "prayer for judgment"—a judicial action that treated my offense as if it never happened. All I had to do was pay the fine. Let me say this: as wonderful as that was, doing me a *big favor* and declaring me *righteous* are two entirely different things—even a prayer for judgment can't compare.

In order for that judge to justify me—in the biblical sense of the word— he would have said, "You've committed a crime, but I'm going to take this police report, erase your name, and write my name in your place. I'll pay your fine and add the penalty to my record. You can have my spotless driving record because I've never broken the law."

This is how Paul defined justification when he wrote to the Colossian believers:

> *When you were dead in your transgressions . . . He* [God the Judge] *made you alive together with Him, having forgiven us all our transgressions, having canceled out the certificate of debt, consisting of decrees against us* [our criminal history] *and He has taken it out of the way . . .* [How?] *having nailed it to the cross* (Colossians 2:13–14).

In other words, God switched the names on the rap sheet. Christ's name was written at the top of the ledger of all our sins. Jesus Christ became the condemned criminal and we became *perfect* law keepers with His *perfect* record attributed to our name:

- He took our vileness and gave us His virtue.

- He took our perversion and gave us His purity.

- He took our record of sin and gave us His record of sinlessness.

This is what is means to be **justified**.

A REMARKABLE REWARD

[S]*o that being justified by His grace we would be made* **heirs** *according to the hope of eternal life* (Titus 3:7).

The aorist tense indicates that this inheritance is already in our possession—bestowed at the moment of regeneration—to be experienced fully and literally in the future. On that date in His kingdom, we will begin to experience the amazing benefits of our kinship to our Father—we will become royal **heirs** of God.

We're not just citizens of the coming [Kingdom] of God, we are co-owners. How's that for grace?![11]

The songwriter penned these lyrics:

> *I once was lost in darkest night,*
> *Yet thought I knew the way.*
> *The sin that promised joy and life*
> *Had led me to the grave.*
> *I had no hope that You would own*
> *A rebel to Your will.*
> *And if You had not loved me first*
> *I would refuse You still.*
>
> *But as I ran my hell-bound race*
> *Indifferent to the cost,*
> *You looked upon my helpless state*
> *And led me to the cross.*
> *And I beheld God's love displayed—*

You suffered in my place.
You bore the wrath reserved for me;
Now all I know is grace.

Hallelujah! All I have is Christ.
Hallelujah! Jesus is my life.[12]

This is the song of those who've been ambushed by goodness and grace.

This is a trustworthy statement; and concerning these things I want you to speak confidently, so that those who have believed God will be careful to engage in good deeds. These things are good and profitable for men.

–Titus 3:8

CHAPTER TWENTY-TWO

BRINGING GOD TO LIFE

Titus 3:8

IS GOD FOR REAL?

Agroup of Americans on a business trip to Russia was shown a building that had been retrofitted during the last century. The typical multicolored onion-shaped turrets and domes signified that it was a church building, and the lobby was similar to any American vestibule, with doors leading into the sanctuary. When the doors were opened, they were absolutely astonished at an unexpected sight. Stacked from floor to ceiling were rows upon rows of chicken coops, all filled with cackling hens.

When asked the reason, the guide made a sweeping gesture around the sanctuary and said with great pride, "Our church building is the finest hatchery in the region." And then he looked at his American guests and sarcastically added, "God is not *real* . . . chickens are."

That viewpoint isn't isolated to other countries. The average person in America today isn't convinced that the God of the Bible is *real*. Random interviews and surveys a few years ago revealed that only seventy-three percent of Americans are convinced that God exists.[1] What used to be an exclamation point is now a question mark.

Jobs are real, houses are real, family is real, suffering is real, money is real, life is real . . . chickens are real—but . . . God?

This isn't a new problem. Here's an editorial comment from the *Atlantic Journal*:

> The world is too big for us . . . too much is going on . . . too
> many crimes . . . too much violence and too much devotion
> to entertainment. Try as you will, you get behind in the race,
> in spite of yourself. It's an incessant strain to keep pace and
> still, you lose ground. Science empties its discoveries on you
> so fast that you stagger beneath them in bewilderment; the
> political world is news seen so rapidly you're out of breath
> trying to keep up with who's in and who's out. Everything
> is high pressure. Human nature cannot endure much more.

And to think that was written on June 16, 1833!

How are we to communicate to our twenty-first century generation that God is real? That Jesus Christ is a safe harbor; that He is the essence of genuine hope; that His Gospel is real and His grace is available?

God has actually left the advertisement campaign to Christians. In a nutshell, here's how we do it: we who have received grace become disseminators . . . distributors of grace.

ADVERTISING A TRULY RELIABLE GOSPEL

This is a trustworthy statement; and concerning these things I want you to* speak confidently, *so that those who have* believed *God will be careful to engage in good deeds.* These things *are good and profitable for men (Titus 3:8).

Paul is now delivering summary statements. He's telling the believers on Crete—and every believer, to this day—that we are, first of all, advertising a Gospel that is truly reliable.

We are to **speak confidently** about **these things**. What is Paul referring to? It is the previous verse—that long sentence which began in *Titus 3:4* and extends through *Titus 3:7*—which encourages remarkable Christians to communicate with confidence the following:

- the truths of God's love and kindness *(v. 4)*;

- faith in Christ alone, apart from good deeds, saves us *(v. 5)*;

- God's Spirit cleaned us up with a complete bath of redemption *(v. 5)*;

- the Holy Spirit is in the process of renewing us day by day *(v. 5)*;
- Jesus Christ—equal to God the Father—is sufficient to save us *(v. 6)*;
- Christ has replaced our sin with His righteousness and all charges brought against us have been thrown out of court *(v. 7)*;
- He graciously made us co-owners of the coming kingdom *(v. 7)*.

The believer doesn't need to beat around the proverbial bush—this isn't wishful thinking or folklore or make believe or a string of old wives tales—this is the Gospel and it is reliable truth from God."[2] Communicate these things with confidence!

And by the way, it was to start with Titus. Notice Paul's personal appeal: *I want you to* **speak confidently** (Titus 3:8*b*). It's possible Titus was holding back. Now I don't know if he was hesitating in the face of cultural opposition or, perhaps, disgruntled pushback in the churches. Paul hinted at this potential hesitation:

> *These things speak and exhort and reprove with all authority. Let no one disregard you* (Titus 2:15).

Like a coach on the sidelines as time is running out, he yells in the ear of his quarterback, "Here's what I want you to do." There's no doubting the play and there's no mistaking the passion, either. Paul says, "Listen, Titus, I know you're young and the culture is evil and the Church might even be resisting these truths, but stay in the game . . . and don't hold back."

Swindoll, in his new *Insights* series on the Book of Titus, delivers his commentary on this text:

> There were so many voices of error on the island of Crete. The same is true everywhere; this is, after all, the primary purpose of a pastor: he is responsible to proclaim grace clearly and emphatically. He cannot allow reluctance to delay him, he must not allow hesitation to interrupt him, and he should not be apologetic. If a pastor stands on the authority of God's Word, he can afford to be bold.[3]

For those of us who preach or teach the Word of God, we've felt the temptation of holding back . . . of not addressing a certain subject . . . of skipping over a few verses and maybe, even, avoiding entire chapters. We know what it's like to stare down the subtle desire to be pleasing to men rather than pleasing to God.

Paul uses the present tense in this challenge; it could be translated this way: *Keep on repeating these things with confidence.*

Paul began with the same thought in ***Titus 3:1***. "**Remind** them, Titus . . . **remind** them . . . and **remind** them again—you need it, and so does the flock. They may not be listening as well as they should."

Pastors, especially, appreciate the following dilemma:

> Three friends—a lawyer, a doctor, and a pastor—went deer hunting. As they were going into the woods, a large buck stepped out of the foliage. It froze and all three men simultaneously raised their rifles and fired. Immediately the buck dropped to the ground and the men ran to it. It was dead, all right, but they couldn't determine whose shot had actually killed the deer. A heated debate ensued, each man claiming his shot had hit the mark. A few minutes later, a game warden came by and asked what all the commotion was about. The doctor told him that he was debating with his friends, the lawyer and the pastor, who actually shot the buck. The officer bent down and after just a few seconds stood up and said, "The preacher shot the buck." "The preacher? How can you be so sure?" The officer said, "Easy . . . the bullet went in one ear and out the other."[4]

The truth is that both the pastor and the flock are prone to forget . . . and Paul wants pastors and parishioners, elders and members to speak, to listen, and to learn these truths over and over again.

Our world must hear these truths from *all* of us:

- We are God's advertisement plan in the community.
- We are His billboard along the interstate of life.
- We are His PowerPoint in the executive suite and classroom.
- We are Exhibit A in the defense of the Gospel.

We are communicating a Gospel that is totally reliable. We can speak with confidence **these things** which Paul has delivered in this letter.

SURRENDERING TO
A TRULY PERSONAL GOD

Let's just make sure we know who we're talking to. Paul specifically identifies *those who have* **believed** *God*. This is Paul's primary audience.

The perfect tense of this verb points to a specific time in their past—the specific time when they were born again . . . when they believed in God their Savior.[5] They've come to know God through Christ, personally. They **believed** at some point in the past, and they are viewed here as those who continue in what they've **believed**.

God is not some life force somewhere out there. He didn't wind up the universe and now watches us from a distance. That might have been a hit song in the past, but God is not watching us from afar. He is personal—so personal that we can place our faith in Him, asking Him to save us.

Paul is saying, "I'm going to call you to a lifestyle of remarkable Christianity, but before I do, let me just clarify who I'm talking to: I'm writing to those who personally know Him, *those who have* **believed** *God*.

And that's critical; the individual Christian who lives with the conviction that God is truly alive and personally involved is the kind of Christian who will be most effective in someone else's life. And that's exactly where Paul is headed.

ENGAGING IN TRULY GOOD DEEDS

Paul has already made it clear that a person isn't saved by means of **good deeds** *(Titus 3:5)*. We don't do **good deeds** to go to heaven. We do them because we're on our way to heaven and we want to take others with us—and **good deeds** get their attention.

This is the advertising campaign for Christianity, demonstrated by *those who have* **believed** *God*.

John Calvin put it this way: we are saved by faith alone, but faith that saves us is never *alone*.[6] That's why Paul saturated this letter with the concept of living out the faith through **good deeds**:

- *be an example of* **good deeds** (Titus 2:7);
- *a people . . . zealous for* **good deeds** (Titus 2:14);
- *be ready for every* **good deed** (Titus 3:1);

- *be careful to engage in* **good deeds** (Titus 3:8);
- *learn to engage in* **good deeds** *to meet pressing needs* (Titus 3:14).

There's more to Christianity than minding our doctrinal p's and q's. Remarkable Christianity isn't just an education in good doctrine—it is the application of good doctrine through **good deeds**.

The kindness and grace of God was never meant to be kept to ourselves . . . we're to open a franchise and become a distributor of kindness and grace to our world.

This, by the way, reflects the character of the Savior we've surrendered our lives to; Luke's Gospel reminds us that our Lord *Himself is kind to ungrateful and evil men* (Luke 6:35).

Paul urges us to **be careful** *to* **engage** *in good deeds* (Titus 3:8*d*). This is the only time in the New Testament that this verb **be careful** appears. It means to think about . . . to be intent upon.[7]

In other words, be intentional; which implies being creative and thorough in our investigation of how and what to do in the form of **good deeds**.

Be careful is in the present tense, which means that Paul is referring not just to a singular isolated good deed but to a way of life. This is to be our mindset.

You know anybody like that? They just seem to live to help; doing something good for someone else is second nature. They're the first ones to take on the extra assignment . . . the distasteful chore—they'll get their hands dirty without complaint. They literally look for good things to do, and they're the exception to the rule. People at school know who they are; the football team knows which players are; the corporate office knows the employees who are. In every facet of life, these are the people who are ready to **engage**.

And Paul is writing here: if anybody's going to be like that, it ought to be the Christian. The word he uses for **engage** is a word that refers to initiative. The person modeling this mentality will make an exceptional mark somewhere, somehow, whether in simple things, mundane duties, behind-the-scene service, or the public square.

INITIATING A TRULY
EXCEPTIONAL LIFESTYLE

Christians who are initiating this lifestyle are truly remarkable. The benefit they are to people and ministry will be like a pebble thrown into a pond, the concentric ripples moving outward long after the first contact.

So it would seem that the one place which would be immediately benefited by Christians and their good deeds would be the Church. Paul wrote:

> [L]*et us do good to all people, and especially those who are of the* **household of the faith** (Galatians 6:10).

If we are people of creativity and energy and willingness and initiative, the first place that benefits is the place we call our **household of the faith**. *That* house will be filled with people eager to do good deeds.

There is a church somewhere that needs you; their efforts are missing your hands and your heart. It's probably the church you already attend. But if they don't need you, find a church that does, roll up your sleeves, and get to work.

As one author put it, stop dating the church. Find one and settle down. You'll never find a perfect one. You used to date that guy or girl and then you got married. Is your spouse perfect? Are you perfect? No, but you stay married.

It's an unfortunate reality that the average church struggles with twenty percent of the people doing eighty percent of the work. Frankly, no matter how unified a church, there is always the need for more volunteers. Find that place where you can do good deeds to all men and especially those of the **household of the faith**. That's God's design. Paul writes that we should *be ready for every good deed* (Titus 3:1*b*).

And watch what might happen when you engage in good deeds in your own personal household, in your immediate **household of the faith**, and in the greater body of Christ as God gives you opportunity.

As a missionary kid, I remember people handing my dad some cash and half-jokingly, half-seriously saying, "Don't tell my pastor about this; he won't be too happy it wasn't given to the church." Yes, there are some churches where the concentric circles become squares because they never extend beyond their four walls.

My three brothers and I spent time each summer on deputation with our missionary parents, traveling up north to churches and individuals who supported our family in the work. We always went through Iowa and stayed in the home of a faithful couple named Mr. and Mrs. Peeper. I'll never forget their name; when we pulled into their driveway, our mother would give us a little lecture not to make fun of their name—she knew us well.

We actually loved going there, because no matter when we arrived, Mrs. Peeper was ready to serve us homemade sourdough cinnamon rolls with extra icing. But first we'd have to sing. So we four boys would sit on the couch, our feet dangling off the edge, and sing some Sunday school choruses like this one:

Why worry, when you can pray?
Trust Jesus, He'll be your stay.
Don't be a doubting Thomas,
Rest fully on His promise.
Why worry, worry, worry, worry
When you can pray? [8]

Yes, I sang for cinnamon rolls . . . you would have, too!

Once our car broke down in Iowa, and the Peepers drove all the way out to get us and bring us back while the car was being repaired. They weren't on a church staff; they weren't former missionaries or parachurch leaders. They were farmers . . . ready to engage in good deeds, especially to the wider **household of the faith**.

The drama of grace and truth is not like a Broadway play where we sit out in the audience and watch. Rather, we get out of our seats and put on a costume and climb up on stage and play a role in the drama [of grace] as God directs us all.[9]

But I want you to notice what Paul says here, particularly to Titus—it goes way beyond our immediate family, our local church family, and even beyond the church family at large:

> ***These things*** [these good deeds] ***are good and profitable for men*** (Titus 3:8*b*).

Paul is reminding us that the demonstration of good deeds will be profitable to *mankind*—not just for the religious elite; not just for those who are converted; not just for people we know; not just for people who are in church—but to people, in general.[10]

During the days of Paul, infanticide was epidemic. Children were left exposed to die; infant girls were especially at risk of being cast aside. Christians began providing care for these abandoned children. One second-century Christian was eventually martyred by the Romans for supporting and protecting a number of deformed and crippled children who had been saved from death after failed abortions and exposure. It was such an affront to Roman customs—violating their cultural norms—bringing down guilt on their heads. There was no recourse but to put him to death.[11]

Seneca, a leading Roman philosopher, communicated the majority opinion when he wrote these tragic words: "We drown children who at birth are weakly and abnormal." Civilization has arrived at that place once again, this time with medical sophistication and prenatal science but the same ethical position as those living on the island of Crete.

Today, couples expecting babies with genetic defects are heavily pressured to end that life. The womb is no longer a safe sanctuary for the imperfect or unwanted.

Christianity views life as precious, no matter how difficult or disabled.

Dionysius, a church leader in the third century, wrote of the plague that swept through Alexandria in AD 250, "The citizens thrust aside anyone who began to be sick, and kept aloof even from their dearest friends, and cast the sufferers out upon the public roads half dead and then left them unburied, treating them with contempt when they died."

How different was the behavior of the Christian? Dionysius continued, "Believers did not spare themselves, but kept by each other, and visited the sick without thought of their own peril, and treated them for their healing, drawing upon themselves their neighbor's diseases, and willingly taking over to their own persons the sufferings of those around them."

The reality of Christianity was demonstrated through sacrificial good deeds.

ARE YOU FOR REAL?

Recently, a *New York Times* editorialist wrote a column remarking on the work of evangelical Christians. Although he was not a Christian, he noted:

In reporting on poverty, disease and oppression, evangelicals are disproportionately likely to donate their income, go to the front lines, at home or abroad, in the battles against hunger, malaria, prison rape, human trafficking, or genocide, and some of the bravest people you meet are these Christians who truly live their faith. I'm not particularly religious myself, but I stand in awe of those I've seen risking their lives in this way.[12]

What an advertisement of the Gospel of grace. We who have received mercy and grace effectively bring God to life before the watching world.

The world says labor is demeaning—the Christian says labor is honorable, and I'll go the extra mile.

The world says children are a burden—the Christian says children are a blessing from the Lord.

The world says climb over people on your way to the top—the Christian says serving others is what truly matters.

The world says they've never seen God—the Christian says, "I can show you what He looks like" . . . and then engages in good deeds that are excellent and profitable to all mankind.

And the world takes note of our good deeds. When they ask us *why*, we tell them about our Gospel and our Savior. Then some of them join us in bringing glory to God.

A Christian journal ran an online article about a Saturday morning effort by one church to revitalize a particular neighborhood near the downtown area of Compton, California:

All the volunteers—nearly fifty in all—were wearing their bright yellow shirts as they streamed out of the site, getting ready to head off to lunch after finishing their renovation project on an old house. One guy was six or eight houses away when he passed a married couple working in their own yard. He paused to compliment the woman on her rose bushes and she noticed his yellow shirt. She asked what they were doing up the street and was told that several churches were working together to serve the city. Her husband had been weed-whacking the other side of the front yard. But when he noticed the stranger, he turned off his trimmer, set it down, and walked toward him. He nodded approvingly toward the renovated house and then looked at the volunteer and said, "I love your heart . . . where can I get a heart like yours?"[13]

Standing there on the edge of the yard, the man was then able to share with them the Gospel of Jesus Christ, explaining that his heart merely reflected God's heart of goodness and kindness.

The greatest *obstacle* to Christianity is a Christian who will not live out his faith. The greatest *advertisement* for Christianity is a Christian who brings faith to life.

The world is fairly convinced that houses are real and money is real; heartache is real and jobs are real. Even chickens are real—you can get real eggs—but God? Maybe He's not for real.

But then a genuine Christian comes along and:

- advertises a reliable Gospel;
- surrenders to a personal God;
- engages in good deeds;
- initiates an exceptional lifestyle.

Why not start something new this week? Somebody will probably be watching . . . and for the first time in their lives, they just might effectively see God brought to life!

But avoid foolish controversies and genealogies and strife and disputes about the Law, for they are unprofitable and worthless.

–Titus 3:9

CHAPTER TWENTY-THREE

LEARNING THE ART OF REFUSAL

Titus 3:9

WHAT'S ON YOUR TRAY?

Buzzards and eagles are similar yet very different. They're both birds; they both soar on the wind; they both have powerful wings and sharp vision. What makes them different is the way they view life below . . . what they focus on . . . what attracts their attention.

To a large degree, whatever Christians are interested in—or not interested in—will determine their spiritual focus and that, by and large, will determine the quality of their lives.

If there's one thing we as believers need to cultivate, it's the spiritual art of refusal: what to pursue and what to ignore.

The Bible refers to it as developing the ability to determine right from wrong *(Hebrews 5:14).*

I can remember as a kid having the rare experience of going out to eat at a local cafeteria. Every time I went, I had the same problem: I wanted more than I could handle.

At the front of the line, the pasta salad looked good, so I'd take some; farther down, the Jell-O salad appealed to me, so I'd take that, too. At least two different kinds of bread (banana bread and sourdough rolls), plus main courses of lasagna and fish were added to my tray, along with those potatoes soaking in butter—besides, I needed a vegetable.

When I finally arrived at the dessert section, how could I decide between chocolate cake, banana pudding, and butterscotch cookies? I took some of each. My meal was a disaster waiting to end in a stomachache, leaving half a tray of food uneaten.

Learning the art of refusal is critical, not only in a cafeteria line but in the Christian life. Just as a young person matures in understanding what to pick and choose regarding physical food, the believer must learn to select his spiritual food—the influences in his life that will make him spiritually healthy.

Let me put it another way: there are just some things in life we really need to learn how to ignore. They're going to distract us from the kind of spiritual growth we need to develop and the kind of life we need to live.

That's exactly what the Apostle Paul is effectively reinforcing in **Titus 3**, where he tells the churches they need to learn the spiritual art of refusal.

In fact, Paul will use the negative to spell out four distractions that *we need to ignore.* They may look interesting . . . they may even seem appealing, but don't put them on your tray—you'll end up with a spiritual stomachache, or worse.

AVOIDING DISTRACTIONS

Let's grab our silverware as we pick up the verse from our previous chapter:

> *This is a trustworthy statement; and concerning these things I want you to speak confidently; so that those who have believed God will be careful to engage in good deeds. These things are good and profitable for men* [or for mankind in general] (Titus 3:8).

We're not ready to make our selections yet because there's an exception:

> **But avoid *foolish controversies, and genealogies and strife and disputes about the Law, for* [note this difference] *they* are unprofitable *and* worthless** (Titus 3:9).

He doesn't say they are unpopular. On the contrary, they were very popular. For that reason, he doesn't want to end his letter to Titus without delivering this warning. Paul lists four distractions that are **unprofitable** and **worthless**. They are not good for you. Don't put them on your tray.

Avoid: to shun; to turn oneself around and literally turn your face away.[1] In other words, while everybody else is captivated, while everybody else is digging in, we turn our face and heart away. And the present tense for this verb means we're going to have to avoid this stuff over and over again.

Foolish Controversies

***But avoid* foolish controversies** (Titus 3:9*a*).

What's Paul talking about? The word he uses for **foolish** is *moras*, which gives us the word *moron*. We get our word *moronic* from this adjective.[2]

The word for **controversies** refers to searching or investigating things that have no basis . . . no substantive meaning. They are merely speculations that occupy the mind without any ability to resolve them. They are fascinating conjectures that waste our time and cause us to get into heated debates and **controversies**.

In chapter one, Paul has already warned Titus about avoiding Jewish fables—they are fruitless and unprofitable.

I was preaching one summer in the beautiful Adirondack Mountains at the home of Word of Life in upper New York. I took them through the Book of Ruth and made several comments on Jewish culture. A man came up to me and asked, "Have you ever read *Jewish Legends*?" I didn't even know the volume existed. It's a comprehensive copy of rabbinical legends and interpretations related to different passages in the Bible that have been handed down from one generation to another.

I ordered the oversized volume with large pages—nearly 1,000 of them. When preparing this message, I came to this verse that, for the second time, warned the Church of legends. I pulled down that volume and began to read many different interpretations and speculations that could have caused arguments and division. Among them were these regarding Noah and the ark:

- Noah and his family barely survived an attempt by all the people on the outside trying to turn over the ark; God sent lions to surround the ark.

- Noah hung a pearl from the roof inside and had no need of the light of the sun because the pearl glowed.

- One large sea creature didn't want to perish, so Noah tied him to the ark. As he swam alongside, he plowed furrows in the water as wide as a sea.

- As the floodwaters swelled, Og, the king of Bashan, sat on one rung of the ark's ladder and promised Noah that he and his sons would be their slaves forever if he would help them survive. Noah punched a hole in the ark and handed out food to the king every day.

- God first brought every raindrop to a boil in the underworld before He carried it out and dropped it on the human race.[3]

- When Noah sent out the dove, she flew to the gates of the Garden of Eden; God opened the gates for her and she was able to bring back an olive leaf freshly picked from the garden.[4]

This is fascinating reading, isn't it?

No wonder Paul would reinforce to the predominantly Jewish congregations on Crete that they should put these things away; they were unprofitable debates and **controversies**.

In the same way, the Church in every generation can get caught up in debatable interpretations about questionable things. The Bible isn't as clear as we'd like it to be, so we take sides . . . and take shots.

Paul delivered the same warning to Timothy when he wrote:

> [Don't] *pay attention to myths and endless genealogies, which give rise to mere speculation rather than furthering the administration of God which is by faith* (1 Timothy 1:4).

In other words, many things don't accomplish the mission of the Church.

Paul wrote further to Timothy:

> *But refuse foolish and ignorant speculations, knowing that they produce quarrels* (2 Timothy 2:23).

If the Bible isn't clear on it, don't argue over it. The Enemy will be more than happy in a church fight to stay neutral and provide both sides with ammunition, which is why Paul will also write:

> [I] *implore you to walk in a manner worthy of your calling . . . being diligent to preserve the unity of the Spirit in the bond of peace* (Ephesians 4:3).

We have a microcosm of the world in our GreenHouse class for potential new members of the church. I typically begin by finding out their church background and ask them to raise their hand when I get to their denomination—Assemblies of God people can raise both hands if they want to. We've had Anglicans, Catholics, Presbyterians, Methodists, Lutherans, Evangelical Free Church, Missionary Alliance, Bible Church, non-denominational, Independent Baptists, Freewill Baptists, Southern Baptists, really confused Baptists—many coming directly from their former church.

They come from all over the country and many ethnic backgrounds. Some are used to their pastor preaching on topics and issues of the day; others had pastors preaching through a book of the Bible for years at a time—they're my favorite students.

Some of their churches sang hymns with organ and piano; others enjoyed newer choruses led by a band. Some still preferred more singing while others wanted longer sermons . . . okay, I made that part up. Some had liturgy and formality while others never knew what was going to happen next.

Some heard the Gospel every time they went to church; others are hearing it for the very first time. The class is filled with older believers and brand-new believers in the Lord. There are singles, married couples, widows, divorcees, couples with children and couples without. Some homeschool their kids; others send them to public school or Christian school. I usually tell the class that my wife and I did all three—and I can say with authority that none of them worked . . . *perfectly*.

All of this variety is represented in just one new members class. How do we think we'll ever get along? Well, we have an ancient textbook that lays it out.

How are the believers on Crete going to come together? There are descendants of Gentile pirates and historic Jewish converts. Some are poor—some are wealthy; some have no education and one of them, as Paul mentions at the end of this letter, is an attorney.

There are going to be people in these churches on Crete who grew up under the influence of the Essenes, a sect that leaned toward formality and ritual. They ate special meals together only after participating in ceremonial cleansing with water. They're now standing in the pew next to Gentiles who barely bathe, much less desire ritual cleansing. The people have religious traditions and pagan ritualistic memories.

Everybody came to Christ the same way and their sins were washed away . . . but opinions tend to stick.

Paul tells Titus that he'll need to remind them that these opinions—these legends—these superstitions—these dearly held preferences that are neither right nor wrong but definitely divisive—will determine what to leave off the table.

At the end of the verse he summarizes what we can do to determine what to keep to ourselves and what to try to convince others to adopt: **they *are* unprofitable *and* worthless**. In other words, certain issues will not bear spiritual fruit even if you win the argument. Without a clear text of Scripture, the interpretation takes on the authority of whoever is dispensing it—like the rabbis of old who created volumes of opinions about Noah, taught as doctrines.

I shared recently with the GreenHouse class my growing opinion that we ought to wear white clothing. I mean, we're told in Revelation that our future wardrobe will be the triumphant robes of white, indicative of victory in battle. And didn't Solomon seem to indicate that he only wore white clothing (*Ecclesiastes 9:8*)? Of course, the class began to smile . . . obviously, I wasn't wearing white clothes, and they knew me well enough by then to know that I was making a standard out of an opinion. Surely no one should take the issue of white clothing seriously.

I then read a quote to them from a church leader who gathered a following in the second century, and he was *absolutely* serious as he demanded:

> Forsake colored clothing; remove everything in your wardrobe that is not white. No longer sleep on a soft pillow nor take warm baths; if you are sincere about following Christ, never shave your beard, for to shave is an attempt to improve on the work of Him who created us.

In any generation, including ours, there are plenty of controversies that are effectively unfruitful:

- if global warming is make-believe;
- if offshore drilling is a good idea;
- if gun control is a bad thing;

- if border patrol is a waste of money;
- if eating only organic foods proves you're taking care of God's vessel;
- if driving an electric car shows you're taking care of God's planet;
- if feeding your cat and dog expensive food that contains vegetables proves you're a loving pet owner.

We could really begin to hash out political views, parenting styles, worship styles, personal experiences, and an array of preferences and opinions and traditions and secondary issues that so easily elevate to the level of "gospel truth."[5]

The Apostle Paul had been around the block several times . . . he knew that Titus faced this kind of threat to an effective and fruitful ministry among the churches on the island of Crete.

Although the non-saving, secondary, non-doctrinal **controversies** change their name over generations, the Church is not so much defeated as she is distracted by pursuing non-essentials—creating foolish **controversies** that diminish our demonstration of the grace of God and with that, the potential spiritual fruit shrivels up and disappears.

Paul reinforces to Titus, "Develop the art of refusal. You're surrounded by a buffet of opinions and speculations. Stick to the Word—and not some strange interpretation of it, either. Protect the Church from loading up on stuff that will do nothing more than make her unprofitable and worthless."

Genealogies

But avoid . . . genealogies (Titus 3:9*b*).

The Jewish people meticulously investigated and documented their family lines since their inheritances and holdings of land were thus determined.[6] This would have been particularly important to a Jewish audience. Genealogies determined status; ancestral dominance would lead to positions of authority. A favoritism earned by prestigious pedigrees could creep into the churches, as well, if they weren't careful.

It would be especially divisive between Gentiles and Jews. Jews would hold over the Gentiles the fact that they had a connection to the apostles—to Jerusalem. They had a familial connection to the prophets—to the former covenants. Certainly God would place them on the top tier, and the Gentiles would become second-class Christians if genealogies were on par with the Gospel.

Jewish believers could claim some kind of spiritual superiority . . . and that would be the end of that. Talk about a distraction in the Church!

Imagine Titus carrying out his orders from Paul *(Titus 1:5)* and appointing an unconnected, unimpressive, unimposing Gentile man as an elder in the Church and bypassing a distant relative from a noble Jewish clan descending from one of the more important tribes of Israel.

There are certainly a number of reasons Paul told Titus and the churches that their genealogies meant nothing in the dispensation of the Church. The only genealogy that mattered was the one that revealed Jesus had, in fact, descended from David, as had Joseph and Mary. Beyond that, the only genealogical record that will matter for eternity is whether we are related to Jesus Christ by faith and in so believing, *we have become children of God . . . who were born, not of blood, nor of the will of the flesh, nor of the will of man, but of God* (John 1:12–13).

That's the only family tree that we should be concerned about. Paul says, "Start living now, in light of the value of *that* family name."

Strife

But avoid . . . strife (Titus 3:9c).

The word **strife** is a categorical term for arguing and quarreling. The implication here is that the churches were already involved in **strife**.

Jim Cymbala, pastor of The Brooklyn Tabernacle, said in an interview that he challenges the new members who join that church not to speak critically or unkindly about any other member. He made this comment:

> To this day, every time we receive new members, I say much the same thing. That's because I know what most easily destroys the church is not crack cocaine, government oppression, or even a lack of funds; rather it is gossip and slander [this kind of **strife**] that grieves the Spirit of God.[7]

Dwight Pentecost, a longtime professor of Bible Exposition, once told of a church split that was so serious each side filed a lawsuit to dispossess the other of the church. The judge threw it out, and it eventually came to a church court convened by denominational leaders. When the court made its decision and awarded the church property to one of the two factions, the losing side withdrew and formed another church in the area. In the course of the proceedings, the court discovered that the conflict had originally begun at a church dinner when an older church member received a smaller slice of meat than the child seated next to him. And it escalated from there.[8]

Accusations were made . . . sides were taken . . . **strife** began.

Strife is an ever present distraction waiting to happen within any body of believers. Paul knew it could uproot any growth Titus had developed as he established the organization of the Church.

Why? Because **strife**:

- reduces the Gospel to personality conflicts;

- dissolves the unity of the Church into cliques and circles;

- refuses to listen to reason and rides on rumor and emotion;

- invites the Enemy of the Church inside, where he is more than delighted to stir up something God hates.

We're told that God despises seven things, and the seventh is *one who spreads* **strife** *among brothers* (Proverbs 6:19*b*).

Strife literally invites the devil to church. And why would the devil ever need to attack a church if he can join it?

Disputes about the Law

But avoid . . . **disputes about the Law** (Titus 3:9*d*).

The Church was embroiled for decades in how the Law of Moses might relate to her. A major division had been avoided at the Jerusalem Council in *Acts 15*—Peter, James, and Paul led the Church toward a decision of grace that no longer required Gentiles to effectively become Jews to be welcomed into the assembly.

Titus was in the middle of these disputes and needed to stand strong against those who wanted the Church to become just a newer outpost of Judaism. And they were just as serious as Titus was.

In the Greek language the root word for **disputes** is the same root word for *sword*.[9] This word had a nuance of violence; it was used for physical combat and, even, for war. Chuck Swindoll, commenting on this verse, wrote that he was aware of two seminary students who were disciplined by the administration after their quarrel over the doctrine of sanctification escalated into a fistfight.[10] How ironic is that? Arguing over surrendering to the Spirit to the point that punches were thrown.

If you don't think the Church today has the same propensity for disputing as they did on Crete, just do an internet search on "church fights" . . . and then batten down the hatches.

It's painfully obvious that:

The Bride of Christ can act horribly while waiting for her Groom.

The Bride of Christ can trip walking down the aisle.

The Bride of Christ can dirty her shoes.

The Bride of Christ can soil and stain her dress.

The Bride of Christ can embarrass her Groom.

I'd love to think that the churches in the first century and the twenty-first century were above any and all of this.

But Paul writes to them and to us: avoid—shun—turn your face away from—don't get involved in—don't put these things on your tray . . . even though they're in the buffet line and everybody else is partaking.

DON'T. DO. IT.

DEVELOPING A STRATEGY OF REFUSAL

There is a reason for avoiding all of that: *for they are* **unprofitable** *and* **worthless** (Titus 3:9e). Let's break that down into two positive statements that will show us how to develop the art of refusal and elude devastating distractions.

Be Discerning

Stay within biblical boundaries. In other words, if the Bible is clear and vocal, then speak up. If the Bible is for the most part quiet, then we ought to follow suit.

Give our energy to good deeds; remember *these things are . . . profitable* (Titus 3:8c)—while these disputes *are* **unprofitable** (Titus 3:9e).

Whether the dove flew to the Garden of Eden or Solomon only wore white clothes won't add to the profitability of the Gospel and the testimony of Christ.

Be Determined

Keep our focus on the mission. Paul uses a word here at the end of the verse that helps us evaluate what we've been arguing about and dividing over: **worthless**: *powerless, fruitless,* or *useless.*[11] Who have we discipled in all this confusion? Who have we won to the Gospel of Christ?

So here's the test: don't get overheated and all bent out of shape to the point of distraction in discussions and opinions and debates that escalate into arguments and cliques and anger and division. At the end of the day, we have produced no tangible eternal spiritual fruit.

No wonder Paul writes to the Church in Ephesus:

> [W]*ith all humility and gentleness, with patience showing tolerance for one another in love, being diligent* **to preserve the unity of the Spirit in the bond of peace** (Ephesians 4:1–3).

Be discerning; stay focused on the mission that God has given us. Be determined; make sure we walk and think and act within biblical boundaries.

When all is said and done, we are **to preserve the unity of the Spirit in the bond of peace.**

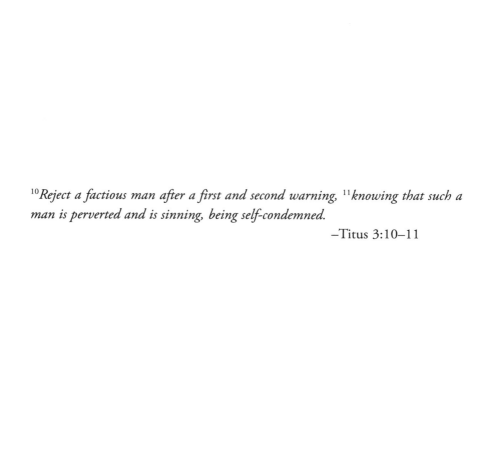

10 Reject a factious man after a first and second warning, 11 knowing that such a man is perverted and is sinning, being self-condemned.

–Titus 3:10–11

CHAPTER TWENTY-FOUR

WARNING: TWO STRIKES AND YOU'RE OUT!

Titus 3:10–11

IGNORING SIGNALS

Nearly one in four Americans will be involved in a lawsuit of some sort during his lifetime. And because our culture is literally inundated with litigation and legal proceedings, it is nearly impossible to buy anything without finding some kind of warning label attached to it.

You can't help but wonder if people don't automatically know this stuff:

- Duraflame© Fire Logs – Caution: Risk of fire.

- sun shield for cars and vans – Do not drive your vehicle with sun shield in place.

- portable baby stroller – Remove infant before folding for storage.[1]

One of the most neglected warning signs is the CHECK ENGINE LIGHT on the dash of a vehicle. According to a Harris Interactive survey, many drivers simply ignore that warning light. The survey revealed:

- Fifty percent of those whose cars were showing signs of an impending breakdown indicated the light had been on for more than three months.

- Those adults surveyed said, "My car seemed to be running just fine."

- Others said, "I didn't have time to have it checked."

- Some admitted, "If I got it checked and they found something wrong with it, I wouldn't have had the money to fix it."[2]

Message received: Ignore the warning sign—hopefully it doesn't mean anything. The truth is life is filled with caution signals and warning signs.

Tim Keller wrote of traveling with his brother-in-law who consistently refused to wear a seatbelt. Pleading didn't help. One day his brother-in-law pulled up to the curb at the airport to pick him up, and he had his seatbelt on. Keller writes:

> I immediately asked him, "What happened? What changed your mind?" He said, "I visited a friend in the hospital who had been in a car accident; he went through the windshield. He had 300 stitches in his face, and as I saw the pain he was suffering, I said to myself, *I need to wear a seatbelt.* Tim asked him, "But didn't you already know that if you don't wear your seatbelt you can go through the windshield if you have an accident?" His brother-in-law said, "Of course I knew that. When I went to the hospital to see my friend, I didn't get new information. I just saw that information applied—and at that moment, the information got real in my own heart and began to affect the way I live."[3]

Wearing seatbelts, following directions, and reading the labels on all the packages are wise exercises. But even then, we won't be able to guarantee the absence of accidents, trouble, and pain. But we *can* minimize the damage and be protected from even greater danger. We have already learned from Paul's warning labels to Titus that:

- Believers responding with humility toward authority can steer clear of certain types of trouble *(Titus 3:1–2)*.

- Grateful Christians remember the pit from which they were dug; they never quite get over their conversion, which keeps them from spiritual lethargy *(Titus 3:3)*.

- Christians who rejoice that they've been ambushed by the goodness and grace of God have a tendency to treat others the same way, protecting themselves and others from potential harm *(Titus 3:4–8)*.

- Wise believers learn the art of refusal—what to avoid putting on their tray in culture's cafeteria that constantly serves up spiritual myths and speculations and unprofitable disputes *(Titus 3:9)*.

And now, Paul tells Titus and these churches the rather surprising news that local churches actually come with a warning label—and here it is: TWO STRIKES AND YOU'RE OUT!

What in the world could Paul be referring to? Hold on to your baseball hat and take a closer look.

CALLING THE STRIKES

Reject a factious man after a first and second warning, *knowing that such a man is perverted and is sinning, being self-condemned* (Titus 3:10–11).

Just as Paul has challenged us to develop the art of refusing unprofitable and fruitless and empty distractions, he now tells us, within the context of a local church, to **reject a factious man** after only two warnings. The word here for **reject** is from a word that literally means to have nothing to do with.[4]

Paul wrote to the Corinthians that they were to remove from their midst the unrepentant man who was, in that particular case, living a life of sexual immorality *(I Corinthians 5)*.

In his letter to the believers in Rome, the Apostle Paul told the believers:

[K]*eep your eye on those who cause dissensions and hindrances contrary to the teaching which you learned, and turn away from them* (Romans 16:17).

The word translated *keep your eye on* is the verb *skopein*, which means to mark and avoid.[5] Our word *scope*, which we use in telescope and microscope, comes from this same verb. In other words, watch carefully for people who cause dissension in the flock—don't let them slip out of your sight.

Here in *Titus 3*, Paul identifies a particular kind of person: a **factious** man. It's the Greek word *hairetikos*, from which our word *heretic* is derived. It's the only time this particular adjective appears in the New Testament, although the noun form appears in *1 Corinthians 11* and *Galatians 5* to refer to factions and divisions in the church body.

While Paul could be warning Titus of heretical teachers hiding within the church community, he is using the word in a broader sense to refer to someone who is contentious and discordant.

One author writes:

> This includes anyone in the church who is divisive and disruptive; the issues may be trivial, but arguing about them is not. Because the consequences of bickering and insubordination can be so destructive of unity among the [flock], the apostle commands that this divisive man, or woman—as the case may be—should be rejected by the church if they do not respond to the warning.[6]

If we combine Paul's warning label here in Titus with other similar passages of Scripture, he is informing the Church to remove from her midst this kind of individual.

And notice that Paul writes, ***Reject a factious man* after a first and second warning**. Two strikes and he's out!

Seriously? I know two men in our church who've been professional baseball umpires. It has to be one of the toughest jobs on the planet, especially when they're calling pitches and yell, "Strike three—you're out!" There's just nowhere to hide after that. I've asked these men what it's like standing there at home plate with half of the crowd yelling at you. They've informed me that it's not a pretty sight.

Titus is going to need a solid chest protector and shin guards—it's about to get ugly at home plate. And by the way, Titus is not to allow three strikes—only two.

Strike One

***Reject a factious man after a first and second warning, knowing that such a man is* perverted *and is* sinning, *being* self-condemned** (Titus 3:10–11).

Paul uses three distinctive words to describe this factious person, beginning with **perverted**. This is the only time we find this word in the New Testament. We might think that he's referring to some kind of sexual perversion, but he's not. The word he's using applies to a person whose mind is turned around or inside out.[7]

We could use the word *slanted* . . . his mind or his perspective is skewed or slanted to one side—and it's to his side only. This is exactly what happens when there are divisive people—and issues—in the Church.

Someone has the facts on *one* side of the issue; since they don't know all the facts and all the issues, everything gets slanted toward their opinion. Then the campaign is on to convince people that their opinion and their perspective is the only correct one . . . and people begin to take sides. Whenever slanted, skewed-thinking people begin directing traffic, collisions are going to take place.

Paul's second description clarifies that this man *is* **sinning**. The word used here means *to miss the mark*. In other words, he thinks he represents the truth, but he has actually wandered off the path, missing the mark entirely.[8]

In conclusion, Paul adds an interesting insight into the mind of this man; he is **self-condemned**. Again, a rare word is used here by Paul, but a word that says it all. John Phillips paraphrases this text to emphasize this particular insight; "This divisive, sinning person is **self-condemned** because he *knows* perfectly well that what he is doing is wrong."[9]

It doesn't mean he'll admit it; but Paul declares, "He knows it." He *knows* when he's causing division; he *knows* when he's gossiping; he *knows* when he's slanting the story without having all the facts. And he doesn't care how much damage he creates.

Strike Two

Reject a factious man after a **first** *and* **second** *warning* (Titus 3:10).

Gene Getz writes in his commentary that this individual only gets two strikes because they get emotional satisfaction from creating controversy in the Church. In dealing with them, there is only one recourse for us and for Titus: radical surgery—they must be stopped.[10] Don't procrastinate.

But give them two warnings first.

Paul makes that clear here in verse ten. In fact, the word he uses for **warning** is a compound in the noun form which means *to put to the mind*.[11] It's the root word we've used to create the term *nouthetic counseling*.

In other words, this isn't a one-sentence **warning** or an email with a cryptic message: "Okay, this is your first **warning**. Quit doing that divisive stuff—you know what I'm talking about—or else."

No, these two **warning**s are more like extended conversations where we "put to their mind"—we counsel them; we expose them to their error and the potential consequences of their divisiveness, according to the Scriptures.

And that's why we only need to give one more **warning** after the first one. They actually got it the first time. They knew what they were doing, and they knew the damage they were creating, and now *they know that we know*—but they've made up their mind they'd rather keep doing it than to listen to their spiritual leaders.

Frankly, they're not going to quit. That's because they actually love the fight. They enjoy the tantalizing controversy. They thrive on being the person in the know and the one who really has the story straight; they love the shock on people's faces when they tell them what so-and-so did or said—their favorite conversations begin with, "You won't believe what I found out."

Left alone, division begins circulating and seeping like a virus through the church body; unsuspecting people come in contact with it and the infection begins to spread.

Chuck Swindoll wrote with seasoned pastoral wisdom as he commented on this text:

> Effective spiritual leadership does everything with compassion but never at the expense of conviction. It never fails to confront when necessary. Just as a surgeon must cut out diseased tissue, so leaders in churches must confront those who would infect the body of Christ with discord and divide congregations into factions. If the [pastor/elder/shepherd] isn't willing to love his congregation enough to risk misunderstanding and criticism, he should step aside and choose another less hazardous occupation.[12]

Well put. That's like saying if a baseball umpire can't quite bring himself to call a batter out, he needs to take up fishing.

Paul makes it painfully clear: remove him from your midst—**reject** him after he disregards a second warning.

YOU'RE OUT!

As ironic as it sounds, Paul's answer to dealing with a divisive person is to create division. There *must* be a division in the Church—but it is to be a division between the flock and that person who persists in his unrepentant, divisive agenda.

He is simply no longer allowed access to the body—literally, his platform and admittance to the congregation is taken away. The flock is thus protected from the divisive spirit and arrogant perspective.

Yes, there will be division; it will be painful and hurtful and emotional and, maybe, even tearful, but the flock will set this **factious** person away from themselves so that he can no longer continue his unrelenting, undermining attempts to create division among them.

By the way, Paul's command to **reject a factious man**, along with other passages dealing with this subject, makes it clear that there is to be no readmission until there is repentance.

The Church becomes an outward demonstration of the loss of fellowship, both on the physical level between church members and on the spiritual level between that person and the Lord. Fellowship has been broken . . . division has occurred. We in the body pray that the breach will be restored, not only between believers but between the unrepentant believer and the Savior.[13]

ON THE BENCH

If we survey the various passages dealing with excluding unrepentant believers from the Church, we discover that action is taken on two different levels. The key word here is excluding *unrepentant* believers—if we excluded all sinners from attending church, who would be able to show up on Sunday?

Paul is writing about a sinning believer who is warned and then warned again for his divisive spirit; he's counseled, he's exhorted, he's brought before leaders on more than one occasion and pled with to change his mind and stop his divisive and disobedient behavior—but he refuses.

At that point, decisive action is to take place on two levels.

Protective Leadership

The primary focus is on being protective and actually attempting to guard the sinning believer from *himself*. Leadership becomes aware at some point that this individual is living a dangerous life of distorted values with a twisted sense of self-importance. Remember, Paul writes that their thinking is upside down.

And leadership knows that this person is going to do nothing more than systematically dismantle his life. He's going to pay a high price, and the price tag could very well play out over the course of the rest of his life. One Christian wrote, "My most painful experiences have been when I've had a problem and no one loved me enough to tell me about it."[14]

Spiritual leadership attempts to protect a brother or sister by exposing their sin and confronting their spirit. This is really just one aspect of discipleship. *Discipline* and *discipleship* are from the same root word.

But when those attempts fail and the person refuses to be discipled, leadership then attempts to protect the flock by creating division. You'll notice that Paul doesn't write the same lengthy steps in **Titus 3** that are found in *Matthew 18* (witnesses and several steps of corroborating evidence and public warning, etc.). Instead, he states that the divisive believer is to be warned twice and then dismissed from the assembly.

It's quite possible that Paul was concerned that Titus and every other shepherd take a quicker path simply because a divisive person is capable of influencing so many people in a short amount of time. If Titus will be decisive, a tremendous amount of intrigue and drama will never make it to center stage.

Put this way, Titus is told—and we are told the same today—to put out the campfire before it turns into a forest fire. Deal with this on the level of leadership before the entire flock ends up engulfed in flames. Shepherds must endure some early heat in order to protect the flock from a flash fire.

In chapter five, I referred to taking a part time job as music pastor and learned that one of the key soloists, a deacon's daughter, was having an adulterous affair with a man in town. When I went to the pastor to tell him about it, I'll never forget his response: he scrunched up his nose, wiped his forehead, and said, "You know, we really can't be sure." I replied, "Well, the entire choir is sure, shouldn't we get to the bottom of it?" He never really followed through, and that one woman (and her enabling father) literally impeded the effective forward movement of the entire church.

Proactive Membership

Dealing with sin involves a second level—the flock gets involved. And the primary focus of the flock is proactive. Paul told one congregation:

> *And let the word of Christ richly dwell within you, with all wisdom teaching and* [note this] *admonishing one another* (Colossians 3:15–16*a*).

Admonish literally means to correct one who is at fault.[15] This is the same root word used by Paul in *Titus 3* for **warning** them. Admonishing is the same thing as **warning**.

Paul is saying to the Colossian believers, and certainly to the Cretan believers, be proactive—be on the lookout—be engaged in **warning** each other. Why? Because in any flock there are myriad issues that can create disgruntlement and disagreement and, even, sinful distraction.

Paul challenges the congregation with a surprising responsibility: don't wait for the issue to work its way from the pasture where the flock is grazing to the attention of the shepherd—don't wait . . . counsel and admonish one another *now*.

The truth is the membership of a church will most often know about a divisive issue or a divisive person *before* the leadership is even aware of the problem.

After three decades of pastoring, I can tell you first-hand that leaders most often find out something only *after* the die is cast—*after* the division has taken root—*after* someone has chosen to leave—*after* a decision was misinterpreted or misunderstood—*after* the gossip has made the rounds and done the damage—*after* the disagreement has reached the boiling point and sides have been taken.

According to Paul (and in the wisdom of God), *proactivity occurs among the parishioners.* They're probably going to spot it before the pastors do. The flock members offer prayer, balanced perspective, the benefit of the doubt, admonition, help, warning, and encouragement to get to the bottom of things without divisiveness or disrespect.

BACK IN THE GAME

John Wesley, the founder of the Methodist movement, developed a series of questions that were posed to people who expressed a desire to join their local Methodist church:

- Does any sin, inward or outward, have dominion over you?

- Do you desire to be told of your faults?

- Do you desire to be told of *all* your faults—and that plain and clear?

- Do you desire that in doing this we should come as close as possible and search your heart to the bottom?

- Do you desire to be on this and all other occasions entirely open, without disguise, and without reserve?

Frankly, who would want to join that kind of church? Only a person who is willing to be warned and admonished and encouraged to pursue a genuine, transparent, unified spirit with fellow believers.

When my younger brother was beginning his second round of intensive chemotherapy for an aggressive brain tumor and was admitted to the hospital, he had to wear a wristband with a warning printed on it: FALL RISK. That was because whenever he stood, he was at risk of falling. The hospital staff and those around him needed to be alert that Tim could fall at any time.

What a wonderful metaphor for every one of us. We are *all* at great risk of tripping, stumbling, and falling. Every one of us can become deformed in our perspective, distorted in our values, disobedient in our actions, divisive in our attitudes, and depraved in our choices.

We can hurt our witness, hindering the joyful unity of the flock, discrediting the testimony of the Gospel and, most importantly, diminishing the awareness of our world to the Gospel and glory of our Lord.

To paraphrase Paul's warnings thus far:

Be *unified*—
although you are incredibly *diversified.*
Be in your doctrine *centralized*
and in your efforts *energized*
to see the Gospel *magnified.*

Let your life be divinely *authorized*
so that the truth through you will be *synthesized,*
and keep your heart entirely *mesmerized*
by your great God, whom you desire—
with all your heart—to see *glorified.*

¹²*When I send Artemas or Tychicus to you, make every effort to come to me at Nicopolis, for I have decided to spend the winter there.* ¹³*Diligently help Zenas the lawyer and Apollos on their way so that nothing is lacking for them.* ¹⁴*Our people must also learn to engage in good deeds to meet pressing needs, so that they will not be unfruitful.* ¹⁵*All who are with me greet you. Greet those who love us in the faith. Grace be with you all*

–Titus 3:12–15

CHAPTER TWENTY-FIVE

WAX-FREE AND SUN-TESTED

Titus 3:12–15

THE REAL DEAL

O ver the years a woman had collected more than two hundred different authentic antique glass jars—all kinds, all shapes, and just about every color. No two bottles were exactly alike. Uneven seams and bubbled glass were understood as marks of distinction, age, and value.

The largest piece was a glass jug made in Eastern Europe; the smallest was a beautiful handcrafted bottle that once held perfume. She had actually dug it up as she searched the ground in an area that had once served as a stopping place for stagecoaches. The small bottle still held a delightful aroma, even though it was more than one hundred years old.

Evidently, antique pieces of glasswork provide different clues that prove whether they are genuine or a recent imitation. Looks alone can be misleading.

A simple test can help to determine the authenticity of antique glass: place it in the sunlight. A genuine antique bottle will change color when exposed to direct sunlight over a period of several weeks. That's because the glass in objects more than one hundred years old often contains a high level of manganese—a metallic chemical added to make the glass a little more transparent. The sun's rays cause a chemical reaction; a pale green glass, for example, will turn brilliant shades of purple.

The genuine antique is revealed when examined, as it were, by the light. In the days of the Apostle Paul, people used pottery for just about everything. And they used a similar test to determine the authenticity of well-made pots, cups, bowls, and many other objects.

Dishonest potters covered cracks and flaws in their pottery by filling them with wax; the person shopping indoors might not detect the wax. Wary shoppers would take a piece of pottery outside and hold it up to the sunlight. As they turned it, any crack covered or filled with wax would show up as a lighter color.

Evidently, this was such a problem that honest merchants would actually stamp their pottery with the Latin words *sine cera*, meaning *without wax*: this pottery is genuine—without wax. Over time, *sine cera* became our English word *sincere*: without any effort to appear to be something you're not.[1]

To be real . . . authentic . . . genuine is the opposite of superficial . . . put-on . . . fake. To be without wax means to be open and honest about the cracks and the flaws and be willing to work it out rather than cover it up.

This is real Christianity—wax-free and sun-tested . . . the resolution for every believer and the entire Church family.

AUTHENTIC CHRISTIANITY

As Paul comes to the close of his letter, it's only fitting that the characteristic of authenticity would make an appearance. What does authentic spiritual character look like? What does a genuine heart for God really look like . . . act like? And how can we really tell if it's the genuine item?

There are people—authors, supposed Bible scholars—who think the Apostle Paul was a know-it-all . . . a dogmatic, unfeeling, unsmiling, never-uncertain leader. Nowhere is that proven more untrue than in the way Paul finishes his letters. They exude warmth and kindness, humility and grace.

All we need to do is take Paul's life and hold it up to the sunlight of truth. What we discover is a life without wax . . . the clarity of a genuine, authentic life.

Honest Dilemmas

When I send Artemas or *Tychicus* to you (Titus 3:12*a*).

Was Paul always sure of himself? Was Paul really the kind of leader who never questioned himself? ***When I send Artemas** or **Tychicus to you . . .*** Wait, what did he just reveal? I'm so grateful for that little English word **or**. In the original language, this is an indefinite clause (*hotan* with the subjunctive) which means Paul hasn't made up his mind—he doesn't quite know.[2] Paul is admitting in total transparency that he wasn't sure what to do.

He doesn't couch his lack of certainty at the moment into more spiritual language such as, "Titus, there are two excellent candidates for the pastorate that I'm currently evaluating." He actually spells it out . . . without wax to fill in the cracks or make the decision any less difficult than it was.

For those of us who lead a ministry or a business or a school or a household, isn't it wonderful to hear Paul say at this point that he's actually not sure which man is the best candidate to send to Crete for further ministry?

He implies, "I'm thinking about it . . . and I'm still praying about it." The Spirit of God is inspiring His text of Scripture through the Apostle Paul, and embedded in it is Paul's humble admission that God hasn't led him clearly in every area of his ministry—at all times!

Even for the great apostle, God didn't fill in all the blanks.

Maybe you're wondering:

- Which college should I attend?
- Which class should I take next?
- Which girl should I marry?
- Which job should I take?
- Which church should we join?
- Which house should we live in?
- Which way should we educate our children?

Let's admit it more often than we dare: we're not sure which way to turn! That's authenticity. And with this kind of admission comes immediate prayer support. Titus would obviously have begun praying for the Lord to give Paul wisdom to choose the right candidate to send to Crete.

In the meantime, what did Paul know about these two candidates?

Artemas was born to parents who considered the birth of their son to be a gift from the goddess of fertility, so they named him the masculine derivative of her name Artemis.[3]

This also informs us that while ***Artemas*** had been born into an idolatrous Gentile home, he evidently came to faith later in life. We can only imagine the drastic changes; we don't know anything about his parents or his past, but we do know that this Gentile young man, named in honor of a goddess, is now one of the trusted assistants of Paul in the early Church.

The other candidate was ***Tychicus***, whose name means "Fortunate." He also is a Gentile who came to faith in Jesus Christ. While Artemas never shows up anywhere else in the New Testament, ***Tychicus*** is present several times. Paul refers to him as *our beloved brother and faithful servant and fellow bond-servant in the Lord* (Colossians 4:7). He's called a *beloved brother and faithful minister in the Lord* (Ephesians 6:21).

Tychicus delivered Paul's letter to the Colossian church and accompanied him on one of his missionary journeys *(Acts 20)*. He was obviously one of Paul's closest companions.

We can quickly see why both men would be candidates for leading the ministry on the island of Crete. Like Titus, they are Gentile believers, well-trained and courageous enough to carry on the ministry among the descendants of pirates.

We don't need to study the mind and ministry of Paul very long before we discover that he was constantly on the search for godly men to invest in and appoint in the ministry.

E.M Bounds would clarify an ongoing search:

> The Church is always looking for better methods; God is looking for better men. What the Church needs today is not more machinery, but more men whom the Holy Spirit can use; and the Holy Spirit does not flow through methods, but through men. God does not anoint plans—He anoints [people].[4]

He wrote that in 1880, and the truth remains today.

If we put the clues together, we discover that Paul decided to send ***Artemas*** to take the place of Titus because we find ***Tychicus*** sent to relieve Timothy in Ephesus *(2 Timothy 4:12)*.[5]

The point I want to make here is this is a mark of authenticity that could be easily missed. Paul openly confesses that he doesn't know which man to send. And he admits it in this inspired letter which will be read all through-out Crete—and the world, two thousand years later.

Paul is real. He doesn't reach for any spiritual wax to fill in the cracks. Study him and discover that he consistently refused to be placed on a ped-estal as one who fully expected to always know what was right, never admit to uncertainty, and never come across as indecisive. Here he does just the opposite by adding this phrase that reveals he doesn't have everything figured out in advance.

Authenticity is disclosed through honest dilemmas.

Personal Deference

[M]*ake every effort to come to me at Nicopolis, for I have decided to spend the winter there* (Titus 3:12*b*).

He hadn't **decided** which man to send to Crete, but he *had* **decided** to spend the winter at **Nicopolis**. Everything else about this letter refers to what Titus has been doing: organizing the churches, appointing elders, challenging every age group toward maturity, and demonstrating remarkable Christianity.

But this paragraph will be somewhat surprising to Titus. Without any advance notice, Paul effectively delivers the news, "Oh, by the way, Titus—you're not going to be staying where you are much longer."

"Wait . . . what? Did I miss something? I'm totally invested here . . . Crete has become home; I've been through power struggles, and I've taken on false teachers. The churches have elders that I appointed, and fruit is just now beginning to appear. What do you mean you're sending Artemas or Tychicus to take my place? This is home!"

I would imagine that these lines in the letter exploded like a bombshell on Titus . . . his plans were about to be entirely interrupted. From what other passages reveal to us, Titus will be sent to Dalmatia—another difficult mis-sion field—but he will evidently go without complaint as the apostle informs him that his ministry on Crete will soon come to an end (*2 Timothy 4:10*).

Hold Titus up to the light and we discover another authentic believer, deferring to the authority of the apostle and being willing to have his life interrupted.

God not only orders the *steps* of His children—He orders their *stops*, too. In fact, what Paul *doesn't* know is that his own plans are about to change.

Notice where Paul expected to spend his winter: ***Nicopolis***. Nicopolis was a city founded by the first Roman emperor, Octavian, to celebrate his victory over Marc Antony and Cleopatra; it flourished on the southern side of Greece.[6]

By comparing Paul's plans here in Titus with his plans revealed to the believers in Rome, he had **decided** to winter in ***Nicopolis***, then travel to serve with the believers in Rome before quickly moving on to serve Christ in Spain *(Romans 15:23–28)*.

Spain was considered the end of the civilized world. It was producing some of the greatest minds of Paul's generation: Seneca, the prime minister of Rome, and Lucan, the poet.

Paul couldn't wait to get to Spain. He effectively writes here, "I may not be sure who I'll send to the island of Crete, Titus, but I do know that I'm going to spend this winter in Nicopolis and then on to Rome and, finally, to Spain."

And God said, "Not quite."

Artemas *did* arrive in Crete and Titus *did* leave for Nicopolis, but while Paul was on his way, his plans would be changed by the Lord's plans: he will be arrested either on his way there or shortly after arriving. He'll be taken to Rome, not to the church—in chains.

Paul will *never* make it to Spain.

Both Titus and Paul—men who put their entire lives into their plans and their ministries—were interrupted. Hold them up to the light; notice the mark of authentic, remarkable Christianity: neither of them did anything but defer to their highest Authority—their Sovereign Lord—as He ordered both their steps and their stops.

Tony Snow, a believer who served as the press secretary for President George W. Bush, battled cancer before passing away. When asked what spiritual lessons he was learning from his fight with colon cancer, he replied with a smile, "We want to live lives of predictable ease—smooth, even trails as far as the eye can see . . . but God likes to go off-road."[7]

Does He ever.

Paul will be arrested the final time, and Titus will have his winter plans changed and go on to an entirely new ministry in Dalmatia. Sudden events will change their plans in a matter of months . . . they just don't know it yet.

But isn't that genuine Christianity? Smooth roads and clear pathways, then a quick turn off-road over bumps and through brush. Before we know it, God has us in rugged terrain . . . no smooth pavement . . . no map . . . no GPS . . . and no Cracker Barrel in sight.

What's on your list of expectations? There is nothing wrong with planning—Paul and Titus were neck-deep in it—but their plans were written in pencil, and when God moved to erase here and rewrite there, they deferred to His wisdom and authority over their lives.

When we say we are following a *sovereign* Lord, we need to understand that it means we will follow Him, even when He takes us on unpaved roads . . . when He doesn't give us an explanation for any of the steps—or the stops—along the way.

Authentic Christianity is demonstrated by personal deference

Selfless Deeds

Diligently help Zenas the lawyer and Apollos on their way so that nothing is lacking for them (Titus 3:13).

Now Paul surprises the Church by calling for a special offering. **Zenas** and **Apollos** are the couriers for this letter and then they're off to other ministry locations. Paul wants Titus to use this opportunity to teach the Church how to give to someone we might refer to today as a missionary. They are serving Christ somewhere else and they need the support of the Church.

This might not have been in the Cretan churches' budgets. And besides that—who is **Zenas**? To this day, we don't know. He isn't mentioned anywhere else in the Bible. His name is Greek, so at least we know he's a converted Gentile.

Paul added that he's *a lawyer* and uses the typical Greek word for an attorney-at-law.[8] He is the only Christian lawyer mentioned in the New Testament—which doesn't mean that only one lawyer got saved in the first century.

What it does mean is that a believer who practiced law was also committed to the Gospel to the point that he built into his life what we might call a mission trip and used the expertise of his career to aid the spread of the Gospel.

What a blessing it is to me to have lawyers in our church family doing the very same thing—using their skills and their connections to help other believers and further the Gospel of Jesus Christ.

Paul also mentions **Apollos**, a rather prominent gifted orator and apologist of the first-century Church. He was so well-known that Paul rebuked the Church in Corinth for dividing into four factions: those following Paul; others following **Apollos**; still others following Peter; and the really spiritual ones following Jesus.

But any way you slice it, these were the leaders that everyone knew and followed. And **Apollos** is not only on the list—he's right next to Paul, getting nearly equal billing.

Here's where Paul's selfless actions come to light: he tells the Church to help **Apollos** and **Zenas** every way they can to encourage them along. Not one word is mentioned about all those petty factions back in Corinth; there's not one disparaging comment about **Apollos**. No politics . . . no power plays.

Authentic Christianity is revealed by selfless deeds

Unified Disciples

***Our people must also* learn *to engage in* good deeds *to meet* pressing needs, *so that they will not be* unfruitful** (Titus 3:14).

Part of an authentic life is selflessly serving others while meeting **pressing needs**. Paul adds a wonderful incentive here: when you live for others, you'll never have to wonder if you're living an **unfruitful** life.

Engaging in **good deeds** refers to a selfless lifestyle, not a momentary flash of service. You don't count out loud your **good deeds**: "Okay, that's one . . . that's two . . . I need to get one more in before bedtime."

Have you ever thought about the fact that God never designed a peach tree to count its peaches? It just bears fruit. Paul is effectively saying to the Church on Crete, "Work together . . . pull together . . . serve together to meet **pressing needs**—that's the way to fruitful living."

He is also implying here that our most fruitful service just might be in helping *someone else* bear fruit.[9] This is not going to come naturally; Paul says that doing **good deeds** would be something the Church would need to **learn** how to do.

We must **learn** how to engage in **good deeds**; our children are going to have to **learn** how to engage in **good deeds**. We don't get this automatically when we turn six or thirteen or twenty-one . . . or any age. It is both instructed and modeled. Authentic Christianity is something we **learn** and relearn, practice . . . and then practice some more.

It seems that Paul comes to the end of his letter to Titus and asks the question, "Who cares?"

- Who's going to care for somebody else?
- Who's going to care for those coming through town who serve Christ?
- Who's going to care for and pray for young men preparing for ministry?
- Who's going to tangibly support people serving Christ in other cultures?
- Who's going to meet the **pressing needs** of others?

Obviously the answer to all of the above is that authentic believers and authentic churches will care!

GET REAL!

These four characteristics of authentic, Son-tested Christianity are what Paul is encouraging in the Church then and now:

1. **None of us should occupy any role with a sense of permanence.** No one. We're to live with our mental suitcase packed and ready, should God choose to change our plans.

2. **None of us is beyond needing helpful assistance.** No one. Even the Apostle Paul needed help and wanted company during the long winter at Nicopolis. If *he* needed assistance, certainly every one of us can ask for it, too.

3. **None of us should avoid being intentionally generous.** No one. Generosity should mark the life of the believer. Engaging in **good deeds**—and learning how to do more of them—is one of the commands of Christ through Paul to the believers in the first century, as well as the twenty-first century.

4. **None of us can make it without the goodness of God's grace.** No one. This is why Paul ends his letter with his signature blessing:

   All who are with me greet you. Greet those who love us in the faith. **Grace** *be with you all* (Titus 3:15).

Paul began this letter by sending **grace** to Titus, and he now ends it with a blessing of **grace** on the entire Church. The text reads, **Grace** *be with you all*. The word *you* is plural. If Paul had been from North Carolina, he would have said, "**Grace** be with y'all."[10] That's the Revised Southern Version.

And what a wonderful point to make: no one is left out—**grace** is extended to *all*.

As this letter concludes, why would the Church need to be reminded of **grace**?

- We'll never pull off this letter without God's **grace**.
- We'll never serve each other without **grace**.
- We'll never submit to authority without **grace**.
- We'll never pursue godly maturity and humility without **grace**.
- We'll never establish homes that honor Christ without **grace**.
- We'll never take the heat and stand up to false teaching without **grace**.
- We'll never stay focused on the truth without **grace**.
- We'll never live with a longing anticipation of the coming of Christ without **grace**.

Genuine Christianity isn't just difficult, it is *impossible* without the work of God's **grace** in our lives. No wonder Paul writes, **Grace** *be with you all*!

And with that, we offer our sincere thanks to Paul and to the Spirit of God through Paul for describing how a genuine Christian life should be lived—how an authentic church is to function—how every unique believer is to daily bathe in and entirely lean upon the enriching, enabling, enduring **grace** of God.

ENDNOTES

CHAPTER ONE

[1] Bruno Chenu, *The Book of Christian Martyrs* (London: SCM Press, 1990), 47.

[2] Ibid., 50.

[3] Adapted from John MacArthur, *Slave: The Hidden Truth About Your Identity in Christ* (Thomas Nelson, 2010), 7.

[4] George W. Knight III, *The New International Greek Testament Commentary: The Pastoral Epistles* (William B. Eerdmans Publishing Co., 1992), 3.

[5] D. Edmond Hiebert, *Titus and Philemon* (Moody Press, 1957), 16.

[6] Charles R. Swindoll, *Swindoll's New Testament Insights: 1 & 2 Timothy and Titus* (Zondervan, 2010), 257.

[7] Robert Black and Ronald McClung, *1 & 2 Timothy, Titus, and Philemon* (Wesleyan Publishing House, 2004), 2011.

[8] Swindoll, 268.

[9] MacArthur, 12.

[10] Ibid., 16.

[11] MacArthur, 20.

[12] Gene A. Getz, *The Measure of a Christian: Studies in Titus* (Regal Books, 1983), 17.

[13] MacArthur, 222.

[14] Jon C. Laansma, *Cornerstone Biblical Commentary: Volume 17* (Tyndale House, 2009), 125.

[15] R. Kent Hughes & Bryan Chapell, *1&2 Timothy and Titus: To Guard the Deposit* (Crossway Books and Bibles, 2000), 278.

[16] *Life Application Bible Commentary: 1 & 2 Timothy and Titus*, Grant R. Osborne, ed. (Tyndale House, 1993), 234.

[17] Swindoll, 258.

[18] David Campbell, *Opening Up Titus* (Day One Publications, 2007), 22.

CHAPTER TWO

[1] Jill Lepore, "The Meaning of Life" *The New Yorker*, May 21, 2007, www.preachingtoday.com, October 24, 2011.

[2] Jonathan Sacks, "Reversing the Decay of London Undone," *The Wall Street Journal*, August 20, 2011.

[3] Ibid.

4   John Kitchen, *The Pastoral Epistles for Pastors* (Kress Christian Publications, 2009), 478.

5   Charles H. Spurgeon, *Morning and Evening; Complete and Unabridged* (Hendrickson Publishers, 1995), 398.

6   Martin Thielen, *What's the Least I Can Believe and Still Be a Christian?* (Westminster John Knox Press, 2011), 49.

7   Howard Hendricks, *Teaching to Change Lives: Seven Proven Ways to Make Your Teaching Come Alive* (Multnomah, 1987), 13.

8   Kitchen, 478.

9   John Benton, *Straightening Out the Self-Centered Church: The Message of Titus* (Evangelical Press, 1997), 30.

CHAPTER THREE

1   Mark Ashton, *Absolute Truth* (Downers Grove, InterVarsity Press, 1996), 9, www.preachingtoday.com.

2   John G. Butler, *Analytical Bible Expositor: Volume 13* (LBC Publications, 2009), 412.

3   John A. Kitchen, *The Pastoral Epistles for Pastors* (Kress Christian Publications, 2009), 479.

4   Howard Taylor, *Hudson Taylor and the China Inland Mission Volume 2: The Growth of a Work of God* (Taylor Books, 1996), 265.

5   Gary W. Demarest, *The Preacher's Commentary: 1&2 Thessalonians / 1&2 Timothy / Titus* (Thomas Nelson, 1984), 311.

6   Ibid.

7   "Pawn Stars," History Channel, February 7, 2007, www.preachingtoday.com.

8   John Benton, *Straightening Out the Self-Centered Church: The Message of Titus* (Evangelical Press, 1997), 32.

9   Kitchen, 480.

10 D. Edmond Hiebert, *Titus and Philemon* (Moody Press, 1957), 22.

11 Charles Ray, *First & Second Timothy, Titus, and Philemon: Goals to Godliness* (AMG Publishers, 2007), 148.

12 James Burton Coffman, *James Burton Coffman Series of New Testament Commentaries: Volume 9* (Abilene Christian University Press, 1986), 302.

13 John MacArthur, *The MacArthur New Testament Commentary: Titus* (Moody Press, 1996), 11.

14 Kitchen, 483.

15 Macarthur, 12.

16 Ibid.

[17] Interview, *Harper's Magazine*, July, 1928.

[18] Ray, 149.

CHAPTER FOUR

[1] Adapted from John MacArthur, www.gty.org/resources/sermons/80–380.

[2] *Life Application Bible Commentary: 1 & 2 Timothy and Titus*, Grant R. Osborne, ed. (Tyndale House, 1993), 246.

[3] D. Edmond Hiebert, *Titus and Philemon* (Moody Press, 1957), 28.

[4] Quoted, www.us.dockers.com/season/landing.aspx.

[5] Charles R. Swindoll, *Swindoll's New Testament Insights: 1 & 2 Timothy and Titus* (Zondervan, 2010), 271.

[6] Hiebert, 30.

[7] John Kitchen, *The Pastoral Epistles for Pastors* (Kress Christian Publications, 2009), 487.

[8] Kitchen, 488.

[9] MacArthur, 13.

[10] Ibid., 9.

[11] Ibid., 27.

[12] Alexander Strauch, *Biblical Eldership* (Lewis and Roth Publishers, 1995), 47.

[13] MacArthur, 27.

[14] Strauch, 18.

[15] Ibid.

CHAPTER FIVE

[1] Alexander Strauch, *Biblical Eldership* (Lewis and Roth Publishers, 1995), 67.

[2] Fritz Rienecker & Cleon Rogers, *Linguistic Key to the Greek New Testament* (Regency, 1976), 720.

[3] David Campbell, *Opening Up Titus* (Day One Publications, 2007), 26.

[4] Charles R. Swindoll, *Swindoll's New Testament Insights: 1 & 2 Timothy and Titus* (Zondervan, 2010), 56.

[5] Charles Ray, *The Books of First & Second Timothy, Titus, and Philemon: Goals to Godliness* (AMG Publishers, 2007), 56.

[6] Adapted from Eugene H. Peterson, *Run with the Horses: The Quest for Life at Its Best* (Inter-Varsity Press, 2009), 15.

[7] D. Edmond Hiebert, *Titus and Philemon* (Moody Press, 1957), 31.

[8] Gene A. Getz, *The Measure of a Christian: Studies in Titus* (Regal Books, 1983), 42.

[9] Jeremy Caplan, "Adultery 2.0" *Time Magazine* (July 20, 2009), 59.

10   R. Kent Hughes, *Disciplines of a Godly Man* (Crossway Books and Bibles, 1991), 39.

11   Strauch, 67.

12   Ibid., 75.

13   Hughes, 44.

14   Strauch, 229.

15   George W. Knight III, *The New International Greek Testament Commentary: The Pastoral Epistles* (Eerdmans Publishing, 1992), 290.

16   John MacArthur, *The MacArthur New Testament Commentary: Titus* (Moody Press, 1996), 31.

17   Warren W. Wiersbe, *Be Faithful: 1–2 Timothy, Titus, Philemon* (Victor Books, 1984), 100.

18   Isaac Watts, "When I Survey the Wondrous Cross," (1707), public domain.

CHAPTER SIX

1   Warren W. Wiersbe, *The Integrity Crisis*, (Oliver Nelson, 1991), 17.

2   Charles R. Swindoll, *Swindoll's New Testament Insights: 1 & 2 Timothy and Titus* (Zondervan, 2010), 279.

3   Walter L. Liefeld, *The NIV Application Commentary: 1 & 2 Timothy/Titus* (Zondervan, 1999), 313.

4   W. E. Vine, *Vine's Expository Dictionary of Old & New Testament Words* (Thomas Nelson, 1997), 1087.

5   James Burton Coffman, *James Burton Coffman Series of New Testament Commentaries: Volume 9* (Abilene Christian University Press, 1986), 305.

6   Adapted from John MacArthur, *The MacArthur New Testament Commentary: Titus* (Moody Press, 1996), 35.

7   Wiersbe, 101.

8   William Barclay, *The Letters to Timothy, Titus, and Philemon* (Westminster John Knox Press, 1975), 236.

9   MacArthur, 36.

10   Ibid., 37.

11   Ibid., 36.

12   Norman Geisler, *A Christian Perspective on Wine-Drinking*, (Bibliotheca Sacra, Volume 139, January, 1982), 50.

13   Ibid.

14   Ibid., 51.

15   Barclay, 237.

[16] Alexander Strauch, *Biblical Eldership* (Lewis and Roth Publishers, 1995), 196.

[17] John Benton, *Straightening Out the Self-Centered Church: The Message of Titus* (Evangelical Press, 1997), 50.

CHAPTER SEVEN

[1] John MacArthur, *The MacArthur New Testament Commentary: 1 Timothy* (Moody Press, 1995), 107.

[2] John A. Kitchen, *The Pastoral Epistles for Pastors* (Kress Christian Publications, 2009), 496.

[3] John MacArthur, *The MacArthur New Testament Commentary: Titus* (Moody Press, 1996), 40.

[4] MacArthur, *The MacArthur New Testament Commentary: 1 Timothy* (Moody Press, 1995), 107.

[5] William Barclay, *The Letters to Timothy, Titus, and Philemon* (Westminster, 1975), 81.

[6] Alvin J. Schmidt, *How Christianity Changed the World* (Zondervan, 2004), 154, quoting A.C. Merrriam, "The Treatment of Patients in the Temple of Aesculapius" *Boston Medical and Surgical Journal* (March 26, 1885), 305.

[7] Schmidt, 159.

[8] Ibid., 157.

[9] Ibid., 153.

[10] George W. Knight III, *The New International Greek Testament Commentary: The Pastoral Epistles* (William B. Eerdmans Publishing Co., 1992), 292.

[11] Warren W. Wiersbe, *Be Faithful: 1–2 Timothy, Titus, Philemon* (Victor Books, 1984), 101.

[12] David Campbell, *Opening Up Titus* (Day One Publications, 2007), 30.

[13] Charles Ray, *The Books of First & Second Timothy, Titus, and Philemon: Goals to Godliness* (AMG Publishers, 2007), 153.

[14] John Benton, *Straightening Out the Self-Centered Church: The Message of Titus* (Evangelical Press, 1997), 51.

[15] Adapted from Alexander Strauch, *Biblical Eldership* (Lewis and Roth Publishers, 1995), 193.

[16] Benton, 51.

[17] Barclay, 239.

[18] *Boston Globe*, November 10, 1993.

[19] Ted W. Engstrom with Robert C. Larson, *Integrity* (Word Books, 1987), 76.

[20] Charles Wesley, *Hymns and Sacred Poems*, 1749.

CHAPTER EIGHT

1   Brother Yun, *Living Water* (Zondervan, 2008), 187.

2   Ibid., 203.

3   John A. Kitchen, *The Pastoral Epistles for Pastors* (Kress Christian Publications, 2009), 497.

4   Ibid.

5   John MacArthur, *The MacArthur New Testament Commentary: Titus* (Moody Press, 1996), 42.

6   Adapted from Charles Ray, *First & Second Timothy, Titus, and Philemon: Goals to Godliness* (AMG Publishers, 2007), 154.

7   MacArthur, 49.

8   Kitchen, 499.

9   Quoted in MacArthur, 47.

10   John Benton, *Straightening Out the Self-Centered Church: The Message of Titus* (Evangelical Press, 1997), 53.

11   Alexander Strauch, *Biblical Eldership* (Lewis and Roth Publishers, 1995), 237.

12   Charles R. Swindoll, *Swindoll's New Testament Insights: 1 & 2 Timothy and Titus* (Zondervan, 2010), 277.

13   Benton, 55.

14   Strauch, 236.

15   Swindoll, 277.

16   Ibid., 281.

CHAPTER NINE

1   Jamie Frater, "Top 10 Famous Con Men" August 28, 2007, http://listverse.com/2007/08/28/top-10-famous-con-men/.

2   Ibid.

3   Charles R. Swindoll, *Swindoll's New Testament Insights: 1 & 2 Timothy and Titus* (Zondervan 2010), 282.

4   Ibid.

5   John A. Kitchen, *The Pastoral Epistles for Pastors* (Kress Christian Publications, 2009), 500.

6   Fritz Rienecker & Cleon Rogers, *Linguistic Key to the Greek New Testament* (Regency, 1976), 652.

7   Robert Black and Ronald McClung, *1 & 2 Timothy, Titus, and Philemon* (Wesleyan Publishing House, 2004), 229.

8   Adapted from Swindoll, 283.

9   Michael Horton, *Christless Christianity: The Alternative Gospel of the American Church* (Baker Books, 2008), 144.

10 Ibid., 101.

11 Ibid., 102.

12 Ibid.

13 Ibid.

14 Jennifer Riley, "Analysis: Why Muslims Follow Jesus" *The Christian Post* (November 16, 2007).

15 John Phillips, *Exploring the Pastoral Epistles: An Expository Commentary* (Kregel Publications, 2003), 249.

16 Ibid.

17 Kitchen, 501.

18 Adapted from Kitchen, 503.

19 Martin Kasindorf and Andrea Stone, "Rescuers Laud California Dad As Hero" *USA Today* (December 8, 2006).

CHAPTER TEN

1   Warren W. Wiersbe, *Be Faithful: 1–2 Timothy, Titus, Philemon* (Victor Books, 1984), 103, 107.

2   William Barclay, *The Letters to Timothy, Titus, and Philemon* (Westminster John Knox Press, 1975), 242.

3   Ibid.

4   D. Edmond Hiebert, *Titus and Philemon* (Moody Press, 1957), 40.

5   Snapshots, *USA Today* (October 16, 2001), B1.

6   Erwin Lutzer, *Twelve Myths Americans Believe* (Moody Press, 1993), 51.

7   Robert Black and Ronald McClung, *1 & 2 Timothy, Titus, and Philemon* (Wesleyan Publishing House, 2004), 230.

8   Charles Ray, *First & Second Timothy, Titus, and Philemon: Goals to Godliness* (AMG Publishers, 2007), 158.

9   Gene A. Getz, *The Measure of a Christian: Studies in Titus* (Regal Books, 1983), 85.

10 Black and McClung, 227.

11 John A. Kitchen, *The Pastoral Epistles for Pastors* (Kress Christian Publications, 2009), 507.

12 Ray, 159.

13 Ibid., 23.

14   Philip Graham Ryken, *1 Timothy: Reformed Expository Commentary* (P & R Publishing, 2007), 9.

15   John Phillips, *Exploring the Pastoral Epistles: An Expository Commentary* (Kregel Publications, 2003), 257.

16   R. Kent Hughes & Bryan Chapell, *1–2 Timothy and Titus: To Guard the Deposit*, Crossway Books and Bibles, 2000), 310.

17   Ibid.

18   Barclay, 245.

19   Kitchen, 510.

20   Barclay, 246.

21   Ibid, 242.

22   John Benton, *Straightening Out the Self-Centered Church: The Message of Titus* (Evangelical Press, 1997), 70.

23   Ibid., 72.

CHAPTER ELEVEN

1   Van Morris, "Three Sisters Age Humorously" http://www.preachingtoday.com/illustrations/2006/october/3100206.html.

2   David Campbell, *Opening Up Titus* (Day One Publications, 2007), 45.

3   John A. Kitchen, *The Pastoral Epistles for Pastors* (Kress Christian Publications, 2009), 513.

4   Fritz Rienecker & Cleon Rogers, *Linguistic Key to the Greek New Testament* (Regency, 1976), 653.

5   John MacArthur, *The MacArthur New Testament Commentary: Titus* (Moody Press, 1996), 70.

6   Adapted from R. Kent Hughes & Bryan Chapell, *1&2 Timothy and Titus: To Guard the Deposit* (Crossway Books and Bibles, 2000), 325.

7   MacArthur, 73.

8   D. Edmond Hiebert, *Titus and Philemon* (Moody Press, 1957), 48.

9   Charles R. Swindoll, *Swindoll's New Testament Insights: 1 & 2 Timothy and Titus* (Zondervan, 2010), 291.

10   John Benton, *Straightening Out the Self-Centered Church: The Message of Titus* (Evangelical Press, 1997), 79.

11   Diana West, *The Death of the Grown-Up: How America's Arrested Development Is Bringing Down Western Civilization* (St. Martin's Press, 2008), 1–3.

12   Kitchen, 515.

13   Hughes & Chapell, 328.

14 Robert Fulghum, *It Was on Fire When I Laid Down on It* (Random House Publishing Group, 1991), 19–22.

CHAPTER TWELVE

1 John MacArthur, *The MacArthur New Testament Commentary: Titus* (Moody Press, 1996), 77.

2 John A. Kitchen, *The Pastoral Epistles for Pastors* (Kress Christian Publications, 2009), 517.

3 John Benton, *Straightening Out the Self-Centered Church: The Message of Titus* (Evangelical Press, 1997), 93.

4 John Phillips, *Exploring the Pastoral Epistles: An Expository Commentary* (Kregel Publications, 2003), 269.

5 Charles Ray, *First & Second Timothy, Titus, and Philemon: Goals to Godliness* (AMG Publishers, 2007), 165.

6 Tony Evans, "Woman to Woman, Part 1" May 10, 2012, oneplace.com.

7 Knute Larson, *Holman New Testament Commentary: 1 & 2 Thessalonians, 1 & 2 Timothy, Titus, Philemon* (Holman, 2000), 360.

8 Gene A. Getz, *The Measure of a Christian: Studies in Titus* (Regal Books, 1983), 111.

9 Kitchen, 517.

10 Ibid.

11 MacArthur, 78.

12 David Campbell, *Opening Up Titus* (Day One Publications, 2007), 58.

13 Walter L. Liefeld, *The NIV Application Commentary: 1 & 2 Timothy/Titus* (Zondervan, 1999), 328.

14 Adapted from Elisa Morgan, Christian Parenting Today (May/June 1999), 64.

CHAPTER THIRTEEN

1 *Life Application Bible Commentary: 1 & 2 Timothy and Titus*, Grant R. Osborne, ed. (Tyndale House, 1993), 260.

2 David Campbell, *Opening Up Titus* (Day One Publications, 2007), 58.

3 Diana West, *The Death of the Grown-Up: How America's Arrested Development Is Bringing Down Western Civilization* (St. Martin's Press, 2008), 3.

4 Ibid.

5 John A. Kitchen, *The Pastoral Epistles for Pastors* (Kress Christian Publications, 2009), 519.

6 Adapted from Gene A. Getz, *The Measure of a Christian: Studies in Titus* (Regal Books, 1983), 114.

7   Chris Francescani, "Chicago Billboard Turns Heads" (May 5, 2007), http://abcnews.go.com/TheLaw/LegalCenter/story?id=3147979.

8   Warren W. Wiersbe, *Be Faithful: 1–2 Timothy, Titus, Philemon* (Victor Books, 1984), 110.

9   Kitchen, 520.

10 Ibid.

CHAPTER FOURTEEN

1   Erwin Lutzer, *Twelve Myths Americans Believe* (Moody Press, 1993), 91.

2   Ibid.

3   John A. Benton, *Straightening Out the Self-Centered Church: The Message of Titus* (Evangelical Press, 1997), 91.

4   Knute Larson, *Holman New Testament Commentary: 1 & 2 Thessalonians, 1 & 2 Timothy, Titus, Philemon* (Holman, 2000), 358.

5   Fritz Rienecker & Cleon Rogers, *Linguistic Key to the Greek New Testament* (Regency, 1976), 654.

6   Charles Ray, *First & Second Timothy, Titus, and Philemon: Goals to Godliness* (AMG Publishers, 2007), 168.

7   Larson, 361.

8   Greg Toppo, "More Women Staying Home with Young Kids" (April 8, 2014), http://www.usatoday.com/story/news/nation/2014/04/08/women-stay-at-home-mothers-work/7468163/.

9   John MacArthur, *The MacArthur New Testament Commentary: Titus* (Moody Press, 1996), 86.

10 Ibid.

11 Heide Lang, "The Trouble with Day Care: Are Scientists Telling Parents the Whole Truth?" *Psychology Today* (May/June 2005), 17.

12 U.S. Census Bureau, "Women by the Numbers" http://www.infoplease.com/spot/womencensus1.html#ixzz1weVTQaWE.

13 Hara Estroff Marano, "Skinny Sweepstakes" *Psychology Today* (January 1, 2008), 89.

14 Ray, 168.

15 Adapted from "The Danvers Statement" http://www.churchcouncil.org/iccp_org/Documents_ICCP/English/17_Male_Female_Distinctives_A&D.pdf.

16 Lutzer, 89.

17 Preaching Notes: Raymond C. Ortland, Jr.

18 MacArthur, 88.

CHAPTER FIFTEEN

1 Kay S. Hymowitz, "Child-Man in the Promised Land," *City Journal* (Winter 2008), http://www.city-journal.org/2008/18_1_single_young_men.html.

2 John A. Kitchen, *The Pastoral Epistles for Pastors* (Kress Christian Publications, 2009), 522.

3 Walter L. Liefeld, *The NIV Application Commentary: 1 & 2 Timothy/Titus* (Zondervan, 1999), 324.

4 John Benton, *Straightening Out the Self-Centered Church: The Message of Titus* (Evangelical Press, 1997), 83.

5 John MacArthur, *The MacArthur New Testament Commentary: Titus* (Moody Press, 1996), 92.

6 William Barclay, *The Letters to Timothy, Titus, and Philemon* (Westminster John Knox Press, 1975), 251.

7 Ibid., 252.

8 Charles R. Swindoll, *Swindoll's New Testament Insights: 1 & 2 Timothy and Titus* (Zondervan, 2010), 295.

9 Gene A. Getz, *The Measure of a Christian: Studies in Titus* (Regal Books, 1983), 102.

10 John Phillips, *Exploring the Pastoral Epistles: An Expository Commentary* (Kregel Publications, 2003), 277.

11 R. Kent Hughes, *Disciplines of a Godly Man* (Crossway Books and Bibles, 1991), 72.

12 Ibid., 77.

13 Ibid., 78.

14 David Campbell, *Opening Up Titus* (Day One Publications, 2007), 50.

15 Kitchen, 525.

16 MacArthur, 95.

CHAPTER SIXTEEN

1 Gene Edward Veith, "The Doctrine of Vocation: How God Hides Himself in Human Work" *Modern Reformation* (May/June, 1999), 4–7.

2 Ibid.

3 John A. Benton, *Straightening Out the Self-Centered Church: The Message of Titus* (Evangelical Press, 1997), 114.

4 Robert Black and Ronald McClung, *1 & 2 Timothy, Titus, and Philemon* (Wesleyan Publishing House, 2004), 241.

5 David Campbell, *Opening Up Titus* (Day One Publications, 2007), 66.

6 R. Kent Hughes, *Ephesians: The Mystery of the Body of Christ* (Crossway Books and Bibles, 1990), 205.

7   Ibid., 206.

8   Black and McClung, 241.

9   John MacArthur, *The MacArthur New Testament Commentary: Titus* (Moody Press, 1996), 98.

10 MacArthur, 100.

11 Campbell, 70.

12 Tullian Tchividjian, "Our Calling, Our Spheres," *Leadership Journal* (Summer 2010), 98.

13 Hughes, 208.

14 MacArthur, 100.

15 Fritz Rienecker & Cleon Rogers, *Linguistic Key to the Greek New Testament* (Regency, 1976), 654.

16 John Phillips, *Exploring the Pastoral Epistles: An Expository Commentary* (Kregel Publications, 2003), 281.

17 Rienecker &Rogers, 654.

18 Black and McClung, 242.

19 Hughes, 211.

20 R. Kent Hughes & Bryan Chapell, *1&2 Timothy and Titus: To Guard the Deposit* (Crossway Books and Bibles, 2000), 321.

CHAPTER SEVENTEEN

1   Max Lucado, *God's Story, Your Story: When His Becomes Yours* (Zondervan, 2011), 93.

2   Adapted from Charles R. Swindoll, *Swindoll's New Testament Insights: 1 & 2 Timothy and Titus* (Zondervan, 2010), 299.

3   John A. Kitchen, *The Pastoral Epistles for Pastors* (Kress Christian Publications, 2009), 532.

4   Charles Ray, *First & Second Timothy, Titus, and Philemon: Goals to Godliness* (AMG Publishers, 2007), 178.

5   Adapted from R. Kent Hughes, *Disciplines of a Godly Man* (Crossway Books and Bibles, 1991), 73.

6   Hughes, 345.

7   Kitchen, 533.

8   Ibid.

9   Adapted from John MacArthur, *The MacArthur New Testament Commentary: Titus* (Moody Press, 1996), 117.

10 Kitchen, 534.

11 Diana West, *The Death of the Grown-Up: How America's Arrested Development Is Bringing Down Western Civilization* (St. Martin's Press, 2007), 71.

12 Quoted in Charles R. Swindoll, *The Tale of the Tardy Oxcart* (Word Publishing, Nashville, 1998), 469.

13 Warren W. Wiersbe, *Be Faithful: 1–2 Timothy, Titus, Philemon* (Victor Books, 1984), 116.

14 Kitchen, 536.

15 MacArthur, 120.

16 Swindoll, 301.

17 Woodrow Kroll, *The Vanishing Ministry in the 21st Century: Calling a New Generation to Lifetime Service* (Kregel Publications, 2002), 40.

18 Ibid., 41.

19 "Huddled up with LISA" *The Wall Street Journal Online* (January 20, 2005), online.wsj.com.

CHAPTER EIGHTEEN

1 Adapted and edited from www.preachingtoday.com/illustrations October 21, 2008.

2 "Water It Down" *World Magazine* (June 15, 2012), 94.

3 John MacArthur, *The MacArthur New Testament Commentary: Titus* (Moody Press, 1996), 132.

4 Charles Ray, *First & Second Timothy, Titus, and Philemon: Goals to Godliness* (AMG Publishers, 2007), 182.

5 MacArthur, 132.

6 John A. Kitchen, *The Pastoral Epistles for Pastors* (Kress Christian Publications, 2009), 539.

7 Richard Lawrence Miller, *Lincoln and His World: Volume 3, The Rise to National Prominence, 1843-1853* (McFarland & Company, Inc., 2011), 219.

8 Fritz Rienecker & Cleon Rogers, *Linguistic Key to the Greek New Testament* (Regency, 1976), 655.

9 Kitchen, 540.

10 Warren W. Wiersbe, *50 People Every Christian Should Know: Learning from Spiritual Giants of the Faith* (Baker Books, 2009), 64.

11 Martin Luther, "Offending the Guilty," *Leadership, Volume 6, no. 3*, www.preachingtoday.com, December 25, 1997.

12 John Benton, *Straightening Out the Self-Centered Church: The Message of Titus* (Evangelical Press, 1997), 141.

13 William Barclay, *The Letters to Timothy, Titus, and Philemon* (Westminster John Knox Press, 1975), 258.

14 Quoted from Charles McCracken, "The Push to Reinvent Christianity," *Israel My Glory* (July/August 2012), 14.

15   Ibid.

16   John Philips, *Exploring the Pastoral Epistles: An Expository Commentary* (Kregel Publications, 2003), 291.

17   James Burton Coffman, *James Burton Coffman Series of New Testament Commentaries: Volume 9* (Abilene Christian University Press, 1986), 322.

CHAPTER NINETEEN

1   Charles R. Swindoll, *Swindoll's New Testament Insights: 1 & 2 Timothy and Titus* (Zondervan, 2010), 304.

2   Glenn Sunshine, "The City of Man," *The Christian Worldview Journal* (September 10, 2012), www.colsoncenter.org.

3   Swindoll, 304.

4   "Water It Down" *World Magazine* (June 16, 2012), 94.

5   John MacArthur, *The MacArthur New Testament Commentary: Titus* (Moody Press, 1996), 137.

6   D. Edmond Hiebert, *Titus and Philemon* (Moody Press, 1957), 65.

7   James Burton Coffman, *James Burton Coffman Series of New Testament Commentaries: Volume 9* (Abilene Christian University Press, 1986), 325.

8   John Benton, *Straightening Out the Self-Centered Church: The Message of Titus* (Evangelical Press, 1997), 147.

9   *Life Application Bible Commentary: 1 & 2 Timothy and Titus*, Grant R. Osborne, ed. (Tyndale House, 1993), 275.

10 Robert Black and Ronald McClung, *1 & 2 Timothy, Titus, and Philemon* (Wesleyan Publishing House, 2004), 252.

11 Swindoll, 305.

12 William Barclay, *The Gospel of Matthew, Volume 1* (Westminster John Knox Press, 1975), 168.

13 Fritz Rienecker & Cleon Rogers, *Linguistic Key to the Greek New Testament* (Regency, 1976), 655.

14 Swindoll, 93.

15 Hiebert, 66.

16 John Phillips, *Exploring the Pastoral Epistles: An Expository Commentary* (Kregel Publications, 2003), 293.

17 Coffman, 325.

18 Robert L. Peterson, Alexander Strauch, *Agape Leadership: Lessons in Spiritual Leadership from the Life of R.C. Chapman* (Lewis & Roth Publishers, 1991), 44.

19 John A. Kitchen, *The Pastoral Epistles for Pastors* (Kress Christian Publications, 2009), 546.

[20] Ronald J. Kernaghan, "Hardball Takes Over Public Life," *Theology, News & Notes* (Winter 2003), www.preachingtoday.com.

[21] Adapted from Swindoll, 306.

[22] Arnold A. Dallimore, *George Whitefield: The Life and Times of the Great Evangelist of the Eighteenth Century, Vol. II* (Banner of Truth, 1980), 94.

CHAPTER TWENTY

[1] James Bryan Smith, *The Good and Beautiful Community: Following the Spirit, Extending Grace, Demonstrating Love* (Inter-Varsity Press, 2010), 28.

[2] Robert Black and Ronald McClung, *1 & 2 Timothy, Titus, and Philemon* (Wesleyan Publishing House, 2004), 254.

[3] Walter L. Liefeld, *The NIV Application Commentary: 1 & 2 Timothy/Titus* (Zondervan, 1999), 350.

[4] Ibid.

[5] Diana West, *The Death of the Grown-Up: How America's Arrested Development Is Bringing Down Western Civilization* (St. Martin's Press, 2007), 67.

[6] Ibid.

[7] Matt Woodley, managing ed., "The Harvard Cheating Scandal" (September 10, 2012), www.preachingtoday.com.

[8] "Brazilian Tangle," *World Magazine* (September 22, 2010), 16.

[9] Black and McClung, 254.

[10] Fritz Rienecker & Cleon Rogers, *Linguistic Key to the Greek New Testament* (Regency, 1976) 656.

[11] John MacArthur, *The MacArthur New Testament Commentary: Titus* (Moody Press, 1996), 149.

[12] John A. Kitchen, *The Pastoral Epistles for Pastors* (Kress Christian Publications, 2009), 549.

[13] John Phillips, *Exploring the Pastoral Epistles: An Expository Commentary* (Kregel Publications, 2003), 297.

[14] West, 85.

[15] Ibid, 86.

[16] John Benton, *Straightening Out the Self-Centered Church: The Message of Titus* (Evangelical Press, 1997), 155.

[17] Adapted from Black and McClung, 254.

[18] Charles R. Swindoll, *Swindoll's New Testament Insights: 1 & 2 Timothy and Titus* (Zondervan, 2010), 307.

19 Adapted from Max Lucado, *In the Eye of the Storm: A Day in the Life of Jesus* (Thomas Nelson Publishers, 1991), quoted by Charles Swindoll, *The Tale of the Tardy Oxcart* (Word Publishing, Nashville, 1998), 486.

CHAPTER TWENTY-ONE

1 John Ortberg, "Anonymous Donor Pays Off Students' Debts" (April 19, 2010), www.preachingtoday.com.

2 Victor Raymond Edman, *But God!* (Zondervan Publishing Company, 1962), 13.

3 John A. Kitchen, *The Pastoral Epistles for Pastors* (Kress Christian Publications, 2009), 551.

4 Ibid.

5 Cleon L. Rogers Jr. & Cleon L. Rogers III, *The New Linguistic and Exegetical Key to the Greek New Testament* (Zondervan, 1998), 511.

6 John Phillips, *Exploring Ephesians* (Loizeaux Brothers, 1993), 64.

7 Adapted from David Campbell, *Opening Up Titus* (Day One Publications, 2007), 102.

8 D. Edmond Hiebert, *Titus and Philemon* (Moody Press, 1957), 70.

9 Kitchen, 533.

10 William Barclay, *The Letters to Timothy, Titus, and Philemon* (Westminster John Knox Press, 1975), 262.

11 Charles R. Swindoll, *Swindoll's New Testament Insights: 1 & 2 Timothy and Titus* (Zondervan, 2010), 308.

12 Jordan Kauflin, "All I Have Is Christ" (© Sovereign Grace Praise, 2008).

CHAPTER TWENTY-TWO

1 http://www.gallup.com/poll/147887/americans-continue-believe-god.aspx.

2 Adapted from John Phillips, *Exploring the Pastoral Epistles: An Expository Commentary* (Kregel Publications 2003), 157.

3 Charles R. Swindoll, *Swindoll's New Testament Insights: 1 & 2 Timothy and Titus* (Zondervan, 2010), 308.

4 P. J. Alindogan, "Hearing" (The Potter's Jar blog, March 4, 2012), www.preachingtoday.com, July 5, 2012.

5 John A. Kitchen, *The Pastoral Epistles for Pastors* (Kress Christian Publications, 2009), 557.

6 Sam Gordon, *The Genius of Grace: The Message of Ephesians* (Ambassador Publications, 2003), 128.

7 Kitchen, 558.

[8] John W. Peterson and Alfred B. Smith, "Why Worry When You Can Pray?" (1949, New Spring (administered by Brentwood-Benson Music Publishing, Inc.).

[9] John Benton, *Straightening Out the Self-Centered Church: The Message of Titus* (Evangelical Press, 1997), 164.

[10] R. Kent Hughes & Bryan Chapell, *1&2 Timothy and Titus: To Guard the Deposit* (Crossway Books and Bibles, 2000), 363.

[11] Alvin J. Schmidt, *How Christianity Changed the World* (Zondervan, 2004), 152.

[12] Nicholas D. Kristof, "Evangelicals without Blowhards," nytimes.com, July 30, 2011.

[13] Bill White, "Community Outreach Moves a Neighbor to Consider Christ," www.preachingtoday.com, November 8, 2010.

CHAPTER TWENTY-THREE

[1] John MacArthur, *Titus* (Moody Publishers, 1996), 161.

[2] John A. Kitchen, *The Pastoral Epistles for Pastors* (Kress Christian Publications, 2009), 560.

[3] *The Book of Legends: Legends from the Talmud and Midrash*, edited by Hayim Nahman Bialik & Yehoshua Ravnitzky (Schocken Books, 1992), 27.

[4] Ibid, 28.

[5] Knute Larson, *Holman New Testament Commentary: 1 & 2 Thessalonians, 1 & 2 Timothy, Titus, Philemon* (Holman, 2000), 385.

[6] Larson, 385.

[7] Jim Cymbala, "Nip It in the Bud," *Leadership Journal* (October 1, 2002), ctlibrary.com.

[8] R. Kent Hughes, *Ephesians* (Crossway Books, 1990), 123.

[9] Robert Black & Ronald McClung, *1 & 2 Timothy, Titus, Philemon* (Wesleyan Publishing House, 2004), 259.

[10] Charles R. Swindoll, *Swindoll's New Testament Insights on 1 & 2 Timothy and Titus* (Zondervan, 2010), 312.

[11] Kitchen, 561.

CHAPTER TWENTY-FOUR

[1] christianitytoday/preachingtoday.com/2012.

[2] Associated Press, "Ten Percent of U.S. Drivers Have Their 'Check Engine' Light On" (www.yahoonews.com (June 10, 2008).

[3] Tim Keller, "Unintentional Preaching Models," Ockenga Institute of Gordon-Conwell Theological Seminary, August 28, 2006.

[4] John MacArthur, *Titus* (Moody Publishers, 1996), 164.

5   Fritz Rienecker & Cleon Rogers, *Linguistic Key to the Greek New Testament* (Regency, 1976), 383.

6   MacArthur, 164.

7   John A. Kitchen, *The Pastoral Epistles for Pastors* (Kress Christian Publications, 2009), 563.

8   John Phillips, *Exploring the Pastoral Epistles: An Expository Commentary* (Kregel Publications, 2003), 309.

9   Ibid.

10 Gene A. Getz, *The Measure of a Christian: Studies in Titus* (Regal Books, 1983), 181.

11 Kitchen, 562.

12 Charles R. Swindoll, *Swindoll's New Testament Insights on 1 & 2 Timothy and Titus* (Zondervan, 2010), 311, 314.

13 Stephen Davey, *In Pursuit of Prodigals: A Primer on Church Discipline & Reconciliation* (Kress Biblical Resources, 2010), 47–48.

14 Paul Cedar, *Leadership*, Volume 5, no. 3 (July 1, 1998), christianitytoday/preachingtoday.com, 2012.

15 Rienecker & Rogers, 581.

CHAPTER TWENTY-FIVE

1   Sam Gordon, *The Genius of Grace: The Message of Ephesians* (Ambassador, 2003), 377.

2   D. Edmond Hiebert, *Titus and Philemon* (Moody Press, 1957), 77.

3   Charles R. Swindoll, *Swindoll's New Testament Insights: 1 & 2 Timothy and Titus* (Zondervan, 2010), 317.

4   E. M. Bounds, *Power Through Prayer* (Moody Publishers, 1979), 9.

5   John Phillips, *Exploring the Pastoral Epistles: An Expository Commentary* (Kregel Publications, 2003), 167.

6   John MacArthur, *Titus* (Moody Publishers, 1996), 167.

7   Tony Snow, "The Up Side," *Guideposts* (January 2008), 20.

8   William Barclay, *The Letters to Timothy, Titus, and Philemon* (Westminster John Knox Press, 1975), 266.

9   John A. Kitchen, *The Pastoral Epistles for Pastors* (Kress Christian Publications, 2009), 568.

10 Swindoll, 318.

SCRIPTURE INDEX